WITHDRAWN

BARCODE overleaf →

PLAY, DRAMA & THOUGHT

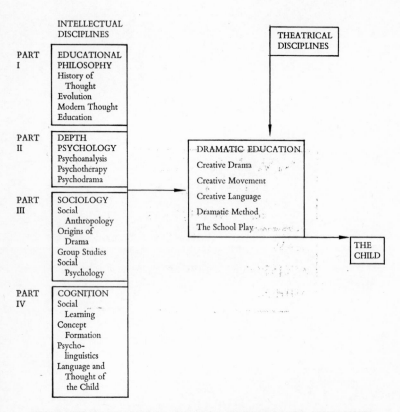

INTELLECTUAL
DISCIPLINES

THEATRICAL
DISCIPLINES

PART
I

EDUCATIONAL
PHILOSOPHY
History of
    Thought
Evolution
Modern Thought
Education

PART
II

DEPTH
PSYCHOLOGY
Psychoanalysis
Psychotherapy
Psychodrama

DRAMATIC EDUCATION
Creative Drama
Creative Movement
Creative Language
Dramatic Method
The School Play

THE
CHILD

PART
III

SOCIOLOGY
Social
    Anthropology
Origins of
    Drama
Group Studies
Social
    Psychology

PART
IV

COGNITION
Social
    Learning
Concept
    Formation
Psycho-
    linguistics
Language and
    Thought of
    the Child

DRAMATIC EDUCATION & RELATED INTELLECTUAL DISCIPLINES

Fig. I

RICHARD COURTNEY

PLAY, DRAMA & THOUGHT

The Intellectual Background to Dramatic Education

CASSELL · LONDON

CASSELL & COMPANY LTD
35 Red Lion Square, London WC1
Melbourne, Sydney, Toronto
Johannesburg, Auckland

S.B.N. 304 93037 7

By the same author
TEACHING DRAMA

THE SCHOOL PLAY
(Cassell)
                    *

THE DRAMA STUDIO
Architecture & Equipment
for Dramatic Education

DRAMA FOR YOUTH
(Pitman)
                    *

COLLEGE DRAMA SPACE
(Editor)
(Institute of Education,
London University)

PRINTED IN GREAT BRITAIN
BY EBENEZER BAYLIS AND SON LTD.
THE TRINITY PRESS, WORCESTER, AND LONDON
F.1267

PREFACE

Dramatic studies have been struggling for many years to establish themselves within the intellectual framework of Europe and North America. Originally in this century they were thought of as 'literature' and so first-degree students took a 'Drama paper' within a degree in English, French, or some other language; post-graduate work was pursued within the same framework. Then, in 1950, degrees in Drama as such were awarded at Bristol University, to be followed in more recent years by Manchester, Hull, Birmingham and, in Scotland, by Glasgow. However, the nature of British university regulations being what they are, these degrees were still soundly based upon 'papers', thus emphasising theory and only regarding practice as a minor part of the discipline. And yet Drama is, by its very nature, a dual discipline with the practical and theoretic elements being of equal importance. In the United States and Canada (and, to a certain extent, in Australia) Drama as a university subject came earlier; in most instances, however, dramatic studies either followed the English pattern by emphasising theory or, in reaction, emphasised practice with a low level of theoretic background. On the continent of Europe, on the other hand, the main emphasis has been upon the study of theatre history.

Meanwhile, other studies have raised a great many related problems which have impinged upon, and widened, the whole scope of Drama as an intellectual discipline. It began with education: thinkers, who had for a long time emphasised 'play', came to see that there was a direct relationship between 'play', 'dramatic play', and 'drama' itself; and so arose the many teaching-of-drama courses in our Colleges of Education. Even more recently, thinkers in a great many fields have discussed the importance of 'dramatic play' and 'drama' within their own specialisms. The process of thought itself was seen to be dramatic in its essence, while identification (the internal impersonation of others) was shown to be the basic way in which man adjusts to his fellow human beings.

And so in recent years the concept of dramatic studies has widened far beyond Literature, beyond Drama, and even beyond the dual emphasis of practice and theory. It has become an all-embracing concept covering the whole growth of man—as an infant, as a school-child, as a student, and as part of the very process of living. It is in this sense that I have used the term Dramatic Education and that I ask that it should be considered as an overall discipline in its own right.

The recent establishment of the degree of B.Ed. in British universities, and of Dramatic Education as a subject within it, was tantamount to the recognition of the subject as a separate intellectual discipline. However, if the degree and the subject within it are to have real academic standing, it is necessary for that field to be defined. This in itself is excessively difficult: not only is there a variety of approaches, but the present syllabuses vary from university to university. Thus the present text ranges widely over the related disciplines and shows their inter-connection within the dramatic field.

The text is written as a source book for students. All sources are carefully indicated so that students can, by reference to the Biblio-graphy, pursue their own specialisms and interests within the subject. I must also indicate that this present text is entirely theoretical as I have approached the practical aspects of the topic elsewhere: classroom work in *Teaching Drama,* 'theatre' in *The School Play,* architecture, space and equipment in *The Drama Studio,* and so on.

Although the establishment of Dramatic Education as a degree subject has led to the writing of this book at the present time, it has been in embryonic form for about twenty years. During this time many modern researches have come to my aid; in recent years whole new areas of thought have been explored which have a direct bearing upon the subject. All these studies are referred to within the text, and some I have been particularly glad to lean upon—as the discerning reader will easily discover for himself.

Owing to the long period of gestation, I owe to a number of people the fact that it was possible to write this book:

Professor Bonamy Dobrée, who first suggested that such a task was possible; Professors G. Wilson Knight and Frederick May for the concept of 'width' in dramatic studies; the late Professor Harvey and Professor J. M. Cameron, Mr A. Laing and Mr Kenneth Ottaway who, in their differing ways, led me to see the implications within the educative process; Dr Kenneth Lovell who invited me to lecture on his course for teachers of backward children at the Institute of Education, Leeds University, in 1962, the material for which forms several sections of Parts I and III; W. A. Hodges, Cyril Crossley, Tom Craven, Les Hunt, the late Dr Newell, T. E. Tyler, Peter Slade, Stanley Evernden, the late Rudolf Laban, Sybil Marshall, Professor George Allen, C.B.E., John Allen, H.M.I., and many others whose thought has, in many ways, stimulated my own;

Dr Harold Nason and Elizabeth Orchard of the Department of Education, Nova Scotia, for the opportunity to lecture and work with Canadian teachers, enabling me to revise my ideas within a wider context; and Don Wetmore and Genevieve Archibald for enabling me to relate Dramatic Education to the Canadian situation while I was lecturing within Dalhousie University where, incidentally, the manuscript was finally completed in the Summer of 1966; and my other Canadian friends (particularly Thomas Simms and Ken Elliot) for their stimulating discussions on related topics;

E. J. Burton, whose erudition in Dramatic Education has been a constant example and who has willingly lent me related papers; fellow members of 'The Steering Committee for Drama in the B.Ed.' within London University (Mrs N. de Montmorency, Barbara Bunch, Marjorie Frances, Beryl Gough and Muriel Judd) and members of the Joint English/Drama 'Steering Committee'(particularly the chairman, Evelyn Carter, and Dr Brooks); T. R. Theakston, Principal of Trent Park College, for his great help and support; Mrs Mary Lane, the Librarian at Trent Park, whose assistance with texts has been invaluable; and John Freeman for his scrutiny of Part III;

Mrs Doreen Harrison, for managing to decipher and type my manuscript; Anne Julia Courtney, for assistance on the Bibliography; John G. Courtney, for his assistance with the Index; and my wife, without whose thought, consideration and perspicacity this book could never have been written.

RICHARD COURTNEY
Associate Professor
Theatre Division
The School of Fine Arts
University of Victoria, B.C.
Canada

for Rosemary

ACKNOWLEDGMENTS

The author and publishers wish to thank the following for permission to reprint copyright material:

Addison-Wesley, Reading, Mass., for four extracts from 'Role Theory' by T. R. Sarbin in *Handbook of Social Psychology, I*, edited by Gardner Lindzey (1954); George Allen & Unwin Ltd, for seven extracts from *Psychoanalytic Explorations in Art* by Ernst Kris, and for two extracts from 'Psychoanalysis and Anthropology' by Géza Róheim in *Psychoanalysis Today*, edited by S. Lorand; Associated Book Publishers Ltd, for an extract from *Child Treatment and the Therapy of Play* by L. Jackson and K. M. Todd (Methuen & Co. Ltd); Basic Books Inc., for nine extracts from *Creativity in the Theater* by Philip Weissman, and for five extracts from the *Collected Papers of Sigmund Freud*, edited by Ernest Jones, published in the United States of America by Basic Books Inc., New York, 1959; Dr Gregory Bateson, Dr Margaret Mead and the New York Academy of Sciences, for four extracts from *Balinese Character* by G. Bateson and M. Mead; Beacon House Inc., for fourteen extracts from *Psychodrama*, Volume I, by Dr Jacob Moreno; The University of Chicago Press, for three extracts from *Language and Culture*, edited by H. Hoijer; Heinemann Educational Books Ltd, for three extracts from *The Education of the Poetic Spirit* by Marjorie Hourd, and William Heinemann Medical Books Ltd, for three extracts from *An Introduction to the Work of Melanie Klein* by Hanna Segal; The Hogarth Press, for two extracts from *Developments in Psychoanalysis*, edited by Joan Rivière (1952), and for an extract from *The Riddle of the Sphinx* by Géza Róheim (1934); The Hogarth Press and International Universities Press Inc., for three extracts from 'Psychoanalysis and Anthropology' by Géza Róheim in *Psychoanalysis and the Social Sciences, I* (Imago, 1947); Holt, Rinehart & Winston Inc., for three extracts from *Social Learning and Personality Development* by A. Bandura and R. H. Walters; International Universities Press Inc., for three extracts from 'The Oedipus Complex, Magic and Culture' by Géza Róheim in *Psychoanalysis and the Social Sciences, II* (1950), for extracts from 'Circuses and Clowns' by S. Tarachow in *Psychoanalysis and the Social Sciences, III* (1951), for two extracts from 'A Psychoanalytic Study of the Fairy Tale' by E. K. Schwartz in *The American Journal of Psychotherapy* (1956, 10), for three extracts by Mark Kanzer from *The Journal of the American Psychoanalytic Association*, and for four extracts from *The Psychoanalyst and the Artist* by D. E. Schneider; Alfred A. Knopf Inc., for an extract from *Moses and Monotheism* by Sigmund Freud, published in the United States of America by Alfred A. Knopf Inc., New York; The Liveright Publishing Corporation, for an extract from *Beyond the Pleasure Principle* by Sigmund Freud, published in the United States of America by Liveright Publishers, New York; Norton & Company Inc., for extracts from *An Outline of Psychoanalysis* and *New Introductory Lectures* by Sigmund Freud, published in the United States of America by W. W. Norton & Company Inc., New York; Penguin Books Ltd, for extracts from *Dreams and Nightmares* by J. A. Hadfield, and from *Group Psychotherapy* by S. H. Foulkes and E. J. Anthony; Prentice-Hall International Inc., for three extracts from *Language and Thought* by John B. Carroll, Copyright © 1964 by Prentice-Hall Inc., Englewood Cliffs, N.J.; *The Psychoanalytic Quarterly*, for four extracts from 'Psychopathetic Characters on the Stage (1904)' by Sigmund Freud, for an extract from 'On preconscious mental processes' by Ernst Kris, and for three extracts from 'A note on Falstaff' by Franz Alexander; The Rationalist Press Association Ltd, for two extracts from *Myth and Ritual in Dance, Game and Rhyme* by Lewis Spence (C. A. Watts & Co. Ltd); The Ronald Press Company, for five extracts from *The Theory of Play* by Elmer D. Mitchell and Bernard S. Mason, Revised Edition Copyright 1948 The Ronald Press Company, New York; Routledge & Kegan Paul Ltd, and Norton & Company Inc., New York, for five extracts from *Play, Dreams and Imitation in Childhood* by Jean Piaget; Sigmund Freud Copyrights Ltd, Mr James Strachey and the Hogarth Press Ltd, for extracts from *An Outline of Psychoanalysis (S.E. 23)*, *Beyond the Pleasure Principle (S.E. 18)*, *New Introductory Lectures (S.E. 22)*, *Moses and Monotheism (S.E. 23)*, *Collected Papers V, Humour (S.E. 21), Collected Papers IV, 'Creative Writers and Day Dreaming' (S.E. 9)*, in the Standard Edition of *The Complete Psychological Works of Sigmund Freud*; John Wiley & Sons Ltd, for four extracts from *Learning Theory and the Symbolic Process* by O. H. Mowrer, for five extracts from *Thought and Language* by L. S. Vygotsky, and for a diagram from 'Language Development in Children' by D. McCarthy in *Manual of Child Psychology*, edited by L. Carmichael.

The extract from Lili E. Peller's 'Libidinal Development as reflected in play' is reprinted from *Psychoanalysis*, Volume 3, No. 3, Spring 1955, through the courtesy of the Editors of *The Psychoanalytic Review*, and the Publisher, the National Psychological Association for Psychoanalysis Inc., New York, N.Y.

CONTENTS

INTRODUCTION

'Why do you teach my child to act?' asked a parent. 'I don't want him to go on the stage.'

'But nor do I.'

'Then why don't you teach him something important—like arithmetic or how to write?'

Years ago, parental opposition of this kind to Dramatic Education was considerable. It exists today, but hardly to the extent that it did twenty years ago. It is based on misconceptions. First, that standing over a child and forcing him to add up or write an essay is to provide him with an education. We have to convince the parent that arithmetic or writing is best taught by the child *wanting* to do them; if we can obtain the same intensity in the child that he has in the playground and channel it towards his lessons, then this is the basis of a real and permanent education. Secondly, that Dramatic Education is 'stage training'. It isn't. Essentially, Dramatic Education is a child playing dramatically. It takes place when the boys in the street are playing 'Cowboys and Indians' or a little girl talks to her dolls as she dresses them. With 6-year-olds, the teacher bangs a tambourine and asks the children what it reminds them of: trains, perhaps—so we're all trains, moving together, impersonating the movements and sounds of trains. With 12-year-olds we may ask them to make up their own play (to improvise), but to concentrate upon the climax; we are still maintaining the elements of dramatic play but now they are channelled towards the creative use of form. By 14 years old, perhaps, we are working on a stage (though we may not be); but essentially we are still asking the child to *play* dramatically. When 'the theatre' enters, it does so incidentally. Thus we must distinguish certain terms:

> *theatre:* performance before an audience;
> *play:* activity pursued merely because we enjoy it;
> *dramatic play:* play which contains impersonation and/or identification;
> *games:* formalisation of play into patterns with rules.

Dramatic Education is based upon dramatic play which is pursued in a school in order to further the development of the child.

But how precisely does 'theatre' enter into the scheme of things? Most children, by adolescence, require 'theatre' to enter their natural make-believe play. The teacher allows this to happen as and when the child requires it. But we are not deliberately and methodically instructing the child in stage technique. This may happen with adults—not with children. As students mature, 'theatre' enters more and more into Dramatic Education until, by college or university, 'theatre' has mingled with dramatic play. In this way we can distinguish the following stages of Dramatic Education:

> *primary* (5—11 years):   dramatic play;
> *secondary* (11—18 years):   dramatic play mingling with 'theatre';
> *tertiary* (18+ years):   'theatre' based on dramatic play.

(These divisions are very approximate and vary considerably from child to child.) But essentially WE START WITH THE CHILD. We do not commence with the idea of where this form of education is going to lead us because, if we did that, we would impose our ideas on the child; rather, we start with the individual child, see him work dramatically, and attempt to lead him slowly on—at his own pace and in his own time. The difference in these two approaches can be seen in the attitude to 'theatre': in the first, the child is instructed in stage technique, diction, theatre movement, and the like, according to a specific syllabus—these items are taught at specific ages and abilities as it is thought 'correct' by an adult; in the second, the child plays dramatically and is introduced to specific technical skills as and when he requires them for his own personal development.

Within the school situation, we must distinguish between the two major parts of Dramatic Education:

1. *Dramatic Method:*   the use of dramatic play in the learning of many subjects (the skills and knowledge of history, geography, mathematics, etc.);

2.   *Drama as such:*   dramatic play pursued for its own sake, purely for the personal development of the child, and as a separate subject on the curriculum; and here we meet the various elements of the subject—
   improvisation (creative drama),
   creative movement,
   creative speech,
   and, with older students, *theatre* (or the school play).

This way of looking at education is comparatively new, yet has evolved naturally and slowly and is in the mainstream of modern European thought. Its origins go back to Plato and Aristotle, Rabelais and Rousseau in philosophy. It is based as much on social anthropology and social psychology as on psychoanalysis and child psychotherapy. It partially stems from modern theories of cognition, from behaviourist theories of imitation, from psycholinguistics and the developmental psychology of Piaget. In this context, it is the centre of modern creative education: all arts spring from it and all scientific methods evolve through it.

PART ONE

PLAY, DRAMA & EDUCATIONAL PHILOSOPHY

1 DRAMA & THE HISTORY OF EDUCATIONAL THOUGHT

The essential characteristic of man is his creative imagination. It is this which enables him to master his environment in such a way that he overcomes the limitations of his brain, his body and the material universe. It is this 'something more' which distinguishes him from the upper primates.

The creative imagination is essentially dramatic in its character. It is the ability to see imaginative possibilities, to comprehend the relationships between two concepts and to see the dynamic force between them. The developing human child has a first year of life which is essentially motor; and then, suddenly with some children, the change comes—he plays, develops humour, and pretends to be himself or someone else. He has gone through other changes before this, some extremely important, but this is the specific development that makes the difference between man and other living creatures—the ability to see another person's point of view, to see the possibilities in a situation which can make it funny, to see the inherent qualities in two ideas and the possible *action* between them. Pretending to be someone else—to act—is part of the process of living; we may actually pretend, physically, when we are young children or we may do it internally when we are adults. We act every day: with our friends, our family, strangers. The most common image for this process is 'the mask and the face': our real self is hidden by the many 'masks' which we assume during the course of each day. Acting is the method by which we live with our environment, finding adjustment in play. The young child, coming upon something within the external world which he does not comprehend, will play with it dramatically until he does. We can observe infants doing this many times a day. As we get older, the process becomes more and more internal until, as adults, it is automatic and we play dramatically in our imagination—so much so, indeed, that we may not even know that we do it.

It follows, therefore, that the dramatic process is one of the most vital to mankind. Without it we would be merely a mass of motor reflexes with scarcely any human qualities.

Each age and each society evolves its own form of education. Where the medieval Church evolved an educational system which kept

the priesthood vital, and the nineteenth century school system incul-
cated specific academic skills in order to provide a clerical force for the
industrial revolution, we must provide education that enables human
beings to develop their human qualities. This is the major need of our
time. The increasing specialisation of our scientific society tends *not* to
concentrate on essentially human qualities. Both in our education and
our leisure we need to cultivate 'the whole man' and concentrate on
the human being's creative abilities. *The dramatic imagination must be
helped and assisted by any modern method of education.*

This attitude to the educative process has evolved slowly over the
centuries. During the history of human thought, the educational
nature of dramatic play has been comprehended by various thinkers at
different times—but in their own terms. Education was related to the
whole framework of thought within which the individual was
thinking. Thus Plato's attitude evolved from Greek thought just as
Ascham's did from Renascence thought.

THE ANCIENT WORLD

Athenian education in the fifth century B.C. was based on literature,
music and physical play. Literature included reading, writing, arithmetic and recitations from the poets—particularly Homer. He was the
overriding authority on religion as well as letters, and whole passages
were learnt by heart and then recited with all the resources of the
stage—inflexion, facial expression and dramatic gesture. Music
included the study of rhythm and harmony, and the playing of the
lyre and the flute, while physical play received great emphasis from
races to ball-games, from wrestling and boxing to riding and dancing.

Dancing was stressed as it was central to every religious and dramatic
ceremony; the form it took was intensely dramatic and it involved
great skill. Wealthy citizens trained the chorus of the religious festival
and the children, often poor, went through a rigorous programme of
poetry, religion, singing and dancing—a coordinated programme, in
fact, which expressed the individual's harmony of thought through
rhythmical exercise.

Further, the theatre itself was a great educational instrument because
it disseminated knowledge and was, for the populace, the only literary
pleasure available. The dramatists themselves were considered by the
teachers to be of equal importance with Homer, and were recited in

much the same way. Drama, in all its aspects, was a major unifying and educational force within the Attic world.

Plato

Plato considered that education must be based upon play and not compulsion, that:

> ... children from their earliest years must take part in all the more lawful forms of play, for if they are not surrounded with such an atmosphere they can never grow up to be well educated and virtuous citizens. [295]

Education must begin early, but 'in a playful manner, and without any air of constraint' primarily so that they can develop 'the natural bent of their characters'.

Plato divides his educational system into two parts: 'musical' and 'gymnastic' His use of the term 'musical' is all embracing:

> ... the young of all creatures cannot be quiet in their bodies or in their voices, they are always wanting to move and cry out; some leaping and skipping, and overflowing with sportiveness and delight at something, others uttering all sorts of cries. But whereas the animals have no perception of order in their movements, that is, rhythm and harmony, as they are called, to us the Gods, who, as we say, have been appointed to be our companions in the dance, have given the pleasurable sense of harmony and rhythm; so they stir us into life, and we follow them joining hands together in dances and songs; and these they call choruses, which is a term naturally expressive of cheerfulness. Shall we begin, then, with the acknowledgement that education is first given us through Apollo and the Muses ... (for) he who is well educated will be able to sing and dance well. [296]

'Musical' education, balanced by physical recreation, includes singing, dancing and literature and should be approached from the tendency to play. His reason for attaching such importance to it is that 'rhythm and harmony sink most deeply into the recesses of the soul' and thus discernment, judgement, goodness and just reason will develop.

But if Plato advocates a liberal education based on play, he can find no place for the theatre in his *Republic*. For him, the ideal is the truth and reality is a copy (or imitation) of it. But the theatre is even further from the truth for it imitates reality. An actor, too, imitates a character —but to imitate is to trespass. Further, an actor might have to imitate a bad character and this might lead him to 'be infected with reality'. The

theatre holds great dangers for an audience: it might lead them to
succumb to emotions it would be better to subdue.

He distinguishes play, which should be the basis of education, and
theatre, which is bad because it is imitation. He is answered by Aristotle, but Plato's influence spread down into the Middle Ages when the
works of Aristotle were lost.

Aristotle

Aristotle, too, emphasised play in education but, being a scientist,
he did so in a specific way. Playful movement should be encouraged to
prevent indolence while play in general 'ought to be neither illiberal,
nor too laborious, nor lazy'. Also, it can be introduced for relaxation
'as a medicine'. He defines these two purposes of play because he
distinguishes activities which are ends in themselves and can be
pursued for their own sake (which is happiness) from those which are
means to an end. As education must provide for the practical life and
leisure at the same time, play is of the utmost importance. Thus far he
would agree with Plato.

But it is in the *Poetics,* with his discussion of the drama, that the
disagreement comes. The *Poetics* stands as one of the major works of
dramatic criticism in world literature although it is both short and
incomplete. It has had a great influence in all periods of history, not
least today, despite the fact that some passages are of doubtful origin.
And it provides a complete answer to Plato's criticism of the theatre.

Plato misunderstood the nature of imitation, says Aristotle. The
theatre does not imitate actualities but abstract ideas—the actor does
not imitate the real Oedipus but an idealised version of his character.
Dramatic characters are not presented as they really are: comedy
makes them worse and tragedy makes them better than they are in real
life. Further, imitation is natural to the human race:

> Imitation is natural to man from childhood, one of his advantages over the
> lower animals being this, that he is the most imitative creature in the world,
> and learns first by imitation. [14]

What is more, learning through imitation is an intellectual pleasure:

> It is also natural for all to delight in works of imitation . . . though the objects
> themselves may be painful to see, we delight to view the most realistic
> representations of them in art . . . (because) to be learning something is the

greatest of pleasures, not only to the philosopher but also to the rest of mankind, however small their capacity. [14]

And to develop his thesis Aristotle introduces his theory of Catharsis: that tragedy provides a 'purgation' of emotions:

> A tragedy . . . is the imitation of an action that is serious and also, as having magnitude, complete in itself, in language and pleasurable accessories, each kind brought in separately in the parts of the work; in a dramatic, not in a narrative form; with incidents arousing pity and fear, wherewith to accomplish its catharsis of such emotions. [14]

His full explanation has not come down to us, and what we have is infuriatingly incomplete. But it is normally assumed that he considered that the emotions which were aroused by tragedy purged the soul like a medicine. In witnessing a tragedy, impure emotions are experienced and so drained away that the noble emotions of pity and fear are enhanced. The influence of the theory of Catharsis was twofold: first, in providing an emotional significance for the drama; and second, in defining the tragic attitude as having the opposing elements of pity and fear. (Kierkegaard chose sorrow and pain, I. A. Richards adopted pity and terror, and other writers have used their own elements.)

Roman Thought

Following Aristotle, the most common Roman concept was that imitation had a direct relationship with art and drama. Cicero described drama as 'a copy of life, a mirror of custom, a reflection of truth' [64], a concept that was to echo down the centuries and eventually reach Shakespeare's idea that drama's aim was 'to hold, as 'twere, the mirror up to nature'. For the Romans, drama was imitation and it had an educational purpose if it was of use and taught moral lessons.

Horace considered that drama must both entertain and educate:

> That poet gets every vote, who unites information with pleasure, at once enlightening and instructing the reader. [176]

He then collated classical opinion into a series of rules for drama, stressing propriety and clearly defined form: comedy and tragedy must be differentiated; characters must be created according to type; violent actions should not be displayed; the structure should be of five acts—and so on. In Rome, rules took the place of Greek speculation.

Seneca condemned the stage because it took people away from the serious business of learning and so he wrote his own dramas not for the theatre but for the study; they were full of bloodshed and long moralisings and, when rediscovered in the Renascence, had an influence far beyond their merit.

Two Roman writers took over the basis of Plato's thought and, from their writings, the opposition to drama was given an intellectual basis for centuries to come. Quintilian's influence was in the late medieval period and early Renascence—on Erasmus and Luther, for example. Plotinus also restated Plato's thought but his influence was mainly on the early Christian fathers, and within Neoplatonism he profoundly affected Catholic thought until the twelfth century.

THE MEDIEVAL PERIOD

The Church fathers condemned the drama out of hand. Ban after ban was issued from Rome forbidding theatre performances and threatening dire punishments for those clergy who entertained actors. Yet, as Allardyce Nicoll points out alongside his long list of papal decrees [276], if the theatre aroused the ire of the Church in such a way, the theatrical tradition must have been particularly strong in the period but, being a verbal tradition, there are no written records of it. The Church based its opposition on three factors: it had grown up in a period when the indecent Roman mime had satirised the Church, and so there was an emotional objection; many of the pagan folk customs had a mimetic and dramatic element (see p. 163 *et seq.*), and so there was a religious objection; and, as their thought was based on Neoplatonism, with its conflict between the world and the spirit as well as the tradition of Plato's own opposition to the theatre, there was a philosophical objection.

But from about the ninth century things slowly began to change. Charlemagne, who was crowned as Holy Roman Emperor in 800, founded schools and monasteries all over Europe; and so, when the works of Aristotle reappeared a little later, the scene was set for a revaluation of drama. This began with St. Thomas Aquinas, who was the first divine to adapt Aristotelian philosophy to the Catholic faith, giving general approval to acting as long as it was recreation, and to games and amusements if they provided relaxation after serious work. It was upon such a basis that Christian drama could grow and so, when the *tropes* of the tenth century became dramatic (see p. 170 *et seq.*), there was an element of Aristotelian thought within the Church that could give it support. What was created was a liturgical drama with a didactic purpose centred on the monastic schools. Its purpose was plainly to help the illiterate comprehend the faith. But, educational or not, once the process had begun dramatic creation went on apace. Hroswitha, the tenth-century Benedictine abbess, could even write secular Latin dramas based on Terence; but the Benedictines had always had a tradition of education in the spoken word and it is probable that they had continued recitations of set conversations right through the Middle Ages.

It was on this turbulent basis that Christian Church drama grew. For five centuries the Mystery and Morality plays provided the only intellectual pleasure for the multitude. Schools and books, after all, were the prerogative of the few. It was the drama that provided the masses with what education they had.

THE RENASCENCE

Drama in Education

In the Renascence, man's world was regenerated by the discovery of classical books. The first large dramatic influence was the Roman Academy of Pomponius Laetus in the middle of the fifteenth century: an association of scholars, they performed Latin plays and reintroduced Plautus into Italy. Similar academies grew up all over Italy and their members, eventually, became schoolmasters and so the dramatic influence reached the children. Most famous was Vittorino da Feltra whose school in fifteenth-century Mantua had a most generous curriculum. Great prominence was given to games, play and, particularly, physical activities.

In addition, there were imitation battles where the boys could take fortresses, set up camps and storm trenches—dramatic play with a vengeance! And he found that those who were most eager in their play were the most zealous in their conduct and learning.

By the late sixteenth century, dramatic activities took place in almost every school. Humanism emphasised the art of speaking, particularly Latin, and much of this was in dialogue; and it reintroduced the study of ancient drama. As a result, school plays were common. But this approach also allowed thinkers to evolve even more liberal forms of education. Rabelais, for example, says that in education Gargantua must be kept occupied, and that book study must be relieved by play and manual occupations. He provides three hundred and sixteen games for exercising the mind and body and, in addition, provides singing, dancing, modelling, painting, nature study and manual training—thus showing a breadth of thought two hundred years ahead of his time [302].

Tudor schools were famous for their music and developed a strong dramatic tradition. In his Statutes for Ipswich School in 1528, Wolsey encouraged drama not merely for classical studies, but also as an exercise in speaking and appreciation. Thus drama was used for developing the mother tongue, a practice exemplified by Nicholas Udall whose school-children, at both Eton and Westminster, performed in high places. He also wrote for the children *Ralph Roister Doister,* the first comedy of any note written in English. The purpose of comedy, he says in the Prologue, is to provide necessary relaxation and a moral lesson:

> For mirth prolongeth life, and causeth health.
> Mirth recreates our spirits and voideth pensiveness,
> Mirth increases amity, not hindering our wealth.
> Mirth is to be used both of more and less,
> Being mixed with virtue in decent comeliness
> As we trust no good nature can gainsay the same:
> Which mirth we intend to use avoiding all blame.

With Udall at Eton were two future headmasters who continued the dramatic tradition: William Malim of Eton who developed movement within plays written in English; and Richard Mulcaster of the Merchant Taylors' School who advocated drawing and music, saw the dramatic method as useful for the teaching of other subjects, and emphasised both play and activity [270]. These were far from isolated examples, for the Tudor tradition of school play production was strong; the Children of the Chapel Royal even became so expert that they rivalled the professional companies during Shakespeare's lifetime.

Drama in the universities of Oxford and Cambridge took place mainly during the Christmas period when Interludes as well as Latin and English plays are recorded. William Stevenson's *Gammer Gurton's Needle* took its place with Udall's drama as one of the earliest English comedies when it was performed by students while, in 1562, the first

English tragedy—Norton and Sackville's *Gorboduc*—was performed by the law students at the Inns of Court. The contribution of education to the larger drama was not complete, however: by the end of the century, Lyly and the University Wits combined the academic drama and the popular theatre, and the plays of Marlowe and Ben Jonson result.

One other interesting educational development was the use of drama by the Jesuits. The Order, founded in 1534 by Ignatius Loyala, had an Aristotelian basis and was concerned with developing Latin as an international language. Although by the early seventeenth century there was an increasing didactic emphasis and magnificence of display, the majority of Jesuit plays in schools were written by the teachers or the children.

Philosophers & Scholars

The bases for humanist thinking on drama were Aristotle and Horace in particular, as well as Cicero's phrase that it was, 'a copy of life, a mirror of custom, a reflection of truth'. From 1498 translations of the *Poetics* were available and by the middle of the next century, several Italian scholars were making original contributions to dramatic thought —particularly Minturno, Scaliger and Castelvetro. Although based on Aristotle and Horace, they retain the moralising tendency of the medieval period. They attempt to codify a series of 'laws' for dramatic composition: tragedy was about kings and ended in disaster; comedy had 'ordinary' characters representing types, and ended happily; five acts and Seneca were models; and, where Aristotle had emphasised a unity of Action, the Renascence scholars added those of Time and Place [279].

In England, Sir Thomas More enjoyed acting at Christmas; his friend Erasmus said drama should refute vice, while a further friend, Sir Thomas Elyot, emphasised dramatic dancing in education. Elyot's pupil Roger Ascham, tutor to the young Elizabeth, would balance two parts of education: dramatic literature, and play, recreation and physical exercise. Bacon makes a clear distinction between professional and educational acting:

> It is a thing indeed, if practised professionally, of low repute; but if it be made a part of discipline, it is of excellent use. I mean stage-playing; an art which strengthens the memory, regulates the tone and effect of the voice and pronunciation, teaches a decent carriage of the countenance and gesture,

gives not a little assurance, and accustoms young men to bear being looked at. [18]

Sir Philip Sidney says that drama should teach and amuse, an idea summed up in Ben Jonson's famous tag:

> The ends of all, who for the stage would write,
> Are, or should be, to profit and delight.

In France, the most original speculations in this field are by Montaigne, who thought that the child 'shall not so much repeat as act his lesson'. He considered that:

> . . . children's plays are not sports and should be deemed their most serious occupations. [263]

More startling, perhaps, is his claim for community theatres supported by the city authorities:

> Well-ordered communities usually endeavour to gather their citizens together, not only in serious devotional services, but also in sports and pleasures. Friendship and good neighbourliness are thereby increased. And then you can hardly allow them better regulated pastimes than those that take place in the presence of everyone, even before the magistrates themselves. And I think it quite reasonable that the princes and the magistrates should sometimes gratify the common people with them, out of their own pockets, in a sort of fatherly affection and generosity. In populated towns there ought to be proper places appointed for these spectacles as a safeguard against worse things carried on in secret. [263]

THE NEO-CLASSIC PERIOD

Drama in Education

The Puritans, basing their thinking on the Mosaic law that one sex should not wear the clothes of another (delightfully ridiculed by Ben Jonson through Zeal-of-the-Land Busy in *Bartholomew Fair*), attacked the theatre in England from the middle of the sixteenth to the middle of the seventeenth century. One after another, Stephen Gosson, John Northbrooke and Philip Stubbes thundered against the theatre. Drama in schools they tolerated—just. But it had to be morally sound and preferably in Latin. Their effect on education was not immediate. Even in 1631 Ben Jonson could make Gossip Censure say of teachers:

> They make all their scholars playboys. Is't not a fine sight to see all our children made interluders? Do we pay money for this?

Even Milton had formed a love of the drama before he joined the Puritans. When in government, they could not stamp it out in theatre or in school. Then, with the Restoration, they were expelled from their parishes, the public schools and universities, but they were allowed to stay in the academies where their influence continued for many years.

By this time, Bacon's system of inductive reasoning had permeated into the schools largely through Comenius. Although they both supported the concept of drama, an educational method which studied natural objects to arrive at the truth was scarcely conducive to dramatic activity. So, too, Latin language rather than literature was emphasised, producing a formal rather than a liberal education. This was reinforced by Locke's belief that education was the formation of habits of mind and that the method, not the content, mattered; thus dead languages were ideal to breed internal discipline. As a result drama in eighteenth-century education is a record of a mere few school plays with boys.

In the latter half of the century, however, the education of English girls was more liberal, including both drama and dancing. *Dido and Aeneas* (1689), by Purcell and Nahum Tate, was written for a girls' school in Chelsea and this, together with the work of Fénelon, gave sufficient precedent for many plays to be performed.

The English girls had a classic example from France. French royalty had long supported the drama: in 1641 Richelieu had attempted to rehabilitate the professional theatre by edict. But the most remarkable event was the formation of the convent of Saint-Cyr for poor but well-bred girls by Mme de Maintenon, wife of Louis XIV. The girls improvised dialogue and conversation, and performed plays by Racine and Corneille. In fact, Racine wrote both *Esther* and *Athalie* especially for them. Associated with the school was Fénelon, Archbishop of Cambrai, whose *Education of Girls* (1687) stated: 'Let them learn through play'. He was more concerned with improvised drama than the repetition of texts and his work had a considerable influence in England. The girls of Saint-Cyr continued to perform, even in front of Marie Antoinette. But, despite the fact that Voltaire supported the theatre and Rousseau advocated play, school drama was being suppressed in France even before the Revolution [67].

2

Thinkers & Scholars

For Descartes, the individual had freedom of thought just as far as the thought was clear and could stand up to the practical test, and critics followed him in analysing the drama. Boileau's *Poetic Art* was Cartesian in that drama was only considered valid when it pleased intellectually, a thought to have considerable influence in the Augustan period. In Germany, Leibnitz supported the theatre if it was instructional, while Lessing considered that the best tragedy purifies pity of selfishness and produces altruism.

Similarly, when Locke said that knowledge came from sense perception, it was concomitant that art should be practical. Thus it was logical for Jeremy Collier to say:

> The business of plays is to recommend virtue and discountenance vice; to show the uncertainty of human greatness, the sudden turns of fate, and unhappy conclusions of violence and injustice; 'tis to expose the singularities of pride and fancy, to make folly and falsehood contemptible and to bring everything that is ill under infamy and neglect. [69]

With these premises he felt that he could condemn the current stage and, with the sole exception of the rejection of Falstaff, the plays of Shakespeare. Thomas Rhymer could do the same, but under the flag of following 'rules' for drama. Dryden, wider and more liberal, could both follow neo-classic rules and recognise merit where the rules were not followed; this was largely because he considered individual plays rather than work in generalities. Yet, even for him, 'delight' is the chief aim of the drama, and it can 'only instruct as it delights'. But George Farquhar, in his *Discourse upon Comedy* (1702), wittily attempted to destroy the concept of the unities as they had been formalised by the academicians, and he led the men of the theatre in their revolt for freedom—Fielding, Sheridan, Goldsmith and Dr Johnson among them. The learned Doctor summarises, in a famous tag:

> The drama's laws, the drama's patrons give,
> For we that live to please, must please to live.

From the middle of the eighteenth century, the 'sentimental' movement arose all over Europe. It is represented by English novels and plays—Richardson's *Pamela* (1740), Lillo's *George Barnwell* (1731) and Moore's *The Gamester* (1753)—as well as by the weighty authority of Goldoni, and philosophic writings in France. Diderot considered that comedy should be serious and deal with 'the duties of man', while Beaumarchais, in his *Essay on the Serious Drama* (1784), pleaded through an appeal to 'nature' for a drama that should deal with 'ordinary' characters and attempt to be 'real'. Sentimentalism is fundamentally different from earlier opinion in that it stated that drama should be neither tragedy nor comedy, that the people and the locality should be drawn from life, that it should be written in prose, and that it should be directed towards a definite social moral. But in the appeal to 'nature' we are clearly drawing near to the world of Rousseau.

THE ROMANTIC PERIOD

Philosophers & Thought

At the end of the eighteenth century, European thought as a whole turned towards Romanticism: in England with Wordsworth, Shelley and Coleridge, in Germany with Goethe, Schiller and Nietzsche, and in France with Rousseau and the revolutionary thinkers. 'Nature' was the basic concept: that which was natural was of value, and that which was unnatural was not. In England, this led to a deeper revaluation of Shakespeare and the Attic dramatists, though, with Coleridge, Hazlitt and Lamb, these considerations were based upon the book read in the study and so tended to become divorced from the practical theatre. Criticism, in many instances, became 'literary'—a tendency which can still be observed today.

Goethe's thought in dramatic education, brilliantly summarised by Coggin [67], distinguished between this and the professional theatre which had no place in education (although Schiller wanted it to be the great popular educator). School plays, he considered, have a beneficial effect on both spectator and actor: they demand considerable skills of memory, gesture and inner discipline. Improvisation is of great value: it shapes the inner thoughts and so releases them, and it develops the imagination:

> In their games, children can make all things out of any: a staff becomes a musket, a splinter of wood a sword, any bunch of clothes a puppet, any crevice a chamber. [67]

Improvisation can use ballads or music to good effect. But all drama should develop ideas: it should arouse emotions and thoughts which the audience *ought* to feel—and this relates to the later concepts of Bergson and Bernard Shaw. Further, he recognises that certain arts, the drama among them, must by the very nature of their size be the responsibility of the community.

A major romantic concept is the duality of the life process: that man is subject to two forces which pull him now this way, now that. Philosophers vary in their approach to this duality. Goethe saw it as a kind of death and resurrection: man must lose part of himself before assimilating the new; the dramatic situation, like life itself, must involve a death and rebirth if the drama is to have meaning. Hegel saw life as dialectical: 'thesis' produces 'antithesis' and the result is 'synthesis'; it was in this sense that Hebbel could say that drama represents the life process. Schopenhauer considered drama to be the result of Will and it represents the Idea of Man; Nietzsche developed this concept to show that drama represents man's will to live, his success in overcoming the transitory nature of existence. For Nietzsche, life and drama are both dominated by two forces: that of Apollo, the idealist, the creator of dreams, who imitates them in art; and that of Dionysos, the primitive, the emotional man, who creates art in ecstasy. For true art, Dionysos must have the help of Apollo—emotion must be shaped by reason. This duality becomes a major concept in subsequent thinking: for Freud it is the Ego and the Id; for Whitehead education is a process of death and resurrection; Dewey sees past and present experience interacting to produce evolving life; and G. Wilson Knight can interpret Shakespeare through the symbols of Apollo and Dionysos.

Educational Thought

Teaching in schools may not have altered much in the eighteenth and early nineteenth centuries, but the philosophy of it did. Rousseau's *Emile* (1762) was the open door through which Froebel, Pestalozzi, Montessori, Dewey and Caldwell Cook could march.

For Rousseau, a child's early education should be almost entirely of play. Just running and skipping and playing are of value. Repression should go and the natural instincts be encouraged:

Love childhood; promote its games, its pleasures, its delightful instincts . . .
you must consider the man in the man and the child in the child . . . Nature

desires children to be children before being men. If we try to pervert the order, we shall produce precocious fruits which will have neither ripeness nor taste, and will soon go bad . . . Childhood has its own ways of seeing, of thinking, of feeling, which are suitable to it; nothing is less reasonable than to substitute our own. [324]

Thus the senses are cultivated and, by 12 years old:

Work and play are alike to him; his plays are his occupations, and he sees no difference between the two. He throws himself into everything with charming earnestness and freedom, which shows the bent of his mind and the range of his knowledge. Who does not love to see a pretty child of his age, with his bright expression of serene content, and laughing, open countenance, playing at the most serious things, or deeply occupied with the most frivolous amusements? He has reached the maturity of childhood, has lived a child's life, not gaining perfection at a cost of his happiness, but developing the one by means of the other. [324]

It is not that Rousseau gives the warrant to all Dramatic Education. In fact, the professional theatre is only justified when it is useful, though he would encourage folk games and dancing. It is rather in that his whole 'natural' thought is based upon the play of the child that he assumes importance for later thinkers.

Basedow, a friend of Goethe, was inspired by Rousseau to start the Philanthropium in Hamburg, a famous school where work and play were to be synonymous. Pestalozzi followed Rousseau in developing what was 'natural' to the child, while Froebel's purpose in setting up his Kindergartens was to provide simple ideas of self-activity and self-expression:

Play is self-active representation of the inner—a representation of the inner from inner necessity and impulse . . .

The plays of childhood are the germinal leaves of all later life; for the whole man is developed and shown in these, in his tenderest dispositions, in his innermost tendencies. The whole later life of man, even to the moment when he shall leave it again, has its source in this period of childhood. [140]

It wanted only Darwin's theory of evolution to provide a scientific basis for what Rousseau and Froebel had already perceived: that the child was a developing organism, that each phase of growth had to be nurtured, and that play was as much part of the developing human being as any other part.

2 DRAMA, PLAY & EVOLUTION

When Darwin's *Origin of Species* was published in 1859, the theory of evolution was not new. But what Charles Darwin did was to place it within such an immense mass of evidence that evolution became the basic philosophical and scientific fact of its age. His theory was twofold: first, that all higher forms of life had evolved from lower forms, and points of similarity were to be observed between the behaviour of men and of animals; and second, that the cause of this evolution was the struggle for existence and the survival of the fittest. While the second part of the theory has been much disputed by biologists, there is, even today, complete acceptance of the theory of evolution as such.

Play, dramatic play and imitation all had to be accounted for within evolutionary theory. If life itself was a process of growth, every action of every living thing had a purpose in this growth and philosophers and thinkers attempted to find evolutionary purposes in play and dramatic play.

THE SCHILLER–SPENCER THEORY

The theory that the play of both animals and men results from the release of 'surplus energy' is generally considered to be the main tenet of Schiller and Herbert Spencer. In fact, the theory had been stated previously by many writers; it was merely incidental with Schiller and was far from original with Spencer.

Schiller

Schiller, the German poet and philosopher, said that play was 'the aimless expenditure of exuberant energy'. This, he considered, would account for some of the apparently aimless activities of birds, animals and insects and, also, for the play of imagination in man:

> No doubt nature has given more than is necessary to unreasoning beings; she has caused a gleam of freedom to shine even in the darkness of animal life. When the lion is not tormented by hunger, and when no wild beast challenges him to fight, his unemployed energy creates an object for himself; full of ardour, he fills the re-echoing desert with his terrible roars and his exuberant force rejoices in itself, showing itself without an object. The insect flits about rejoicing in the sunlight, and it is certainly not the cry of want that makes itself heard in the melodious song of the bird; there is undeniably

freedom in these movements, though it is not emancipation from want in general, but from a determinate external necessity.

The animal *works* when a privation is the motor of its activity, and it *plays* when the plentitude of force is this motor, when an exuberant life is excited to action. [329]

The animal, Schiller considers, has more energy than he needs for the serious purposes of life; so he develops a reserve store of energy which finds its natural outlet in play. Young animals and children, because they are fed and protected by their parents, are not concerned with self-preservation and thus all their energy is 'surplus' in the sense that they use it entirely for play.

This first part of Schiller's theory is clearly suspect. The apparently aimless activities of insects and birds often have a serious purpose, and modern zoologists have shown that all activity by insects, birds and animals that might seem, at first sight, to be purposeless, has a clear and definite end. As far as children are concerned, those who have complete freedom to play will do so until they drop—avoiding calls for meals and oblivious to the passage of time; even when they tire of one game they will happily transfer their gusto to another. The energy they use could hardly be termed 'surplus'.

But Schiller also relates the unhindered use of 'surplus energy' to his idea of the play of imagination in man:

The imagination, like the bodily organs, has in man its free movement and its material play, a play in which, without reference to form, it simply takes pleasure in its arbitary power, and in the absence of all hindrance. These plays of fancy . . . belong exclusively to animal life, and only prove one thing . . . that he is delivered of all external sensuous constraint . . . without our being entitled to infer that there is in it an independent plastic form. [329]

This play has much in common with art which, as he said elsewhere, was the most effective influence in raising man from savagery to civilisation.

The 'surplus energy' theory in no way *accounts* for play, but it can, under certain conditions, describe one of the features of some types of it. The animal or child, free from economic or parental pressures, tends to be active at what he likes to do. All animal life tends to be active which may, indeed, account for the tendency to play.

Spencer

Herbert Spencer's *Principles of Psychology,* published in 1855, was based upon evolutionary theory but was bitterly attacked for stating that acquired characteristics could be inherited. Although it is still a matter of some controversy, some modern psychologists would go so far as to admit that each individual inherits racial characteristics; thus Spencer, to a certain extent, is regarded in a better light than he was some years ago.

Although Spencer subscribes to the 'surplus energy' theory, he does so in his own way, discussing the problem from several points of view, rather than as a rational and logical thinker who analyses facts right out until he reaches a conclusion.

First, he discusses 'surplus energy' and says that species that are no longer struggling for existence have an excess of both time and energy:

> Thus it happens in the more-evolved creatures, there often recurs an energy somewhat in excess of the immediate needs, and there comes also such rest, now of this faculty* and now of that, as permits the bringing of it up to a state of high efficiency by the repair which follows waste. [347]

Living nerve cells in the nervous system are constantly going through a dual process: as activity tears them down, they rebuild themselves and are ready again for action. They become increasingly sensitive to stimulation and, because they are constantly receiving stimuli from the sense organs, there is an overwhelming desire to act whenever the nerve centres are rested. Nerve currents tend to discharge along the lines of least resistance and Spencer says that play activity (driven by 'surplus energy') is directed towards those activities which have a prominent part in the organism's life. Functioning becomes a definite organic need because the 'faculties' are stored with energy:

> Hence play of all kinds . . . Hence this tendency to superfluous and useless exercise of faculties that have been quiescent. Hence, too, the fact that these uncalled-for exertions are most displayed by those faculties which take the most prominent parts in the creature's life. [347]

But he did not consider that 'surplus energy' was the only explanation for play. He discusses, secondly, the fact that there seems to be an

---

* Spencer's use of the word 'faculty' is, historically, in terms of *faculty psychology* where certain faculties (like memory, will, etc.) were seen as entities, rather than (as in modern usage) more general terms for various groups of mental phenomena.

instinctive basis for it. Many later thinkers, particularly McDougall, elaborated on Spencer's concept that the urge for playful activity seems to rest upon instinct.

Thirdly, he finds in play activity a strong tendency to imitate:

> Play is equally an artificial exercise of powers which in default of their natural exercise become so ready to discharge that they relieve themselves by simulated actions. [347]

Thus, if the organism can find no serious activity to engage in, an imitative activity is substituted. The form of imitation, certainly in the higher animals and mankind, is a dramatisation of adult activities: girls playing with dolls and boys playing soldiers are, in fact, playing at what they will be doing seriously at a later time in their lives. Groos later takes up the point about play being training for later life, but denies that play depends on imitation. Play, for Groos, seems spontaneous.

Fourthly, Spencer held that there is a close relationship between art and play—indeed, that art is but one form of play. Their similarity is seen, he said, in that:

> . . . neither subserve, in any direct way, the processes conducive to life. [347]

That is, neither:

> . . . have maintenance of the organic equilibrium of the individual, or else maintenance of the species, as their immediate or remote ends. [347]

While it is true that there is a clear relationship between art and play, it is difficult to hold that they are synonymous, as Ebbinghaus pointed out:

> But play is not identical with art, because it is still too serious a matter. The boy who plays robber and police is not like an actor playing the role of a robber. He really is the robber so far as the advantages, the freedom, and the power of a robber are concerned; and he enjoys these advantages, while the actor does not even think of them. The actor, even while playing the role of a king, desires to play the king, not to be the king. Play, that is, the instinctive activity of play, is intermediate between art and life, a gateway to the former.
> [92]

It is in connection with the relationship of art and play, that Spencer anticipates Groos' theory of practice—by practice in art and play activities, the individual improves his ability to function, and so play becomes a training for later life—but Spencer indicates that it is an incomplete explanation of the play phenomenon: although the exercise of any 'faculty' improves that 'faculty', this is not a distinguishing feature of play for him.

Spencer's fifth main point is that the form which play takes depends on the level of development of the player.* An increased complexity of structural formation brings an increased diversity of play behaviour so that, with man, the forms are almost unlimited. He distinguishes the following broad divisions of play forms:

(a) Superfluous activity of the sensory-motor apparatus. Most commonly this is imitation of the types of activity which an organ carries on when it is pursuing the serious business of life. Play is, therefore, carried on by the parts of the body most significant in the creature's survival:

> And still more interesting in the giraffe, which when free is all day long using its tongue to pull down branches of trees, there arises, when in confinement, so great a need for some kindred exercise that it perpetually grasps with its tongue such parts of the top of its house as can be laid hold of . . . so wearing out the upper angles of the doors, etc. The useless activity of unused organs, which in these cases hardly arises to what we call play, passed into play ordinarily so called where there is more manifest union of feeling with action. [347]

(b) The exercise of higher coordinating powers in both games and exercises.

(c) Mimicry. As the structure of an animal determines what form its play shall take, lower animals will play at the mimic chase and mimic fight. This relates to the mimic dances and accompanying chants of savages.

(d) The highly developed aesthetic products of ancient civilisations resulting in substitute gratification.

(e) Superfluous activity of the sympathies and altruistic sentiments which give rise to fine art, the highest form of play.

He further tries to classify games in three ways: sensory-motor play, games with rules, and artistic-aesthetic play.

Sixth, Spencer pointed out that play can act as a compensatory satisfaction. In this he anticipated the work of later social psychologists who would not doubt that play can be a compensatory device through which satisfaction can be obtained (see pp. 196–7).

* Compare, Lehman and Witty [233] p. 648 et al.

Clearly, Spencer's importance does not merely rest on the 'surplus energy' theory. His interests ranged widely over the whole field of play, anticipating much of other thinkers' work as we shall see. And he stated categorically that, as evolution continued, play was destined to take an increasingly important part in human life.

THE INSTINCT THEORY

Heredity was a basic concept of early evolutionists. The fact that human beings have innate powers, or instincts, which they inherit from generation to generation was a popular concept in the nineteenth century; then, attacked by behaviourist critics (particularly Watson), it was generally discredited in the U.S.A.; despite similar attacks in Britain by such scholars as P. E. Vernon, it has remained a popular theory in this country. To all followers of the instinct theory, play is an instinct: impulses which are inherently part of man's personality and behaviour.

Karl Groos & 'Pre-exercise'

Karl Groos' two detailed books, *The Play of Animals* and *The Play of Man,* provided a complete and elaborate classification of the play of living organisms from the instinctive point of view. The body of his work is still the most scientific and comprehensive examination based upon evolutionary theory. So, too, it produced in its time a most profound effect upon educational thinking by showing how wide is the range covered by play and, also, its value for children, both at the time of the play itself and as training for later life.

Groos first rejects previous concepts, particularly the 'surplus energy' theory; it is insufficient because it cannot explain the different forms of play—that the play of each species differs from every other, and that the play of individuals of any one species shows different forms. Although he takes up Spencer's point about play being a training for later life (and develops it as a main feature of his theory), he denies that it hinges upon imitation:

... the most important and elementary kinds of play can be attributed neither to imitative repetition of the individual's former acts, nor to imitation of the performances of others. [154]

Yet, imitation is still important:

> ... imitation is strongest in the more intelligent animals, such as highly
> developed birds and monkeys, and . . . man may be called the imitative
> animal *par excellence* . . .
>
> Playful imitation, however, must always be connected with 'pleasurable
> interest', and indeed it seems probable that such feelings of pleasure rest on
> the basis common to all play, which a searching examination will discover to
> be experimentation in this case, as well as in the others that we have con-
> sidered. [154]

Imitation 'is an instinct', but it appears spontaneous: the young bird
trying its wings in the nest, or the young antelope, which was born in
captivity, nevertheless trying to leap at six weeks old before it had ever
witnessed such a thing, are given as examples.

Groos provides two quite revolutionary concepts, both of which
have directly affected education. First, he considers that the purpose of
childhood is to provide a period of play. Play, which trains the higher
animals and man for serious living, must take place in a long period of
immaturity in order for it to have its full effect:

> The higher the attainment required, the longer the time of preparation. This
> being the case, the investigation of play assumes great importance. Hitherto
> we have been in the habit of referring to the period of youth as a matter of
> fact only important at all because some instincts of biological significance
> appear then. Now we see that youth probably exists for the sake of play.
> Animals can not be said to play because they are young and frolicsome, *but
> rather they have a period of youth in order to play;* for only by doing so can they
> supplement the insufficient hereditary endowment with individual ex-
> perience, in view of the coming tasks of life.
>
> The animals do not play because they are young, but they have their youth
> because they must play. [154]

Second, he states that play is directly related to the development of
intelligence. Play arises in youth when certain important instincts
appear, and before they are of serious need to the individual and, in this
way, play is necessary for the development of higher intelligence. And
imitation is related to this development:

> The imitative impulse is thus found to be an instinct directly useful in the
> serious work of life among most, and presumably among all, of the higher
> gregarious animals. Its simplest manifestation is the taking flight of a whole
> herd as soon as one member shows fear . . . So we have here an hereditary
> instinct that is even more especially adapted than that of play to render many

other instincts unnecessary, and thus open the way for the development of intelligence along hereditary lines that can be turned to account for the attainment of qualities not inherited . . . many instincts are becoming rudimentary in the higher animals because they are being supplanted by another instinct—imitative impulse. And this substitution is of direct utility, for it furthers the development of intelligence. [154]

It is clear that in his attitude to instinct, Groos takes up a neo-Darwinian position and considers natural selection alone as the principle of development; he denies the inheritance of acquired characteristics, as was held by Lamarck and Spencer. But he uses Spencer's definition of instinct ('complex reflex acts') and argues that, in the course of time, these develop into complex reflex actions which are instinctive. It is this adaptability of instincts which has made this theory important for education. Wood further explains:

Now instincts, according to Groos, are mostly connected with the struggle for life and the preservation of the species. Without play practice it would be impossible for these instincts to develop in the very young. In the lower animals there are undoubtedly some complicated instinctive acts, which are necessary to the existence of the animal, and which are performed by in-herited mechanism without practice. With children, however, instincts appear undeveloped, and with their development goes also the development of intelligence and moral character. In regarding play as the natural and best field for the exercise of instinct we come to its full biological significance. Childhood is in man a proportionately prolonged period because man has to reach a higher development than any other animal.
. . . instincts are not sufficient equipment for life, and the child has to acquire imitatively, and experimentally, a number of capacities adapted to his individual needs. These capacities are variable and inherited, and are capable of a development far surpassing the most perfect instinct.
These capacities are both acquired and developed through play. [394]

Groos' basic position, that play is a preparation (or 'practice') for adult activities and work, certainly applies in the animal kingdom, and in many cases, with primitive man. But it has been attacked in its application to modern man. Patrick says:

If the serious life of today consisted in escaping from enemies by foot, horse, or paddle, in living in close proximity to domestic animals, in pursuit of game with bow or gun, in subsisting on fish caught singly by hand, in personal combat with fist or sword, in throwing missiles, striking with a club or pursuing an enemy, in seeking safety in trees or caves, in living in tents or tree houses, in sleeping and cooking by a campfire, then we might venture to explain the play life of the child as 'an instinctive activity existing for purposes of practice or exercise with serious intent'. [290]

From such a literal standpoint, Groos' view must appear fallacious. If, however, we take the view that play leads to a mastery of the self, both physical and psychological, and develops these abilities to an all-round efficiency in adulthood, then Groos' interpretation of children's play is sound. But he does not account for the play forms of adult life.

It is difficult to see what the idea of 'pre-exercise' adds to the idea of 'exercise'. Play exercises the individual, physically and psychologically; what is exercised is any new acquirement. As Piaget puts it:

> For instance, when at about the age of one the child discovers free fall, he amuses himself by throwing everything to the ground. In this way he exercises his new power, which will one day be integrated in his knowledge of the laws of the physical world, but there is certainly no pre-exercise of his future understanding of physics. [294]

But, if Groos' basic hypothesis may not meet with general approval from empirical psychologists, his vast collection of observations of the play activities of both animals, and men [155], is unrivalled as a basic source of material. Coordinating this material, he evolved the following system of classification:

ANIMAL PLAY:
1. Experimentation (controlling the body and developing perception).
2. Movement plays (practice in locomotion as such).
3. Hunting plays.
4. Fighting plays (teasing, tussling, and playful fighting).
5. Love plays (among young animals, rhythmical movements, display of colours and forms, calls and notes, and coquetry).
6. Constructive arts (building nests, etc.).
7. Nursing plays (fostering).
8. Imitative plays.
9. Curiosity ('the only purely intellectual form of playfulness . . . in the animal world').

HUMAN PLAY
A. *Experimental play,* involving games of general functions such as perception, ideation and emotion. These are divided into:

1. Sensory plays, like those of young children which exercise the sense organs.
2. Motor plays—
   (a) of the body (running, jumping, etc.).
   (b) with a foreign body (like throwing with a ball).
3. Plays involving higher mental powers—
   (a) Intellectual play, making use of memory, recognition, imagination, attention, reasoning (like riddles, chess, etc.).
   (b) Emotional plays, like those involving surprise (hide-and-seek, etc.).
   (c) Volitional plays, involving direct experiment with the will (many contests, games of skill).
B. *Sociometric play,* involving games of special functions like fighting, chasing, courting, social and family games, and imitative play.

This system of classification is according to the content of the game and hinges upon the concept of 'practice', or 'pre-exercise'. Classification according to content, however, has its drawbacks. It is a descriptive method rather than an explanatory one. Although certain elementary games can be classified quite easily (like the sensory games of the baby a few months old, or the purely motor games like throwing stones), the older the child the more difficult it is to place a game in a specific class. Marbles, as Piaget pointed out, may be sensory-motor in its actions, but from 7 or 8 years old it is also a competitive game and, therefore, social. Groos' classification of play and imitation, like his explanation, may have drawbacks but they both provide us with a considerable amount of basic material with which to understand the phenomenon.

'Pre-exercise' & Education

Groos' influence upon teachers is illustrated by Joseph Lee's *Play in Education* which takes the basic tenets of the theory and applies them to education. Lee's preliminary position might be that of Rousseau and of Froebel:

> If the lesson has struck home, the result is not merely more knowledge or more intelligence, but more boy or girl—more of a person there for all purposes. If his arithmetic has truly reached him, he will play better football; if his football has been the real thing, he will do better arithmetic. That is the

nature of a true educational experience—that it leaves a larger personality behind. [231]

To this he relates the theory of 'pre-exercise'. Play is part of the law of growth, in four ways: first, it exercises body and mind in the actions towards which their growth is directed (education in the humanities is that 'which most fully liberates the great human instincts which govern children's play'); second, play activity follows the order of growth and the mental powers are established, instinctively, as play calls for them; third, children develop more fully and normally if they have the opportunity to play than if they have not; and lastly, play always aims beyond existing powers—the child 'practises walking in spite of bumps and failures, not because he can walk but because he can't'—and thus play is a method of learning. But 'the great play instincts' do not all appear at once, nor do they remain static; rather they develop as the organism develops:

> And the first form of an instinct may be very different from that which it is destined finally to become . . . The future architect may find his sense of form first in music or in dancing. The infant statesman is very probably exercising his eloquence in showing that he was not out at first . . . [231]

Dramatic play and impersonation is the child's way of understanding his world, of understanding others:

> The best way to be anybody—to get the feel of him as he is from the inside— is to act out his character and function . . . I believe that the impersonating impulse bequeaths sympathetic insight—the power to see people as they really are, the intuitive sympathy that sees with another's eyes . . . [231]

Rhythm is important: it combines drama, song and dance; it brings a fusion to physical actions and, through repetition, an economy of mental effort; it is our way of recognising units of any sort (like time, number, etc.); it is the basis of social fusion; and it is the common factor in all the arts. With the young adolescent, dramatic play is a method of projecting an ideal of life and conduct:

> . . . if you can get King Arthur to actually enter your soul, and fight for you in the schoolroom and in the playground, he is as valuable an ally as any boy need have . . . (Dramatic imagination) is the first reaching out of the spirit, the first shaping of aspiration . . . [231]

Lee adds nothing to Groos' basic position that play is purposeful; he merely illustrates. Just as in early hunting games when the fun is to get away, later team games concentrate on the end—getting a man out or putting the ball over the line. To them both, play is achievement and it was through instances such as Lee gives that Groos' tenets came into modern education.

The Theory of Catharsis

Followers of the instinct theory, in the early part of this century, took Aristotle's theory of catharsis (as developed by Freud, see pp. 73-4) and applied it to play. Carr [56] said that play was a safety-valve for pent-up emotions. An instinct is associated with an emotion, like fighting with anger or hate, but society may not allow the emotions free reign and they become inhibited; play, by allowing fighting, can release these emotions which will then subside. Karl Groos in a later work [156] adhered to this theory but considered it to have 'a relatively limited importance, in comparison with the purpose of self-development'. That there is a physiological basis to catharsis is illustrated by Mitchell and Mason:

> Another respect in which play can be thought of as having a cathartic effect, although very different from the other, has to do with internal bodily changes which take place in the presence of a fighting situation. Glandular secretions such as adrenalin are inserted into the blood stream which make the individual a better fighting animal, preparing him for great muscular effort, and conditioning his blood to clot more readily if wounded. If self-control is exercised and the accompanying emotions are inhibited, irritability results because of the changes in the organism which these secretions have produced. Engaging in strenuous fighting games serves as a substitute for actual fighting, and the organism is relieved. [260]

This particular aspect of instinct theory has importance for it leads to later concepts of the compensatory factor in play, it has direct relevance to 'child drama', and is related to many concepts of 'depth' psychology.

Later Instinct Theory

Critics of Groos had said, if play was an early ripening of instincts, we would expect that a puppy's fighting play would involve real fighting and an attempt to hurt the playmate. William McDougall [252] stated anew the basic position on instincts and then went on to

answer Groos' critics by saying that play instincts are modified versions
of the original instincts: a puppy playing at fighting is exhibiting
different behaviour from one who is fighting—the affective state of
the basic instinct (in this case, anger) is absent. Thus each instinct exists
in its pure state and, also, in a modified form.

We should note that the instinct theory of motivation has, amongst
its modern adherents, a number of distinguished educationalists and
educational psychologists—including Percy Nunn, Cyril Burt, J. S.
Ross and C. W. Valentine—and that some modern zoological studies
[358] have increased interest in instinct.

PHYSIOLOGICAL THEORIES

The theory of evolution is a biological concept and, in its time, was
one of a whole host of zoological, biological and physiological studies.
Physiology was clearly related to psychology, in that man thinks with
his brain, and in 1830 a major book of physiology was to have considerable effect upon psychological studies. This was Charles Bell's
Nervous System of the Human Body which showed that motor and
sensory functions are performed by different nerve fibres. This not only
enabled later psychologists to present life as a stimulus-response
relationship (Pavlov, Thorndike, Clark Hull, etc.), but it gave a factual
basis to the theory of psycho-physical parallelism or interaction. The
concepts of evolution and a psycho-physical relationship formed a basis
for a number of play theories which, if they did not give as much
emphasis to imitation as the instinct theories, did provide a 'common-
sense' basis for the play phenomenon and a theoretical foundation for
sports and physical play in education.

The Recreation Theory

This theory suggests that play refreshes and restores the physically
and mentally tired. Although the origins for this theory might be
found with Lord Kames, the eighteenth-century English philosopher,
who said:

Play is necessary for man in order to refresh himself after labour [260]

—the more immediate forerunner of this theory was Guts Muths. This
German teacher (called 'the father of physical training') considered that

the natural impulse to activity was the creator of play, the value of which he saw, not only for physical development and training, but also for its recreational results [260]. His twofold classification was between movement plays and rest plays.

The main advocate of the Recreation Theory was Moritz Lazarus, Professor of Philosophy at Berlin in the late nineteenth century, who urged man to:

flee from empty idleness to active recreation in play. [229 & 260]

His basic theory is twofold: first, that after hard work a certain amount of rest and sleep is necessary; and second, that:

When mental and physical powers are tired, man turns to play to recuperate.
[229 & 394]

This simply tells us that when the brain is tired it needs a change, particularly in the form of physical exercise, and this may restore some nervous energy. But, if there is physical fatigue, sleep and rest are required; mental exertion will not help because mental fatigue depends on bodily fatigue. Obviously, this theory is limited; it has little of growth about it; it can apply only to certain types of adult activity; it can scarcely be relevant to children since so much of their life is play.

The theory has some relevance to later sociological theories, and was extended by Patrick into the Relaxation Theory.

The Relaxation Theory

Patrick deliberately concerns himself with adult play forms, for children's play is hardly relaxing. He defines play as activities which are:

... free and spontaneous and which are pursued for their own sake alone. The interest in them is self-developing and they are not continued under any internal or external compulsion. [290]

This he opposes to work where man holds himself down to a given task for the sake of an end to be attained other than through the activity itself. He says that there are similarities between the play of children, the sports of men, and the pursuits of primitive men. This is because:

... *those mental powers upon which advancing civilisation depends, especially voluntary and sustained attention, concentration, analysis, and abstraction, are undeveloped in the child and subject to rapid fatigue in the adult. Hence the child's activities and the play activities of the adult tend always to take the form of old racial pursuits.* [290]

Higher mental processes are fatiguing and relaxation is to be found in 'racially old activities' which 'involve brain tracts that are old, well-worn, and previous'. This type of activity he defines as that which gives exercise to the larger muscles and 'the more elemental forms of mentality'.

Although he questions the validity of the Theory of Recapitulation, his own work bears some resemblance to it in his insistence upon 'race habits' and 'racial memory' as the explanation of play motivation. Primitive man depended on wild and domestic animals and this is reflected in the child's animal books, animal plays and Teddy Bears, and:

> The child's first musical instruments, the rattle, the drum and the horn, were the first musical instruments of primitive man. [290]

He explains popular sport as a memory of the ancient battlefield: football is a mimic battle and the spectators, by inner imitation, both participate and give unrestrained expression to their emotions. This view has much ethnological support, as have his views that dancing involves the fundamental muscles and, therefore, the brain patterns which have been the earliest developed.

His argument is that ball-games, dancing, and similar activities relax the higher brain by activating the basic brain patterns. While this, in itself, may or may not be true, his comments upon racial memory, the nature of sports and dancing, and the relationship of the brain to activity in the larger muscles, all have significance to the sociological theories of play and drama.

The Recapitulation Theory

More a speculation than a theory, G. Stanley Hall's concept of Recapitulation is both physiological and evolutionary. It rests on heredity. He says that man inherits tendencies of muscular coordination that have been of racial utility, and in play:

> ... we rehearse the activities of our ancestors, back we know not how far, and repeat their life work in summative and adumbrated ways. It is reminiscent, albeit unconsciously, of our line of descent ... [165]

He directly opposes Groos' concept that play is 'practice' for the future. Rather, the boy who fights when he is young will not have a strong urge to fight when he is a man (as this has some relationship to catharsis, it is interesting to note that Hall was the first man to invite Freud to lecture in the U.S.A.).

There are three essential points to Recapitulation. First, play content changes as age progresses; each age group has a different set of games the content of which is relatively constant; and each stage is reached by the child at relatively constant ages. Second, play content corresponds to ancestral activities which have followed one another in the same order throughout evolution; third, play frees man from ancestral residues and, at the same time, hastens his development towards higher stages.

The successive culture patterns in man's history which are echoed in children's play have been developed by various American writers, and are:

1. Animal Stage—children imitating, climbing, swinging, hanging, paddling.
2. Savage Stage—hunting plays, tag, hide-and-seek, throwing with a stick (baseball and cricket).
3. Nomad Stage—keeping pets, running away, playing in huts at the bottom of the garden.
4. Agricultural/Patriarchal/Early Settlement Stage—dolls, gardening, digging sand, modelling.
5. Tribal life—team games.

Clearly, any classification of this type is based upon the interpretation of play itself, and cannot be separated from it.

Like his contemporaries G. T. W. Patrick and Joseph Lee, G. Stanley Hall emphasised the importance of rhythm, its link with the dance, and the importance of both for education:

> In the dark background of history there is now much evidence that at some point, art and work were not divorced. They all may have sprung from rhythmic movement which is so deep-seated in biology because it secures most joy of life with least expense . . .
>
> Dancing is one of the best expressions of pure play and of the motor needs of youth. Perhaps it is the most liberal of all forms of motor education . . . (and), not excepting music, the completest language of the emotions. [165]

It is fair to say that the basis for the Theory of Recapitulation is regarded as fallacious. It is not considered that play content evolves: Lehman and Witty have shown [233] that the content of games varies with the environment. The theory that play recapitulates cultural epochs is not regarded as proven: known primitive tribes do not progress uniformly; nor can it be shown that man lives over, in such a precise way, the order of evolution. Hall's is a static theory, too, looking more to the past than towards growth.

At the same time, man cannot separate himself from the past and there are some patterns of behaviour which bear resemblances to racially old behaviours. The sociological approach to dramatic education considers these to be of considerable importance.

Later Physiological Theory

Recapitulation, like many imaginative but fallacious ideas, brought about a great many detailed and valuable experimental studies. Some were carried out in direct liaison with Stanley Hall—like those of Gulick, Croswell, and McGhee [165]—while others grew out of the theory itself, like that of Appleton.

L. Estella Appleton produced *A Comparative Study of the Play Activities of Adult Savages and Civilised Children* [13], using five representative savage tribes and five representative groups of American children. She found: that savages and children both play in violent exercise and with the whole body, but that the children had a keener sensitivity and more specialised muscular control; that the character of savage play compares to that of children between the ages of 7 and 15, for both contain 'sensory elements', 'rhythm', 'mimicry', 'dramatic representation', 'skill',' the practical judgement', and 'individual competition'; but that, intellectually, savage play compares to the play of American children between the ages of 6 and 10.

As a result of her findings, Appleton modified Hall's concept to a theory of play based on physiological growth: 'Play is an instinct'; it is the 'impulse to act' which must satisfy the needs of the growing body, and play precedes the ability to function and gives rise to it. Thus play leads to growth. But the emphasis differs from that of Groos: he considered instincts led to activity which is practice for life; Appleton thought that the hunger for growth (play) led to action which stimulated growth and is, also, practice for life.

While it is true that play depends upon the nature of the body, a thorough-going physiological theory is virtually untenable, as we can see from the work of typological psychologists like Kretschmer [222] and Sheldon [338] who attempt to maintain that behaviour varies with certain types of body structure. On the other hand, human activity is physiologically based and all theories of motivation must take the findings of neurophysiology into account, as well as up-to-date information from encephalography and cybernetics.

Genetic Theory

Modern studies in the genetics of behaviour show that behaviour patterns are transmitted over generations. The basic units of heredity are genes, located on the chromosomes, which are found in pairs on the nucleus of each cell. The specific genetic constitution of the individual (genotype) interacts with the environment to produce the phenotype with specific characteristics of height, intelligence, emotionality, etc. It is genes that are inherited, not the phenotypes. The genotype determines the potentialities of the individual; the environment determines which, or how much, of these potentialities shall be realised during development.

Johan Huizinga's *Homo Ludens* examines the genetic aspect of play [186]. Genes transmit the *tendency* to play and the organism has need for this. But play is more than a mere physical phenomenon and a psychological reflex: it has a serious element and is significant for the genetic development of the species.

Huizinga considers that modern civilisation has separated play from life. It is no longer part of every man's cultural activities but is relegated to mere sport and similar occupations which are isolated from the fabric of the process of living. Genetically, play is an integral part of life and to isolate it as modern man has done is to destroy the true, natural spirit and the ultimate value of play to man and society.

It will be seen that the concept of evolution has led to two major theories of motivation—instinct and physiology. Both see play as a tendency, to which imitation and dramatic play are related, whose action is to further the growth of the organism. Some thinkers offer a partial explanation of play (like surplus energy, pre-exercise, recreation or relaxation) or an imaginative interpretation of it (like recapitulation). But none of these philosophic concepts can provide us with a complete definition of the terms play, dramatic play, and imitation. More information must be sought from the psychological and sociological sciences before such definitions can be attempted.

3 DRAMA & PLAY IN MODERN EDUCATION

It was not until the middle of the nineteenth century that drama came to play a significant part in education once more. Much of this change was due to evolutionary theories which indicated that growth was natural, and that each stage of growth had to be completed before the next could be begun. Historically, the resuscitation of drama in education occurred when the children of Queen Victoria and Albert performed *Athalie* and other plays in their original languages. From then on, it grew more common for grammar schools to aid language study through the performance of plays in those languages: for example, Bradfield's triennial Greek play, first performed in 1881, still continues. But there were also performances of Shakespeare, and other theatrical entertainments. The professional theatre, too, had been given the chance to grow once the monopoly of the Patent Theatres had been broken in 1843 and, from that date, the story is one of continuous development—from Macready to Irving, from Robertson through Gilbert, Henry Arthur Jones, Pinero and Wilde to Bernard Shaw. But educationally, the great advance came with the twentieth century.

STAGES IN PAIDOCENTRIC EDUCATION

'Learning by Doing' & 'Learning by Drama'

Paidocentric education, or education from the child's point of view, was a term coined by Sir John Adams. From just before the turn of the century, a series of new methods and ideas came to amplify Rousseau's dictum: 'Consider the man in the man and the child in the child'. This was the point of view of John Dewey in America:

> ... the primary root of all educative activity is in the instinctive, impulsive attitudes and activities of the child, and not in the presentation and application of external material, whether through the ideas of others or through the senses; and that, accordingly, numberless spontaneous activities of children, plays, games, mimic efforts ... are capable of educational use, nay, are the foundation-stones of educational methods. [87]

As a result, many schools came to experiment with such methods: Dewey's own Laboratory School; the Porter School, near Kirksville,

Missouri, where Marie Harvey worked with groups, on projects, and used a little free dramatisation; and the Dalton School, New York, established in 1916, where much of the girls' 'learning by doing' (Dewey's catch phrase) reached its culmination in some form of dramatic activity.

The formulation of the basic idea that dramatic activity was a very effective method of learning, was largely due to Caldwell Cook. Working at the Perse School, Cambridge, before the First World War, his 'play way' approach gave the name to the movement. About the same time, John Merrill was working with similar methods at the Francis W. Parker School in the United States: oral work and simple improvisations were seen as methods for teaching language and literature, but not in such a comprehensive way as that of Cook. About the same time, William Wirt developed the Gary, Indiana, Plan which emphasised the use of a school auditorium for the 'work-study-play' concept of education—oral communication was developed through dramatic activities.

Education Through Play

The next stage was the concept that natural play was educationally important just for itself. Although this was said by thinkers as far apart as Plato, Rabelais, Rousseau and Dewey, the putting of it into practice had to wait until the second half of the twentieth century. By the 1920s and '30s, schools were experimenting with free play, particularly with 5—7-year-old children: in Britain with teachers like E. R. Boyce, who wrote *Play in the Infants' School* [38]; and in the United States with Winifred Ward, who wrote *Creative Dramatics* [374]. The latter gave its name to the whole movement in the U.S.A. [339] and is basically a combination of 'the play way', free play and children's theatre. In the 1930s, the movement went on apace with many 5—11-year-old children both having free dramatic activity and using 'the play way'. Interesting developments took place in other fields—as with the unemployed men in industrial conurbations by Robert G. Newton [275]—but it was not until after the Second World War, with the reorganisation of British education, that the next stage of the evolution came.

Meanwhile, this sort of creative development had been paralleled in the other arts. The concept of 'child art' enabled teachers to stop

instructing 9-year-olds in perspective and to let them 'express themselves' in paint. Unfortunately, 'free expression' became for a while a
synonym for freedom from discipline and for some time the general
creative movement was frowned on by conservative teachers. However, it slowly became obvious that spontaneous activity did not
necessarily mean the child returned to his animal activity, that the
teacher could lead the child towards an inner discipline and still
maintain the benefits of spontaneity training. And so, the creative arts
began to take their place as an essential part of education. Like Rousseau,
the creative movement looked at the child as a child. Like Dewey, it
saw that experience, 'doing', was an essential element in the process.
But all was then seemingly solved under the all-inclusive banner of
'self-expression'. If the question was asked, 'Self-expression of what?',
workers in the field as experienced as Caldwell Cook, Harriet Finlay-
Johnson, Winifred Ward, or Robert G. Newton, could only provide
a partial answer.

Drama Today

The answer came after the Second World War, but was based on a
concept of Sir Percy Nunn in 1922. He had said:

> Imitation is the first stage in the creation of individuality, and the richer the
> scope for imitation the richer the developed individuality will be. [280]

That dramatic play is the individual, human quality led two teachers to
develop concepts that were to alter the whole structure of dramatic
activity in schools: Peter Slade postulated that 'child drama' was an art
form in its own right, with its own place as a subject within a school;
and E. J. Burton said that dramatic activity was the human being's
method of assimilating experience and was, therefore, basic to all
education. Here were two ways of looking at the problem, diverse yet
complementary, which have enabled the education system in Britain
and America to forge ahead in the most striking manner.

In British schools today, most of the time of 5—7-year-olds is spent
in play, and many Juniors (7—11) have special periods for dramatic
play and others for the dramatic method. In Secondary schools (11+)
there is a steady growth: there were few specialist drama teachers in
1948 but, in 1966, there was a whole host of schools with special periods
of Drama on the timetable. In America, the story is similar amongst

younger children though, as Winifred Ward said in 1961 [378], free
dramatic play has not made great inroads into Junior High Schools.

    The same development is observable in the training of teachers. In
1955, there were ninety-two colleges offering complete courses in
'creative dramatics' in the United States, as well as many other courses
where the subject was part [297]. In 1964 one quarter of all English
Colleges of Education were offering Drama as a main subject [73].

    But, because dramatic activity is such an individual thing, there are
many approaches in education. At the same time, they do all coalesce
into one entire concept—Dramatic Education.

DRAMATIC APPROACHES TO EDUCATION

The Play Way (The Dramatic Method)

    The earliest statement of the dramatic method was that of Caldwell
Cook in *The Play Way* (1917). Previously, dramatic work in a school
had been concerned with the production of a play or the use of simple,
read dialogue in a Latin or French lesson. Cook looked at the matter
differently: he said that acting was a sure way to learn. In the study of
History, for example, the method was to use the text-book as a
stimulus (as the basis for a history story) which the children then acted
—their 'make-believe' enabled them to really understand (and thus
learn) the facts of history. Cook's method was founded on three basic
principles:

> 1. Proficiency and learning come not from reading and listening but from
> action, from *doing,* and from experience.
> 2. Good work is more often the result of spontaneous effort and free interest
> than of compulsion and forced application.
> 3. The natural means of study in youth is play. [70]

With Shakespeare, the boys had already had the chance to see over
their parts, the stage managers were appointed, the property men
organised, and the boy with the knobkerry (who banged it loudly if a
mistake was made) was detailed, before the lesson. Then, in the classroom, Shakespeare was acted, with real actions and objects on the
imitation stage; Cook's boys did not read the play round the class, nor
did they just learn lines by heart and use hired costumes. They acted it
spontaneously before their peers. Although he thought ballads were

best for boys under 10, and Shakespeare after that age, the children were led to write their own plays—and from there he led to painting, modelling, drawing, language teaching, and small lectures. The teacher was not there to impart instructions but, basically, was a leader assisting the boys to develop their expressive abilities and their inherent self-discipline.

From that time, the play way method of teaching all subjects in the curriculum gathered pace. The various editions of the *Handbooks for Teachers* (first from the Board of Education and, later, the Ministry of Education) advocated the dramatic method for speech, history, literature, art, and other subjects. In 1950 *The Story of a School* handbook [160], described how A. L. Stone geared the whole work of a specific Junior school to dramatic movement: expressive movement became dance, movement producing vocal expression became drama, movement for strength or skill became physical education, and movement in relation to objects and things became the basis of the arts and crafts.

The play method of teaching is the basic element in all English Infant schools today and, in many Junior schools, the majority of lessons are taken in this manner. The extent to which it is used with children of eleven years and older varies considerably: in the more formal, academic school it hardly exists; in the freer, more experimental schools quite a large proportion of the curriculum can be taken up with such activities.

Creative Drama

In 1954, Peter Slade published his *Child Drama,* based on experimental work he had been doing for twenty years. His thesis was that there was an art form, 'child drama', in the same sense that 'child art' exists in its own right, and that it could take its place in the curriculum alongside Music, Art, Literature and the like. Here, then, was a claim, not that dramatic activity could be used as a method of teaching other things, but that it was a separate 'subject' with its own place on a school timetable.

The baby's early experiments with movement and sound are embryonic forms of drama, art and music, and the child is more absorbed than in mere copying. By one year of age, Slade says, there are signs of the game appearing, often accompanied by a sense of

humour, and this develops into forms of impersonation. Examples of
the embryo art forms are:

> ... sucking a finger whilst at table and describing a circle with a wet finger
> on the table ... is more obviously Art. Clenching the wet fist and banging
> the table with meaning (e.g. 'more food') is more obviously Drama, whilst
> banging the table with a clear interest in the sound value and time beat only,
> is more obviously Music. [342]

The toddler begins to move in a circle, often round and round on a
given spot by means of a dancing step—'This is our first clear link with
the dance of primitive communities'. It is at this time, too, that the
child experiments with rhythm and time beat, often differentiating
between the two in his experiments. As this is related to action there
are embryonic Music and Drama developing together.

He distinguishes between two forms of play, both of them dramatic:
personal and projected play. In personal play, the whole person is used
in movement and characterisation; there is a tendency towards noises
and physical exertion, and the child is acting in a real sense—developing
towards running and ball-games, fighting and dance, swimming and
acting. In projected play, the mind is used more than the body, and the
child 'projects' an imagined dramatic situation outwards onto objects
with great absorption; there is a tendency towards quietness and
stillness—developing towards art and the playing of music, reading
and writing, observation and patience.

Amongst the many values that drama has is an emotional one, and
Slade is firmly committed to the fact that dramatic play provides a
child with 'a great safety-valve'—an emotional catharsis:

> It offers continual opportunities for playing out evil in a legal framework ...
> [342]

In providing emotional release, it also offers opportunity for emotional
control, and thus it provides an inner self-discipline. 'Child drama' is
characterised by 'language flow': spontaneous speech sound which is
stimulated by the improvisation, and enriched by the acting. The
natural dramatic play of children develops in terms of space: the
youngest child plays in a circle, by about eight years old in a horse-shoe
shape, and only with adolescence does he act at one end (sometimes on
a stage). Thus 'theatrical' values are of secondary consideration and only
introduced to children as they are old enough to absorb them. As the

child grows older he gradually needs an audience. Thus there is a kind
of drama for every child at a particular age, and education must
provide him with a developing dramatic experience.

Slade's concepts have been developed and re-exploited by himself
and other members of the Educational Drama Association over recent
years. Brian Way, in particular, has developed this approach [400] in
many educational areas with the most exciting and stimulating work
even, in his Theatre Centre, relating a professional company to the
educational situation. Stanley Evernden, at Loughborough College of
Education, has pioneered 'child drama' in teacher-training and summarises its aims as:

1. to move and speak confidently and appropriately in a wide variety of
   situations;
2. to explore situation, character and mood, etc. (preparing for life by
   rehearsing it—growth of the sympathetic imagination);
3. to 'play out' distorted and immature notions, in order to make room for
   sounder and maturer ones;
4. to gain practice in self-discipline and cooperation with others in the
   creative use of freedom (incidental social training);
5. to gain specific training in social behaviour (e.g. directing strangers,
   ordering a meal, interviews, etc.);
6. to expend their own resources and so become ready for fresh learning
   ('enrichment from without');
7. to base their acting, if and when they come to theatre, on sincere being and
   doing, rather than on techniques for seeming and showing. [101]

With 'child drama' the key question is: does dramatic play provide
an emotional catharsis? This hinges upon the relationship between
dramatic play and the unconscious, and the relationship of play and
imitation—both factors we shall examine below.

It is interesting to compare 'child drama' with Winifred Ward's
'creative dramatics', for their ideas have had considerable impact in
Britain and the Commonwealth, on the one hand, and in the United
States on the other. In a recent statement [378] Ward showed that with
5—7-year-olds there was not much difference in approach: she used
rhythms for children's creative play and impersonation; there was an
emphasis upon sense awareness, and the children freely created simple
plays from stories. However, by the Intermediate stage (approx.
7—11 years old) Ward places more emphasis upon dramatic activity

as a method—as motivation for social studies, oral communication and language. In many ways, her approach is similar to Slade's:

> Though it is not considered questionable to share a creative play occasionally with parents and the school, the nature of improvised work is such that if exhibition is its objective, the educational purpose is largely defeated. [378]

Yet she places much more emphasis upon drama as a method and many of her followers emphasise the Children's Theatre to a much larger extent than does Slade.

The common element in this approach is improvisation, creative drama. The children are creating their own stories and impersonations as *they* require them. If improvisation concerns story and impersonation, it also involves creative movement and speech—two elements that have had particular emphasis in recent years.

Creative Movement

Movement experience provided for children in school includes physical education, games, athletics, swimming, outdoor pursuits, dance and drama. All of these, except the last two, concentrate upon functional movement. In dance and drama the child is concerned with expressive movement and, in recent years, the educational connection between them has been stressed. This has largely been due to the pioneer work of Rudolf Laban whose 'modern educational dance' has had a large impact in some educational quarters.

Laban saw that dance played a considerable role in everyday life in ancient times but that primitive forms of communal dancing, as with natives from other continents, are strange to us and cannot serve as a model or an inspiration. And so, basing his ideas upon the free flow of movement inherent in the dancing of Isadora Duncan, Laban attempted to evolve a form of movement expression which contained:

> . . . the richness of liberated movement-forms, gestures and steps, as well as in the use of movements which contemporary man uses in his everyday life.
> [226]

He saw that the first task for education was to foster the urge for movement and, thereafter, that dance consists of movement-sequences in which a definite effort of the moving person underlies each movement. He distinguished eight basic efforts—wring, press, glide, float, flick, slash, punch and dab—each of which contains three of the six movement elements: strong, light, sustained, quick, direct, and flexible. These distinctions, he considered, should not in any way destroy the spontaneity of movement which is essential in the awakening of a broad outlook on human activities through the observation of the flow of movement used in them.

That there is a direct link between 'modern educational dance' and drama is obvious. Perhaps the most influential work in this field is *Leap to Life* [390] which describes the work of Alan Garrard with adolescents. Based on Laban's analysis of movement, Garrard evolved a form of Dance Drama where the purely creative movement of the children spontaneously grew into creative drama. Not that this was new: many teachers had been working in this field for many years—indeed, much of Slade's work describes spontaneous movement drama with young children. The difference lay in Garrard's use of Laban's technique, and allowing the children to work within such a technical frame in order to produce spontaneous drama.

In recent years there has been much work in this field. Lisa Ullmann at the Movement Studio at Addlestone, Surrey, has broadened the whole scope of Laban's work. There have been most interesting experiments in the relationship between Physical Education, Movement and Drama in many areas of the country: Devonshire, for example, have built special Studios to combine these activities in a number of their schools. And many teachers of Dramatic Education have utilised creative movement as part of their syllabus.

Creative Language

That there is a direct relationship between the dramatic imagination and creative writing, language and speech has been recognised throughout this century: Caldwell Cook's play way included not only the acting of Shakespeare, painting and craft work, but also creative playmaking and the writing of poetry; Slade stressed the 'language flow' resulting from child drama; and Laban said that movement was the foundation for all expression—whether it be speaking, writing, singing, painting or dancing. Even so traditional a vehicle as the *Handbook for Teachers in Elementary Schools* could say:

... it is certain that drama is a most effective method for improving the

3

clarity and fluency of children's speech. It should be realised that drama is a
good deal more than this. In the school it may be appropriately defined as a
training, a study, and an art. It is excellent discipline in speech and self-
confidence. It affords remarkable opportunities for active literary study and
it is a natural and effective mode of artistic expression for a child. [159]

Foremost amongst those who see the relationship of drama to
creative language is Marjorie Hourd. She points out that the under-5-
year-old at play is using identification:

> The child at this age identifies things with people (it is a Mother stick and a
> Father stick), and people with himself. It seems as though it is not until this
> identification with objects and people has taken place that the child is able to
> sever himself from them . . . This is where dramatisation comes in. It is one
> of the means by which the child gradually learns to isolate himself . . .
> Dramatisation is at once the means by which he ventures out into the
> characters and lives of others, and the means by which he draws these back as
> symbols into the person of himself. [181]

This she sees as the basis for the imaginative sympathy by which the
older child identifies with many different kinds of people in poems and
stories, novels and plays. From this basis she traces the development of
all types of creative writing, but particularly playmaking and 'creative
writing' of poetry and prose [182].

She develops the following scheme of human expression:

CREATIVE ENERGY

(Rising from instinctual sources chiefly libidinous)

SPONTANEITY
(The accessibility of this power
for personality)

AESTHETIC EXPERIENCE
(The contemplation of the
patterns and forms of existence)

IMAGINATION
(A unifying function based upon:
(a) the cognition processes of relation and correlation;
(b) the conative urge towards
reconciliation, especially of
opposite emotions and feelings)

ORIGINALITY
(The highest operation of the
cognitive function of imagination, essential to any significant
work of art)

SUBLIMATION	FORM
(The use of the energy of a sexual impulse in the conquest of reality)	(Medium yields its incompleteness to the generating impulses of ideas; and through the poet's artistry acting upon it, form results)

IDENTIFICATION   FANTASY   DRAMATISATION
            SYMBOLISM   METAPHOR

(These are the means by which the individual seeks to unite his own ego needs with the demands of reality, hence they are all closely connected with sublimation.) [181]

This interesting scheme of the creative process underlies her approach to creative education as a whole and creative language in particular. But the initial 'spark' with young children is dramatic. Not that literature as a whole is dramatic—there is a clear difference between the play and poetry, the novel, and other forms—but the dramatic sense is always there for young children whether they are reading silently or being read to. Often dramatisation of a most powerful and mentally active kind takes place in the classroom where an untrained observer might only be conscious of a passive listening. She further points out that, as Freud had indicated, the latent content of dreams is dramatically created into the condensed form of dream thought (see p. 65) and it is the sublimated release of this dramatic material through form that results in the creative work of art.

The School Play

Throughout this century the popularity of the school play has been growing. Formerly it was an annual event and, even today in certain schools, this is all it may remain. Yet there has been an increasing movement towards more than one play in a year presented to the public and, often, there are house plays and even form plays in addition. To begin with it was largely the prerogative of the public and grammar schools who usually performed a standard classic. However, with the broadening of English education, the movement has become widespread and all types of drama are presented—from classics in the original language to Shakespeare, and from modern plays to improvised dramas. All types of presentation are used: not merely the

proscenium or end stage, but in arena and open shapes, as well as many
of their variants.

In addition, there are two other developments of importance. First,
fewer younger children are performing in front of the public. Thirty
years ago it was common to see 5—6-year-olds performing a Nativity
play at Christmas time. But psychological theory has shown that for a
child to perform in front of an audience before he is ready for it may do
him positive harm—may produce 'showing off' instead of the spirit of
cooperation and team-spirit which is essential to absorbed dramatic
play—and, as a result, young children are acting in public productions
far less frequently than used to be the case. Second, the school play is
seen as one part only of dramatic education. At the beginning of this
century, it may have been the *only* dramatic activity of the school.
Today it runs alongside classroom work—the formal 'theatre' grows
naturally out of creative drama and play [76].

Beyond the school, three types of theatrical work have developed:
the youth theatre, the children's theatre, and the community theatre.
After initial experiments in many countries, a number of youth
theatres were begun in Yorkshire after the end of the Second World
War and voluntary groups of young people came together, under
trained leaders, to present plays to the public. There is now a National
Youth Theatre, under Michael Croft, and many large conurbations
are providing similar facilities: the Enfield Youth Theatre, for example,
exists alongside a dramatic education programme organised by the
local education authority. Children's theatres are companies performing specifically to audiences of children; the majority are professional
players, but some consist of children performing to children. In
Britain, this movement began in London under Sir Ben Greet in 1918,
while Bertha Waddell founded her famous Scots company in 1927.
Léon Chancerel initiated a similar movement in France, and there have
been many experiments in the U.S.A., Canada, New Zealand, Russia,
Sweden, and elsewhere [67]. Community theatres serve the local area
and are common in Russia and Eastern Europe while, in the United
States, they are often associated with universities. In the United
Kingdom, there has been a slow but steady growth of such theatres
since 1955, particularly in large conurbations; perhaps the largest of
such schemes is that of John English for the City of Birmingham.

The Philosophic Basis

At the same time that the various dramatic approaches have been made to practical classwork in recent years, a philosophic basis has been evolving. It has grown naturally out of previous thought. It is paidocentric, and in the direct line from Rousseau and Dewey. It is Nietzschian in that it denies the reality of abstract laws and bases itself upon the process of living. It is related to, though not the same as, Existentialism—even Herbert Read [306] can oppose functional education by an appeal to Heidegger (who considered that our essence is in our existence)—and at the same time, in making its judgements from known facts and its denial of 'system', Dramatic Education is based on an empirical method of thought.

H. J. Blackman, James Britton and E. J. Burton said:

> The danger of classification of any kind is that, starting as a convenient generalization, it comes to be pursued in place of the living complexity it attempted to summarize, and working is dictated by the generalization instead of by the actual existing situations. [32]

Burton extended this by saying it is impossible for us to create a 'philosophy', as previously known, for we are within the scheme we are trying to assess:

> . . . it is not for us to say that human beings should, or should not, respond in this or that way. They *do*—or *do* not. And this acceptance of life in totality is our starting principle. [52]

These thinkers reject education when it is seen as a training in reason, will, conscience, taste, or sensibilities and emotions. Rather, activity is the centre. Education must be concerned with the attitudes and ideas which the child has about any activity in which he is engaged. It is through these ideas that the child uses initiative in developing his activities or in profiting from them, exercising himself by organising and learning from his experience so that the whole activity becomes a personal project, continuous, cumulative, and multi-dimensional.

It is in this sense that, for Burton, drama is the vital part of all education. If life itself is:

> . . . . total experience, assessed, tested, and recognised, and established in its own terms by (a) previous (b) other and (c) further experience . . . [52]

—then the material of drama only has validity within the 'living process':

> . . . the dramatic activities and approaches of mankind, including those of
> children, can only be assessed *in terms of the areas of experience they cover,* their
> *own* manifestations, and their *own* results . . . In other words, theatre (and for
> that matter all art) and the basic activities, such as dramatic play . . . can be
> assessed and described only *in their own terms* . . . What one cannot do is, in
> the name of some theory, to prescribe assured boundaries or to try to compre-
> hend all within categorical terms drawn *from some other branch of human study.*
> . . . Drama is greater than any studies based upon it; and life is greater than
> drama which depends on, lives within, and seeks to learn from it, as an active
> and ever developing process. [52]

Thus all branches of learning are subordinate to the total experience. But, as life is ideally a matter of total awareness and the adjustment of each individual to the total environment:

> Dramatisation, simulated doing, to record, assess, and to experiment further,
> whether by individual, group or community, is a means by which this total
> awareness and continuing and repeated adjustment is more nearly approached
> and gradually . . . achieved. [52]

Total awareness is something towards which we grow, and drama is the method by which we do it, for it is:

> . . . a large-scale laboratory of life examination and study. [52]

Drama is involved in all educational processes. It underlies all primitive education, in the form of trying out the affairs of life; when formalised in the initiation ceremony it brought the adolescent (by 'doing' within the sphere of culture patterns, actions performed, and words said and remembered) into a relationship with the community and the tasks of the environment. Through all human existence, drama is:

> . . . the universal method of 'trying out' and planning the future enterprises,
> from the dance to be attended, the interview to be suffered, the lesson to be
> planned—even though in the more sophisticated adult the 'trying out' is
> merely 'visualised' *as a series of actions.* [52]

This is not a concept which is as literal as Groos' 'pre-exercise': rather, it is that drama is an experiment with life, here and now. The infant improvising, playing dramatically, is experimenting with the nature of objects, the probabilities and limiting factors of the event, and the details of the process:

Every action challenges thought and recollection, precision . . . [47]

Where the infant 'pretends' to make a garden, and plays at it dramatically, the adult faced with the reality does the same thing imaginatively but without the externalised play. Thus the development of cognition is related to dramatic action:

> . . . the ability to work in abstractions can itself be conceived as derivative of working in 'imaginative' doing. [52]

The higher mental processes have their roots in sense experience and the relationship between the senses and intelligence must be maintained. What are we doing when we ask a child to improvise a scene in a desert? We are asking him to recollect his earlier observations: what sand is like, how does it feel to be walking in it, to recollect hot sunshine, thirst, and being overwhelmingly tired; the process of recall leads to imaginative experience. Imaginative experience is based on memory which, in itself, is based on observation—exactly the same process as that involved in abstract thought. But dramatic action is also the basis for later sensitivity and artistic experience, for the appreciation of the conditions of existence and of human needs. And it is also the mainspring from which 'arts' and 'sciences' originate:

> Drama, whether child play or the most advanced production, bases on observation, experience, and what we esteem 'truth'. (i) We observe and experience. Perceiving relationships, patterns, and rhythms, from such observation and experience the artist, in whatever medium, achieves his 'work of art'. (ii) Again, we observe and experience. We examine in more detail, following closely related phenomena, disregarding irrelevancies, and establishing through measurement and experiment certain patterns of behaviour and events. So we reach—through the ability to explore and to accept the world as experienced, and to coordinate observation—the disciplines and achievements of science. [47]

The Scope of Dramatic Education

Dramatic Education is paidocentric, it begins with the child. It recognises him for who he is. It does not, as in the eighteenth century, see him as a miniature adult. Nor does it, as in some American approaches, begin with the concept and then bring this down to the child. Rather, it recognises that the child *is* what he is—that his creative

₅₅

matic in character. It starts with the child as he is and
complete and whole; it recognises that the child's play
itself, of its own value. It is an evolutionary approach
t necessarily instinctual, considers that there is a physio-
sychological basis for it.

ces all creative dramatic approaches to education. It ack-
nowledges that child drama exists and is the method whereby the
child grows up and matures. It recognises that the dramatic imagination
enables the child (and the adult in a different way) to see the relationship between ideas and to see their mutual inter-*action,* and that,
through impersonation and identification, he can comprehend and
realise the world around him. Thus it is important that he can express
himself through creative movement and spontaneous speech and language and, also, use these within identification to relate himself to his
environment. Further, Dramatic Education considers that theatrical
disciplines enable the adolescent and the adult, under certain conditions,
to grow and develop in the same way that dramatic play assists the
younger child.

Drama is the basis of all creative education. From it all arts flow.
Earliest man expressed himself dramatically first: he danced in mimesis,
creating sounds. Thereafter he needed art to paint himself, or cover
himself with animal skins, or magically represent his actions on cave
walls; and music was essential to provide the rhythm and time for his
dramatic dance. The child 'pretends' and in his 'make-believe' he
needs the arts of music, dance, art and crafts. Dramatic expression
provides the other arts with meaning and purpose for the child.
Spontaneous creativity is based upon sense experience and, whether we
approach it psychodramatically or synectically, spontaneity is based
upon the dramatic imagination.

The dramatic imagination lies behind all human learning, both
social learning and 'academic' learning. It is the way in which man
relates himself to life, the infant dramatically in his external play, and
the adult internally in his imagination. This is what Freud means when
he says that dramatic play enables the child to 'master' his environment,
and what Burton means when he says that drama is an experiment with
life here and now. It teaches us to think, to examine and explore, to
test hypotheses and discover 'truth'. Thus it is the basis of science as well
as art. But, also, because it relates us dramatically to knowledge,
providing us with a significant and realisable relationship to 'content',

Dramatic Education uses the method which enables us when we are young to learn 'academically'—a method we retain when we are adults even though we may not know it.

Dramatic Education is a way of looking at education as a whole. It sees that the dramatic imagination is the most vital part of human development, and so it fosters this and helps it grow. It asks that we re-examine our whole educational system—the curricula, the syllabuses, the methods and the philosophies by which these develop. In all aspects, we must start from acting: not acting which implies an audience, but acting as improvisation—the spontaneous make-believe inherent in all children. For nothing is alive to us, nothing has reality in its utmost sense, unless it is quickened and vitalised when we *live* it— when we *act* it. Then it becomes part of our inner selves. Dramatic Education is at the basis of all education that is child centred. It is the way in which the life process develops and, without it, man is merely one of the upper primates.

Further, it provides a necessary 'new look' to the educational process of the twentieth century. Many of our methods and treatments are derived from systems conceived a century or more ago. Throughout Western civilisation, our young people are facing problems (social, intellectual, emotional) the answers to which our present educational system does not have. From 1945 onwards, British education has undergone revolution after revolution, some more challenging than others; but none has produced a basis for a permanent structure. Above all else, the curricula, syllabuses and methods throughout Europe and North America do not satisfy the child: there are few schools that provide a real meaning and 'end' that the child can realise and from which he can obtain satisfaction. Dramatic Education provides a solution whereby real meaning is given *to the child*—he has an 'end' to his lessons which is of importance for him because he *lives* it.

The Intellectual Discipline of Dramatic Education

Modern academic studies have been diversified to an alarming extent. Intellectual studies have been fragmented into a great many specialisations, each of which pursues its own knowledge within its limited framework to its logical conclusion. Yet the modern world needs such specialisation, it needs the detailed knowledge to master a universe that is expanding in ways unthought of only a few years ago.

And, as a result, we are in danger of not seeing the wood for the trees. Ultimately, categorical systems of knowledge are merely the way by which we are helped to understand the life process. Their laws are not the laws of life but the laws of the disciplines concerned. Within their own references they may be completely valid. But, in terms of life itself and the educational processes which enable life to grow and evolve, they can only provide a partial answer.

Although it is impossible to have ultimate categorical systems, this does not mean to say that such disciplines cannot be of use. Far from it. Such systems can be used constructively although we recognise that the process of life itself is the only ultimate arbiter. While all branches of learning are subordinate to the total experience, they are *at the same time* the working tools by which we can comprehend life.

It follows that Dramatic Education is an all-inclusive academic discipline. It uses as tools all branches of learning that bear upon the dramatic impulse. It utilises eclectically each and every single discipline into one unified body of knowledge so that it can help us comprehend the nature of experience. It brings together many aspects of hitherto unrelated studies: aspects of philosophy, for we must examine why we educate our children in this way; psychoanalysis, to understand the symbols the child uses, and the underlying motives, within the content of his play; sociology, for acting is a social activity implying the interaction of individuals; social psychology, because imitation, identification, role playing and the like are directly related to man acting within his environment; cognition and psycholinguistics, for the relationship of concept formation and language impinges directly upon the dramatic method of learning. And in approaching the theatre, aspects of mathematics, physics, engineering, aesthetics and other fields of study become grist to our mill.

If we commence our thinking about education with the child as a child, developing and evolving within the life process, then all other studies become the tools by which we apprehend existence. It is in this context that we approach those fields that most immediately bear upon Dramatic Education.

PART TWO

PLAY, DRAMA & THE UNCONSCIOUS

4 DRAMATIC PLAY & THE ELEMENTS OF PSYCHOANALYSIS

To the question, 'Why does a girl play with her dolls?' or 'Why does a boy play at Cowboys and Indians?' the psychoanalyst would reply that, in one way or another, the child is expressing his or her unconscious. He would go on to say that *how* and *what* the child plays are reflections of unconscious drives which, although basically common to everyone, vary according to the development of the individual's unconscious. Although far from new, it was Freud's concept of the unconscious that has most influenced subsequent thought. Admiring Darwin, he conceived it as evolutionary and biological; but it was dynamic, with its energy drawn from instinctual drives. And it was this concept which has so revolutionised man's way of looking at himself.

SCHOOLS OF 'DEPTH' PSYCHOLOGY

'Psychoanalysis', strictly speaking, refers to Freud's theories and the methods of psychotherapy based upon them. Those who broke from Freud to use different systems used other names: Adler's was called 'Individual Psychology' and Jung's 'Analytical Psychology'.

Despite obvious differences, they have certain features in common. First, they all stress the importance of the unconscious in our mental life—it is repressed emotions for Freud, unverbalised attitudes for Adler, and unrealised potentialities for Jung—but all agree that behaviour is constantly influenced by motives of which we are normally unaware. Secondly, the same principles govern 'normal' and 'abnormal' behaviour. The motives and processes of the disordered are of the same kind as those of the normal; the difference is one of degree. If psychoanalysts' examples are from the abnormal it is because these provide more vivid illustrations which can be comprehended more easily. Thirdly, they all stress the importance of infancy as the formative period for the developing personality. Freud's approach is evolutionary, developmental and historical: our unconscious reactions to our parents in our earliest years have lasting effects on our motives, and the situations which cause trouble in later life are those which revive the unresolved conflicts of childhood. For Adler, a man's 'life style' (his

habitual way of feeling, acting and dealing with difficulties) is derived
from childhood, when he habitually tried to achieve some sense of
adequacy; in adult life he repeats his childhood pattern. To Jung,
childhood experiences are not so important as the present yet they
determine which of the individual's potentialities are realised and which
remain dormant. Fourthly, there is an underlying belief that no mental
happenings are accidental: irrational happenings are meaningful—to
Freud, for example, they represent painful memories repressed into
the unconscious and striving for expression.

For 'depth' psychologists, dreams, hypnotic recollections and word
associations are important in the understanding of human life, but
certain aspects of normal behaviour are significant. Thus child analysts
have evolved techniques for understanding a child's unconscious
through play and games of make-believe which, therefore, take on
enormous significance, not only for the present adjustment to themselves, to others and to their environment, but for their future adult
living.

The Basic Theories of Freud

For the understanding of children's play, Freud's basic concepts of
the unconscious are very important. At first he postulated two instincts:
self-preservation and the preservation of the species (the ego and sexual
instincts). The former leads man to seek pleasure and avoid pain—this
is the Pleasure Principle (or urge to seek sense gratification). It is
opposed to the Reality Principle which sees the consequences of
seeking mere pleasure. However, the Repetition Compulsion can go
beyond both principles: a past traumatic experience may have to be
re-enacted (by dreams, in play, or overtly) in order to assimilate it. The
sexual instinct is based on libido (sexual energy). If this is unsatisfied it
can lead to substitute gratifications dominated by the pleasure principle
(like day-dreaming); or, if libido is withdrawn from one area, it must
inevitably produce its effects somewhere else.

Freud postulates three maturational stages in infancy: oral, anal and
genital. In the oral stage the mouth is the primary organ for pleasure,
and the child is mentally incorporating, or introjecting: putting things
into his mouth he incorporates what he loves—wishing to be like the
other person he identifies with them. (Thus Freud shows the primacy
of identification, the first step to impersonation.) At about six months,

when first cutting teeth, the child may be frustrated if the breast is not available; thus he attempts gratification by aggression (biting) says Abraham [2]. But, as he still identifies with the mother, the image of the aggressive mother who will eat him up occurs. The anal stage (the wish to expel aggressively) Abraham also divides into: anal-expulsive, when the child enjoys sadistic expulsion; and anal-retentive (coinciding with sphincter control about one year) when he only parts with his faeces out of love for the person who cares for him. The genital phase occurs about the third year when interest centres on the penis; then, about the fourth year, occurs the Oedipus complex. Sophocles tells how Oedipus unwittingly kills his father and marries his mother, then punishes himself by putting out his eyes. Freud says that the child is sexually attracted to his mother and resents his father, then fears punishment for his wish (symbolic castration). Later abnormal results might be: passivity concealing hatred and fear of the father (later, all men in authority); over-affection and dependence on the mother (the need to be loved); or, repressing desires for the mother, a passive desire for the father may develop (homosexuality). Girls develop the Electra complex: the clitoris is the 'inferior' counterpart of the penis and 'penis envy' develops. Thus she may: be hostile to the mother (who 'denied' the child a penis) and so desire the father's penis; identify with the mother and desire a baby (a penis substitute) and develop normal female sexuality; or, if clinging to her penis desire, she may become dominating and aggressive (developing masculine tendencies). Should libido development be arrested somewhere in the oral, anal and genital stages this is a fixation; this increases the danger that, when facing obstacles later, the libido may have a regression to that fixation.

Freud later modified his instinct theory. In 1914 he defined narcissism as love for oneself: primary narcissism is natural to the baby but secondary, morbid, narcissism may develop in later life if the individual's love is thwarted. In 1920 he postulated the life and death instincts: the tendencies to bind together and to destroy.

Freud's first theory of personality differentiated: the conscious, or present awareness; the unconscious of which we are not normally aware; and the preconscious which, although unconscious now, can easily be recalled—slips of the tongue are in this category. It was in 1922 that he made his famous division between the ego, the superego and the id. The id is the primitive mass of impulses of the newborn child: it demands immediate satisfaction, knows no precautions to ensure survival, is unconscious, is governed by the pleasure principle, knows no logic, and stores the entire mental energy. Part of the id separates out to become the ego, or self. Initially narcissistic, it establishes itself by becoming:

> ... aware of the stimuli from without, by storing up experiences of them (in memory), by avoiding excessive stimuli (through adaption) and, finally, by learning to bring about appropriate modifications in the external world to its own advantage (through activity). [122]

Where the ego is conscious, the superego (roughly equivalent to conscience) is only partly conscious. It originates in the Oedipus complex and the fear of punishment:

> Parental attitudes are taken over by the personality, one part of which (the superego) assumes the same attitude towards the rest as the parents did previously towards the child. [7]

The ego wards off the demands of the id and the striving of the super-ego by defence mechanisms: (1) rationalising the irrational demands of the id (covering up mistakes); (2) magical undoing—the belief that former irrational deeds can be 'blown away'; (3) denial—the ego withdraws from a too painful reality (as in some pathology); (4) introjection—the ego incorporates the loved object and identifies with him; (5) projection—the ego gets rid of something unpleasant which belongs to the outside world; (6) isolation—separation of the emotion and the idea of the experience (sometimes leading to compulsion neurosis and 'dual personality'); (7) reaction formation—too firm a repression of a forbidden drive produces opposite tendencies, presenting the ego to society in a pleasant light (as with the excessive puritan); (8) sublimation—the normal and successful mechanism, channelling energy into substitute goals acceptable to society (the basis of the arts and successful work).

The child sees that forbidden acts lead to punishment or loss of the mother's love, and it is the relationship with the mother (based on identification) that is the foundation for the child's later imitations and socio-emotional attachments [136]. Although adult anxieties are of social ostracism and rejection by society, they are based on childhood residues in the unconscious, for separation from the mother is the prototype of all later anxieties. The analyst attempts to understand the unconscious drives and to achieve sublimation (with adults through free association and dreams, and with children through play). But neither dreams nor play portray anxieties *exactly*: they work by symbolism.

To Freud, dreams are the highroad to the adult's unconscious, for they deal with wishes which cannot be accepted by the conscious in a waking state. But their manifest content (what the dreamer perceives) conceals a deep latent content. As the unconscious desire has been repressed, the latent content cannot be directly perceived by the dreamer; and so the manifest content is created—the symbolic realisation of a repressed desire. (As play serves a similar purpose to dreams, play too has a manifest and latent content.) Methods of symbol creation are: (1) condensation—a dream figure may be a composite image of several people; (2) displacement—significant emotional elements are made insignificant; (3) plastic representation—the sound of a word may create the image ('a view' stimulated by the word 'review'); (4) secondary elaboration—the dreamer attempts to impose order on the images; (5) fixed symbols, common to all humanity, which are normally sexual in character. Fixed symbols are pictorial and in early life they are 'comparable to stage settings' [121]. A house represents a body: if smooth, a man; with ledges, a woman. Parents are kings and queens, siblings are little animals, birth is water, death a journey. Hollow objects and containers are female symbols and so are snails, mussels, chapels and churches; apples, peaches and oranges are breasts; a landscape with rocks, woods and water symbolises female organs. Male symbols are a cloak, a hat, or anything long and pointed (stick, steeple, pistols, knives, etc.); aeroplanes and balloons symbolise erection, while the magic number three represents penis and testicles. A spider symbolises the aggressive mother, but spider fear is fear of incest; rhythmical or violent motions (riding, climbing ladders) represent intercourse, while teeth falling indicate castration fears. Dream symbols are the result of infantile experience, 'from the relics of the prehistoric period (age one to three)' [201] and symbols representing recent action may well be similar to those representing past action. In fact, we are determined by the whole of our past.

Both dreams and dramatic play are ego attempts to relate the id to reality and so, in play too, there are symbols which disguise the latent content. Freud says:

> The saying that in play we can learn a person's character may be admitted if we can add 'the repressed character'. [121]

Yet play symbolism is never simple: 'polysymbolism' occurs because
the intertwining of tendencies, conflicts and repressions gives rise to a
variety of meanings. The symbol, Freud says, at first, is a disguise.
Later, under the influence of Adler, Silberer and Jung, he said it was a
language as well as a disguise. But, clearly, the understanding of play
symbolism and, therefore, the unconscious meaning inherent in
dramatic play is of considerable importance to education.

Adler

It was Adler who originated the popular concept of the 'inferiority
complex'. As all men feel inferior, the young child develops his own
method to compensate for this [4]. This becomes a man's 'life style':
the habitual attitudes which compensate for inferiority feelings and aim
at superiority. This goal is seen in a number of ways:

> It may be crystalised as the ideal either of useful achievement, of personal
> prestige, of the domination of others, of the defence against danger, or of
> sexual victories. [384]

The ways in which a child can attempt to overcome his sense of
inferiority are: compensation—attacking the difficulties and adjusting
well to the three challenges of life (society, work, sex); overcom-
pensation—assertion in an alternative way in which the striving is too
apparent (like the weakling who becomes a gangster); and the retreat
into fantasy, or psychogenic illness, as a means of obtaining power.

The symbols of make-believe are, for Adler, reflections of inferiority
or the desire for expansion; they represent the individual's present
attitude.

In later works Adler stressed cultural factors, and saw 'social interest'
in place of the power motive. His influence is found in Horney,
Suttie, Stekel, Reaney and social psychology generally, as we shall see
on pp. 131–3, 196–7.

Jung

For Jung there are three levels of the personality: the conscious, the
personal unconscious, and the collective unconscious. This can be
comprehended by the famous analogy of a chain of islands rising from
the sea. The land above the ocean is the conscious, the ego, the knowing,

the 'I'. Just below the surface of the water is the personal unconscious containing 'repressed infantile impulses and wishes, subliminal perceptions, and countless forgotten experiences' [111]; these can be recalled by will, chance associations, dreams (when they are disguised) or, with neurosis, have to be forced out. Deep down on the sea bed, where all the islands are joined, is the collective unconscious containing the common beliefs and myths of humanity. In fact, there are really two deep levels: the racial unconscious containing the collective symbols of the race of the individual; and the universal unconscious, common to all humanity. The individual unconscious consists of memories varying from individual to individual, but the collective unconscious is made up of elements common to everyone. Jung deduces the existence of the collective unconscious from four factors: instinct, which is inherited; the unanimity of theme in the mythologies from different cultures; the common occurrence of 'primitive and universal symbols such as are found in myths and legends'; and the delusions of the insane which contain many symbols (like those of death and rebirth) which are also found in mythology. The image patterns of dreams, hallucinations, mythology, magic, alchemy and religion are the same for all members of a race, therefore they must be inherited. Not that the specific details are the same: what is inherited is the underlying pattern of symbol formation. The concept of the collective unconscious is generally rejected by Freudians and social psychologists, though Freud did say that it:

> ... includes not only dispositions, but also ideational contents, memory traces of the experiences of former generations. [132]

The concept also relates to several physiological theories of play, particularly that of Stanley Hall.

To Freud, a symbol (in a dream or play) was a generalised expression of a particular, usually sexual in character: thus pencils and swords are generalised symbols of the phallus. But Jung saw the symbol as a particular representing the generalised idea: when an adult dreams of his mother the symbol represents the generalised concept of the Great Mother of all living common to all men at all times. But dreams are of two kinds: personal, from the personal unconscious, concerned with particular events in the dreamer's life; and collective, from the collective unconscious, having significance for others apart from the dreamer and to be interpreted through mythological analogies. Jung delineates a series of major symbols ranging from conscious to unconscious: the Persona, or the mask we assume in social relationships; the Shadow, the symbol of forbidden urges which is our 'other self'; the Anima (for men) and the Animus (for women), of opposite sex to ourselves, and the symbolic representation of our view of the opposite sex; and the great Archetypes which are symbols of various aspects of the collective unconscious. For Jung, collective symbolism is the real language of the human soul. Collective symbolic thought corresponds to an initial phase of human thought when man was not concerned with the conquest of the external world and was turned inwards: then he sought to express in myth the discoveries of psyche. Here was a new explanation for myth: the same archetypes in a single collective unconscious innate in all men; and there are many images which have an 'over-all' significance in this way. Water is an example: it is connected with the 'original environment'; is essential for crops and, thus, agricultural civilisations; is a constant oneiric symbol; mythological gods and men come out of water; in baptismal rites it represents both rebirth and purification; in the imaginary stories told by children concerning birth, it plays a major part. This is clearly related to modern anthropology which tells us that myth is the chosen cloak for abstract thought:

> The irrational aspect of myth becomes especially clear when we remember that the ancients were not content merely to recount their myths as stories conveying information. They dramatised them, acknowledging in them a special virtue which could be activated by recital . . .
>
> Myth is a form of poetry which transcends poetry in that it proclaims a truth; a form of reasoning which transcends reasoning in that it wants to bring about the truth it proclaims; a form of action, of ritual behaviour, which does not find its fulfilment in the act but must proclaim and elaborate a poetic form of truth. [114]

The suppositions and methods of Greek physics are similar to the rational thought of a child of seven to ten years, and Piaget would say that the same genetic mechanisms which account for the development of thought of the child today were in action also in the minds of men who, like the pre-Socratics, were just emerging from mythological and pre-logical thought. It can be said that the more primitive the society, the more lasting the influence of the child's thought on the individual's development. But this, for Jung, would not be enough. Rather, the child's thought and mythological symbols, oneiric representations and pre-logical science, are all part of the collective unconscious—common to all men. (See also p. 246.)

SYMBOLIC THOUGHT

The understanding of the unconscious symbolism inherent in dramatic play, and in drama itself, is of considerable import. Jung distinguished the symbol and the sign. The arbitrary sign, like numbers and words, makes possible the formation of rational thought. But there is some resemblance between a symbol and that which it signifies: a metaphor, for example, expresses a relationship between the image and the object—a relationship comprehended by the mind of the individual. Thus symbolism is used in emotional language (like poetry) while signs are used for intellectual and rational concepts.

But in poetry the overt symbolism is conscious and Freud distinguishes this from the unconscious symbol where the meaning is hidden from the individual creating the symbol. Symbolism is a form of thought, symbolic thought, which is individual and intimate, with its roots and its direct expression in the unconscious. But when expressed in dramatic play (or by the dreamer describing his dream in words) it becomes a form of secondary symbolism: the attempt to express consciously the unconscious symbolic thought.

But the nature of symbolic thought is the subject of some disagreement. Freud's critics say the unconscious impulses cannot be reduced to sex and aggression—that the 'desire for glory' is the chief unconscious motive [180], or that aggression is not an impulse but a reaction to frustration [90]. Stekel rejects the unconscious and repression, postulating scotomization (man turns a blind eye to his conflicts) [349]. Otto Rank regarded birth as the most traumatic event in human life [304] and the major source of anxiety; adult anxiety was the outcome of the basic birth anxiety—birth is separation from the mother and later separation revives this anxiety. Thus there are two basic anxieties: Life Fear, or 'fear of having to live as an isolated individual'; and Death Fear, or fear of losing individuality and being swallowed up in the whole [305]. The maternal symbol (vessels, receptacles, etc.) is the major expression of man and it is associated with paternal symbols (like the sun). We shall examine the social significance of these on pp. 128-9.

Although Freud rejected Rank, they both conceive symbolism as deriving from the past, from infancy, while Adler, Jung, Silberer and

Rivers emphasise the present. Silberer examined the point at which, in the half-sleeping state, thought abandons coherent and logical structure for imaged symbolism. As the first images are often a continuation of the last conscious idea, he postulated: material symbols, representing particular objects or events (like Freud's unconscious symbols); and functional symbols, showing the functioning of thought in the present, thus allowing for the possibility of anagogic interpretation (supported by Jung but denied by Freud). Unconscious symbolism, therefore, represents both past and present. That symbolic thought could derive from recent events was supported by Rivers' findings with neurotics in the First World War: symbols resulted from physiological regression to more primitive levels in the nervous system under the influence of sleep, thus there are a 'series of levels in the nervous system' [315]. But whether past and present, or just past, symbolic thought is the basis for the content of dramatic play: it is this which gives play its meaning for the individual.

BRITISH PSYCHOANALYSIS

Later British 'depth' psychologists, like Crichton Miller, J. A. Hadfield and Ian Suttie, accepted the main hypotheses of Freudian theory but, in the tradition of the Tavistock clinic, were essentially individualists.

Suttie agreed with Rank's emphasis upon the mother and stressed the importance of love (as opposed to sex, as with Freud). There is a primal attachment-to-mother and this results in the need for company, attention, protectiveness and the like, but in addition:

> I think that play, cooperation, competition and culture interests generally are substitutes, for the mutually caressing relationship of child and mother. *By these substitutes we put the whole social environment in the place once occupied by mother*—maintaining with it a mental or cultural rapport in lieu of caresses, etc., formerly enjoyed with the mother. [351]

Thus, too, culture is derived from play—both are substitutes for nurture.

J. A. Hadfield

Hadfield considers that the function of dreams and play is to reproduce the unsolved experiences of life and attempt solutions. Dreams and play stand in place of experience: by reliving experiences in imagination they can examine the problems of life by trial-and-error and warn of the consequences. Repetition in play and dream thrusts forward unsolved problems until they are solved, and serves the same purpose as ideational processes: the forming of mental images (as memory, if of the past; as imagination, if of events that have not taken place) so that problems can be solved without actually being experienced. A child's play is often the working out of problems using concrete symbols: she is imagining situations and taking up attitudes (as with a 'naughty doll') without knowing she is dealing with her personal problems, that she is trying to adjust to her own naughtiness. In condemning the sins of a doll the child is condemning her own sins, which has the effect of settling the problem in her mind. This relates to the child's need to repeat a fairy-tale again and again:

> It is indeed because we do *not* understand our deeper emotional problems that we have to work these out by analogy, by myth, and by parable, and that is precisely the function of dreams. [163]

Hadfield sees the symbols of play and dream as both disguise (like Freud) and as an analogy of an idea or emotion (like Jung); they may, in fact, have a double meaning. And while some fixed symbols (such as the snake for the male sex organ) might justify an arbitrary interpretation, it is always possible that the symbol may refer to something specific to the particular individual.

Hadfield agrees with Jung that symbolic language is primitive language for this has a physiological basis: the latest developed part of the brain (the cortical area) goes to sleep first, and any mental activity is carried on in the lower (thalmic) areas, primarily the seat of feelings and emotions. Primitive thought (and that of the lower centres of the brain) is emotional, expresses itself in concrete symbols rather than words, works by sensations rather than ideas, and follows an associational rather than a logical order of events: dreams and play follow all these strictures. Symbolic language is illogical, works by analogy and is animistic. To primitive man all material things are living: there is no change and no determinism—everything is caused by living agents. In dreams, thoughts and feelings are personalised (as they are in fairy-tales or the films of Walt Disney) and so our rage may be personalised as a fury, or our feelings of revenge may be personalised and projected as a witch.

As a result, Hadfield sees 'dream as a drama':

We come therefore to realise that the dream is a drama in which all the
actors represented in the dream are parts of oneself. Our personalities have
many attributes; we have our kindly side, our arrogant side, our ingratiating
side, our lazy side. These are often in conflict, and therefore create problems
in the personality which may be reproduced in dreams. Because of the
tendency of the human to animism, all these aspects of the personality are
personalised, and in the dream may be represented as persons, whether of
our acquaintance or an imaginary person of that same character, all having an
argument or discussion—as they might in a play. [163]

In a dream:

. . . all the people are *dramatis personae,* representing, as they do on the stage,
certain ideas or types of mind, not the people themselves. In a play a man of
self-sufficient character stands for self-sufficiency in the abstract, a priggish
man for priggishness, a prostitute for the sensual part of ourselves, a parish
priest for consideration for others. These are all characteristics we ourselves
possess and the dream presents a drama in which all these characteristics in us
are represented by people fighting it out, debating the question, playing out
the problem in dramatic form and therefore tending towards a solution. The
value of a theatre is that we see ourselves as we see others; in a dream we see
ourselves as our subconscious sees us. In treating patients, the technique of
psycho-drama, in which the patients play out certain roles, is used for much
the same purpose. [163]

And play serves the same biological function as dreams, sorting out the
unsolved problems of the day [164]. He sees it as surplus energy (like
Schiller), as an instinct (like Spencer and Groos), and finds forms of
racial play in peep-bo and hide-and-seek; and (like Groos) he sees that
imitation is related to the development of intelligence:

Imaginative play . . . owing to identification . . . serves another interesting
purpose, namely *the development of ideas.* Play is often symbolic . . . [164]

But its essential quality is that it expresses the unconscious symbolic
language in secondary symbolism in order to reproduce the unsolved
experiences of life and attempt solutions.

5 DRAMATIC PLAY & CHILD PSYCHOTHERAPY

FREUD & THE PLAY MECHANISMS

We have seen that Freud considered dramatic play as an attempt by the ego to relate the id to reality, that from play we can learn of a person's 'repressed' character through his symbolic language, and that the foundation for imitative behaviours lies in the relationship between the child and his mother. In 1908 he said:

> We ought to look in the child for the first traces of imaginative activity. The child's best loved and most absorbing occupation is play. Perhaps we may say that every child at play behaves like an imaginative writer, in that he creates a world of his own or, more truly, he arranges the things of his world and orders it in a new way that pleases him better. It would be incorrect to say that he does not take his world seriously; on the contrary, he takes his play very seriously and expends a great deal of emotion on it. The opposite of play is not serious occupation, but reality. Notwithstanding the large affective cathexis of his play world, the child distinguishes it perfectly from reality; only he likes to borrow the objects and circumstances that he imagines from the tangible and real world. It is only this linking of it to reality that still distinguishes a child's 'play' from 'daydreaming'. [135]

The child's creation of a world of his own in play is the foundation for the arts. But play is also the natural language of the child: the symbols he uses are replicas of the life situation and, through them, the child approaches his world of reality.

> By dealing with things that are small and inanimate, he can master situations that to him are overwhelming. [135]

For Freud, play elaborates material already experienced: it is a form of secondary symbolism with which the child attempts to order reality in accordance with the symbolic thought of his unconscious.

The point then arises, how is it done? Freud gave two different answers: catharsis and the repetition compulsion.

Catharsis

In his early work with Breuer [39] he had emphasised the cathartic effect of play. Play allows the child to 'act out' situations which are disturbing and confusing to him:

. . . free play in and of itself has decided cathartic value, over and above the
therapeutic implications ascribed to it by the therapist. [393]

Modern techniques, however, differ from earlier approaches when:

The child was encouraged to express his difficulties in the interests of a rather
aimless catharsis. It is now realised that the essentially therapeutic element in
play is that through it the child learns to *control* in fantasy, impulses which are
as yet difficult for him to control in reality. It is often his preferred mode of
coming to terms with some aspect of reality which presents insuperable
difficulties for a direct approach. In this kind of situation the participation of
other children and of the teacher is often a vital factor. [24]

Freud himself discarded the theory that catharsis by itself could lead to
a lasting therapeutic change (as we see from his 'On the history of the
psychoanalytic movement') but although catharsis by itself is inadequate, it has some relevance. It implies enactment in effigy—just as the
savage sticks pins in a model of his enemy—and thus the content of
play is important. It can show the therapist or the teacher some facts
about the symbolic language of the child. But, as Levy illustrated [235],
it can only be shown to be effective when the symptoms follow a
specific event or events, and when they are of short duration and in the
recent historic past of the child.

Repetition

Freud was himself dissatisfied with the theory of catharsis and, in
1922, postulated the repetition compulsion as the mechanism of play:

We see that children repeat in their play everything that has made a great
impression on them in actual life, that they thereby abreact the strength of
the impression and so to speak make themselves masters of the situation . . .
In the play of children we seem to arrive at the conclusion that the child
repeats even the unpleasant experiences because through his own activity he
gains a far more thorough mastery of the strong impression than was possible
by mere passive experience. Every fresh repetition seems to strengthen this
mastery for which the child strives. [125]

The repetition compulsion occurs when the individual has been
through an experience which was too difficult, or too large, for him to
assimilate immediately; as a result, it calls for re-experience. The ego
then attempts:

. . . to assimilate the experience more completely through renewing and thereby gaining the mastery over it. [370]

A passively received impression provokes an active response (play) in the child: and this may be a series of painstaking repetitions of impressions which, because of their unpleasant content, the child has every reason to avoid. In the original difficult situation, the child has been passive within the experience—as when the dentist has been prying into his mouth. In his play, however, the child himself pretends to be the dentist and repeats the vigorous procedure on a small sister or brother, who is then as helpless as the original child had been with the real dentist. The repetition compulsion, in fact, is the mechanism which makes the child attempt to assimilate experience—the purpose of play is to master reality.

THE ELEMENTS OF PLAY THERAPY

The child psychotherapist allows his patient to play and attempts, through 'reading' the secondary symbolism of play, to understand his symbolic language and, so, the unconscious problems that beset him. Although there are many applications and practices in psychotherapy, there is a certain amount of common ground.

First, most analysts would agree with Lowenfeld that play consists of all activities of children that are:

. . . spontaneous and self-generating, that are ends in themselves, and that are unrelated to 'lessons' or to the normal physiological needs of the child. [244]

And if they are spontaneous they also help the child to assimilate reality, as Freud said, even if their experience is traumatic. Walder states:

To the psychic organism just establishing its existence, for which everything is still novel—some things attractively pleasant, many things painful and menacing—excessive stimulation (trauma as it might be called in a certain sense) is plainly a normal experience, while in the life of the adult it surely constitutes the exception. This, probably, is one of the reasons why the abreaction of traumatic experiences by games plays so important a role precisely in childhood. [370]

Second, play activities are seen as projections: expressions of the child's innermost thoughts, drives and motivations which express private meanings:

. . . what a subject does in a projective situation may be directly expressing his private world and characteristic personality processes. [113]

Although the projections inherent in play configurations are conditioned by age, previous experience, intelligence, physical and social maturity, other abilities of the child, and the nature of the toy material, essentially play is a surface manifestation of the unconscious [393]. Analysis, therefore, make inferences from overt observations to the latent content and structure of play.

Third, play shows the child's relationship to the world. Erickson [98] says succinctly that play is the microcosm through which children deal with the macrocosm of the adult world.

Fourth, 'make-believe' is an inherent part of the play situation and, for all practical purposes, dramatic play is indistinguishable from play itself. The dramatic element, in fact, provides the great variety within play configurations:

Inherent in play activity is the make-believe element. A child cannot drive a car, fly an aeroplane, or go into outer space. Reversal of roles in the parent-child or teacher-pupil relationships can be achieved by the child only in a play situation. Overt expressions of hostility, of aggression, and of the desire to punish are not tolerated by the adult world, but are possible for the child in play . . . [393]

The dramatic element relates children one to another:

Playing together means the sharing of a phantasy life. Through play children tell one another these phantasy truths. Through the sharing of these intimate truths, they become realities and they fall into their proper perspective, and the children become real people to one another. [20]

And the drama helps the child to come to terms with his environment:

Sometimes he transforms the whole playroom into his house, street, or school, and often he re-enacts adult roles he has observed: his mother, teacher, the milkman, mailman, etc. Developmentally speaking, this play serves as a means for the child to explore and understand the social world around him in relation to himself. [169]

And, further, it is an inherent part of constructional play:

When a child employs a work bench and uses tools, he is mastering material and creating a replica of what he has seen in the adult world. In such construction, the child not only imitates an adult world as in the representational activity; he becomes identified with the grown-up person who produces his own objects . . . [169]

Jackson and Todd state that the rudiments of imitative and dramatic play begin to appear at about ten months, and summarise as follows:

Dramatic play is the type which interests us especially because of its therapeutic possibilities.

The function of dramatic or imaginative play is very complex for it may be an expression of a variety of needs. When we see a child play at being a coachman and whipping his 'horse' unmercifully, or at being a car driver and running people over in the street, we might be tempted to take a superficial view that he is merely 'imitating' what he had seen or heard. We might also jump to the hasty conclusion that he is a cruel or 'sadistic' child, who enjoys inflicting pain in imagination. Both these views may be partially true. Yet it may also be true that the child is seeking to satisfy a craving for power, which he has little chance of exercising in real life. He may be 'doing unto others' what he has had 'done unto himself', passing on to the imaginary horse or the imaginary person, the pain, the fear, the crushing sense of impotence, which others had inflicted upon him. He may, by working himself up into a state of angry excitement or of highly pleasurable sense of mastery, seek the experience, and learn the control of emotions which he is obliged to repress, in his everyday relationships. He may be even imagining himself as the chastised horse or the crushed pedestrian, thus allaying, through punishment, his guilt in connexion with his own 'naughtiness' or badness, and at the same time finding reassurance in the discovery that, after all, punishment does not annihilate the culprit—something that he had unconsciously feared . . . by 'playing through' his emotional attitudes towards himself, the child puts himself in the place of the persons in his environment, tests the strength and quality of his emotions, as well as his control over them, and builds up his personality in the process, emerging finally as a more complete and better integrated individual. [194]

SCHOOLS OF PSYCHOTHERAPY

The differences in child psychotherapy are basically in approach and we can distinguish five main types centred round particular analysts.

Anna Freud

Freud's daughter, Anna, was particularly concerned with the relationship between the ego and the superego in children. She differed

from Melanie Klein in that she analysed slightly older children and took
into account information from parents.

In 1928 [118] she said that helping the child to accept the growing
demands of the superego calls for educational rather than analytic
measures, and that direct interpretations should be used sparingly. By
1936 she was stressing [119] that greater importance should be given to
the conscious mind than had hitherto been the case. Dream analysis
provides information about the id, but not about the individual existing
here and now; this can only be provided by information about the ego's
unconscious defence mechanisms (as seen in play) and these show the
transformations which the basic drives have undergone. In addition
to the defence mechanisms delineated by Freudian theory (see p. 64)
she postulated five others: (1) denial in fantasy—the painful fact is
denied and turned into its opposite; (2) denial in word and act—
reassurance to protect ego from the knowledge of its own helplessness;
(3) restriction of the ego—as when a young girl, frustrated socially in
her mixing with the opposite sex, restricts her feminine interests to
excel intellectually; (4) identification with the aggressor—assumption
of the opponent's qualities through introjection (the child playing
'dentists' after having an extraction); (5) a form of altruism, or satisfying one's own desires through the lives of others (like Cyrano).

Essentially she considers that Kleinian analysis of the very youngest
children, and their concept of symbol formation, is not possible. For
Anna Freud, life is governed by the desire for instinctual gratification
in which perception of the object is achieved only slowly.

Margaret Lowenfeld

Lowenfeld uses specific materials, particularly trays of sand, so that
within a realistic background the child builds imaginary worlds [245].
The child plays 'world games' wherein he demonstrates his own
emotional and mental state without the interference of an adult—there
is no direct interpretation or transference. This approach is taken further
by Bender and Schilder:

> Spontaneous play in children is essentially a means of investigation and
> experimentation in the laws of nature and human relationships . . . The
> emotional problems and the formal problems cannot be completely separated.
> The child's experimentation with form and configuration is an expression of

his tendency to come to a better handling of objects by action. By trial and error the child comes to an insight into the structure of objects. [26]

The child plays with form, configuration and construction and, from this, Lowenfeld can build up a picture of the child's symbolic thought but does not provide an interpretation.

Erik Erickson

Erickson combines spatial configurations and psychoanalytic interpretation [98]. An analysis of play is made in four areas of be-haviour: (1) affective—the child's emotional interest in, and withdrawal from, the object of behaviour; (2) ideational—verbalised content and acted-out themes; (3) spatial—configuration in the three-dimensional sphere; and (4) verbal—expression, through voice and manner of speech, in terms of pitch and rhythm. But Erickson also draws on other material (past impressions and data from parents) before making an analysis.

He defines play as a function of the ego, an attempt to synchronize the bodily and social processes with the self. In play, man's ego feels free from, and superior to, the confinement of space, time and social reality—free from the compulsions of conscience and the impulsions of irrationality. It is no wonder, says Erickson, that man feels 'only human when he plays':

> This dramatisation takes place in the play sphere. Utilizing his mastery over objects, the child can arrange them in such a way that they permit him to imagine that he is master of the life predicament as well . . . He has, as Freud put it, *turned passivity into activity;* he plays at doing something that was in reality done to him. [99]

He distinguishes three levels of play material: that which has a *common meaning* to all children in a community, that which has a *special meaning* to some, and that which has a *unique meaning* to the individual —and the same play formation may have meanings on all levels. Further, play is directly related to social learning:

> I propose the theory that the child's play is the infantile form of the human ability to deal with experience by creating model situations and to master reality by experiment and planning. It is in certain phases of his work that the adult projects past experience into dimensions which seem manageable. In the laboratory, on the stage, and on the drawing-board, he relives the past

and thus relieves leftover effects; in reconstructing the model situation, he redeems his failures and strengthens his hopes. He anticipates the future from the point of view of a corrected and shared past. [99]

In this sense, play is seen as a dramatic experience and is directly related to Burton's concept that dramatic play is 'a large-scale laboratory of life examination and study': i.e., the use of the past in reconstructing a model situation related to the present and the future by experiment and planning.

Non-Directive Therapy

Virginia Mae Axline [17] and others consider that the individual has within himself the ability to solve his own problems; and that this natural growth makes mature behaviour more satisfying than immature behaviour. This method is totally different from the others for all of them, to one degree or another, attempt to help the individual actively. Non-Directive Therapy, on the other hand, accepts the child as he is and attempts to encourage self-expression by natural catharsis.

Melanie Klein & 'The English School'

Melanie Klein originated a technique of analysing the play of children between two and six years of age and, as a result, considered that the beginnings of the superego and symbol formation were much earlier than was once thought—going back, indeed to the first days of life. In this she was supported by a number of distinguished analysts: Susan Isaacs, Joan Rivière, Géza Róheim, T. E. Money-Kyrle and Freud's biographer, Dr Ernest Jones.

Klein tells us much about the formation of identification, and symbol formation (the basis for impersonation) in the child's first months.

The early ego, when exposed to the instincts and reality, does two things: (1) it imagines an ideal breast; and (2) the ego splits, projecting the death instinct outwards towards the original object, the breast, which becomes the centre of the fear of persecution. Thus arise two fantasies: the ideal breast and the persecutory one, the 'good breast' and the 'bad breast'. These fantasies merge with real experience of love and feeding, pain and deprivation. The infant then reaches the 'Paranoid-Schizoid Position', the chief anxiety being that the persecutory object will 'get inside' the ego overwhelming the self. Fantasy can influence a child's reaction to reality: that of the persecutory breast can lead a hungry child to turn away from the breast; a hungry child imagining a 'good breast' may, if fed, merge feelings of his own goodness and the good object and so have feelings of strength but, if not fed, he feels the 'bad breast' is stronger than his own love and the 'good breast'. Projective identification occurs; ego parts are split off and projected into the external object which is then controlled by, and identified with, the projected parts. But:

> Projective identification . . . has its valuable aspects. To begin with, it is the earliest form of empathy and it is on projective as well as introjective identification that is based the capacity to 'put oneself in another person's shoes'. Projective identification also provides the basis of the earliest form of symbol-formation. By projecting parts of itself into the object and identifying parts of the object with parts of the self, the ego forms its most primitive symbols. [337]

The child's feelings about external objects are attributed by him to the objects themselves: and so there are 'good objects' and 'bad objects'. But a slight change in the situation and the child can love and hate the same object in rapid succession—thus he lives in a world inhabited by gods and devils (Money-Kyrle suggested that these concepts are derived from such early memories).

As the infant grows, the ego feels stronger and the power of the bad objects is felt to be smaller. It is then that he reaches the 'Depressive Position':

> . . . in which the infant recognises a whole object and relates himself to this object. This is a crucial moment in the infant's development, and one which is clearly recognised by laymen. Everyone who surrounds him will perceive a change and recognise it as an enormous step in his development—they will notice and comment on the fact that the infant now recognises his mother.
> [337]

He sees his mother as a whole person, rather than relating himself to her breast, hands, eyes, and so on—he recognises her as an individual living her own life. It is then he realises his own helplessness and dependence. Believing he is in danger of destroying the person he most needs and loves, he undergoes depression. He mourns for the good object, destroyed and lost. At the same time, he begins to distinguish reality and fantasy: his mother's reappearance after an absence means he tests his impulses against reality, and this modifies his belief in the

4

omnipotence of his destructive impulses. The superego changes and
becomes more integrated: from persecuting objects, it centres on the
good and loved parents. Also, the pain of mourning, and the reparative
drives to restore the loved objects, are the basis of creativity and
sublimation. Thus comes about the major development in symbol
formation: to spare the loved object, the infant partly inhibits his
instincts and partly displaces them on substitutes. Hanna Segal says:

> One of Freud's greatest contributions to psychology was the discovery that
> sublimation is the outcome of a successful renunciation of an instinctual aim;
> I would like to suggest here that such a successful renunciation can only
> happen through a process of mourning. The giving up of an instinctual aim,
> or object, is a repetition and at the same time a reliving of the giving up of
> the breast. It can be successful, like this first situation, if the object to be given
> up can be assimilated in the ego, by the process of loss and internal restoration.
> I suggest that such an assimilation object becomes a symbol within the ego.
> Every aspect of the object, every situation that has to be given up in the
> process of growing, gives rise to symbol formation.
> In this view symbol formation is the outcome of loss, it is a creative work
> involving the pain and the whole work of mourning. [337]

So the infant develops capacities for linking and abstraction, forming
the basis for mature thinking. In adult life, all good external objects
symbolise the 'good breast' and so any loss in later life re-awakens the
anxiety of the good internal object. Play itself also reflects this: Melanie
Klein sees the peep-bo games at about six months as overcoming
feelings of loss and depressive anxiety, and the later play of throwing
down a rattle and having it picked up as regaining lost objects and
overcoming depression [219].

It is within the later Depressive Position, when the infant can distinguish both mother and father, that the Oedipus complex begins to
develop. But, as Paula Heimann indicates, it differs from the 'developed'
complex because of the infant's primitive mental condition:

> . . . oral impulses go together with phantasies of sucking, squeezing, biting,
> tearing, cutting, emptying and exhausting, swallowing, devouring and
> incorporating the object; the urethral/anal aims concern burning, flooding,
> drowning, expelling and exploding, or sitting upon or dominating the
> object. [219]

Fantasies of this kind are the material upon which the infant draws when
concerned with his parents' inter-relationship. Klein traces the origin

of the phallic woman fantasy (the terrifying figure who will tear, rend and destroy like the witch in fairy-tales) to the beginning of the Oedipus complex when incorporation fantasies, being oral, are supreme.

There is a close relationship between fantasy (a function of the ego) and symbol formation. The ego consists of introjected objects: at first, part objects like the breast; later, whole objects like the mother, father or parental couple. Some objects become identified with the ego, but some remain as separate internal objects and the ego maintains relationships with them—and this is what happens with the superego (the internalised principles derived from the parent figures). Thus the structure of the personality is made up of the more permanent fantasies the ego has about itself. The internal symbols allow fantasy to be elaborated by the ego, and this enables sublimations to develop in play. Susan Isaacs says that make-believe play between the ages of two and seven arises from unconscious fantasies within practical situations calling for knowledge of the external world; and the situations may then be pursued for their own sake, as problems of learning and understanding, and thus lead to actual discoveries of external fact, or verbal judgement, or reasoning:

> In particular, observation made it clear that spontaneous make-believe play creates and fosters the first forms of 'as if' thinking. In such play, the child re-creates selectively those elements in past situations which can embody his emotional or intellectual need of the present, and adapt the details, moment by moment, to the present play situation. This ability to evoke the *past* in imaginative play seems to be closely connected with the growth of the power to evoke *the future* in constructive hypothesis, and to develop the consequences of 'ifs'. The child's make-believe play is thus significant not only for the adaptive and creative intentions which when fully developed mark out the artist, the novelist and the poet, but also for the sense of reality, the scientific attitude and the growth of hypothetical reasoning. [219]

Susan Isaacs indicated [192] the importance of children's growth through play in the manipulative skills, imaginative art and discovery, reasoning and thought; further, the cooperative expression of fantasy in dramatic play leads a child from anxieties to real satisfactions in social play [193]. She went on to indicate that there is a direct relationship between the learning process and make-believe:

> In this view of creative learning the therapeutic and the educational aspects

are almost indistinguishable. It is a view point with far-reaching implications for our basic theory of learning, implications which we are only now beginning to explore. It emphasises that there is a continuity in the child's relationship with things as there is in his relationship with people. Just as our personal relationships contain echoes from our relations with our parents, so our adult interests in the world of things are impregnated by our infantile interests, for example, our earliest interest in our bodies, the products of our bodies and the bodies of our parents. There is also a continuity of development between the magical omnipotent wish of the child (and the primitive adult) and the controlled imagination of the poet and the reasoned argument of the scientist. We have to see all learning as primarily motivated by unconscious fantasy. [219]

Quite clearly there is a direct relationship between these concepts and the concepts of 'creative education' as indicated by such thinkers as Marjorie Hourd:

The skilful teacher can do much to help children to discover and to come to terms with, usually unconsciously, the hidden meanings which activities and subjects have for them. [181]

The Kleinian school follows the development of dramatic play, not merely with infants, but throughout life. From eight to eleven years old there is an unconscious attempt to repress fantasy, deny emotions, and show contempt for tender feelings. The fantasy is still there, but in real terms: his activities must have definite, concrete results. His love of secrecy expresses love and hate in a socialised sphere, and many fantasies are expressed in terms of possessions, as with personal collections. The school situation echoes the original feeding situation (the child is 'taking from' and 'giving to' someone) and learning is:

. . . a means of reparation; on the other hand, it may be invested with meanings of attack and destruction, often resulting in inhibition and failure. [81]

Free dramatic play at this age depends on others playing different roles in support of him, and he can often express his fantasies more directly than in other activities. Unconscious fears of certain situations are shown: the school or hospital drama can show underlying feelings of the relationship between mother and child; or plays on the pattern of 'Cowboys and Indians' can indicate a desire to overpower and replace the father. At the same time, the manner in which the role is played

indicates an unconscious pattern: the strict teacher, rude pupil, dominating nurse, patient in pain, a retributive enemy—all may be representations of fantasy figures. There are many dramatic reflections of
reparation—devoted nurses or mothers (being the good person on
whom people depend) or shopkeepers (the mother overflowing with
good things, or frustrating when not having what is wanted). And
however blood-curdling some of their dramas may be they represent
'in a modified form fantasies still more terrifying' [81].

Further, the Kleinian analyst finds that adult play contains the same
basic patterns as that of the child. Lili Peller says:

> The libidinal core providing the leitmotiv fantasy remains, while the growth
> of the ego works radical changes in the play activity itself. To indicate just a
> few forms of adult play: there are the so-called hobbies—an almost infinite
> variety of pastimes in which the range of libidinal investment runs from
> dilly-dallying to passion. The name seems derived from 'hobby-horse'. A
> hobby-horse was, before the motor-car's arrival, the main toy of little boys,
> providing masculine pride besides its play value and adult approved zonal
> gratification. The boy's play with his hobby-horse belonged to narcissistic
> play (the paraphrasing or aggrandizing of body parts or functions), and
> today's hobbies belong in the same group. The body play of infants is a
> private affair in all aspects, while the adult's hobby is solitary in its libidinal
> core, but socialised in its ego aspects. Fellow hobbyists share and enhance their
> pleasure through many channels, like journals, exhibitions, conventions. In
> any case, even for the secluded collector, his interest is communicable—
> whether he chooses to do so or not . . .
>
> The keeping of pets may be a more remote reflection of the preoedipal tie,
> the tie between two beings, of whom one is inarticulate, helpless and direct
> in his body wants and body gratifications, while the other appears omni-
> potent . . .
>
> In the vast realm of art we may see adult counterparts of oedipal play.
> (I have mentioned before that in oedipal play the emphasis is on content; in
> games, on formal elements. For true art, a successful marriage of formal
> elements and content seems to be a prerequisite.)
>
> While all the earlier mentioned groups of play undergo such radical
> metamorphosis, postoedipal play, e.g. games, changes comparatively little.
> When the mature ego embodies a deep and unconscious libidal fantasy in a
> play activity, the resulting structure differs, almost beyond recognition, from
> the play forms of infant and child. After the decline of the oedipus complex,
> the foundations of the ego are here to stay, and games, like other postoedipal
> addenda to the personality, change slowly and almost imperceptibly from
> decade to decade. [291]

THE PHENOMENON OF 'ACTING-OUT'

Some of Freud's psychotic patients showed a specific phenomenon: 'acting-out'. They did not discuss their problem, or represent it symbolically, they actually *did* it. They acted-out the actual situation that had created the anxiety over again, just as it had occurred originally. Recently, psychoanalysts have come to recognise that not only is acting-out an activity of psychotics, but it also occurs naturally with young children at certain stages of their development.

Freud said that acting-out was a representation of the past through action instead of memory. Both children and psychotics in the process of acting-out are intolerant of delay, they demand immediate object possession, and show a desparate clinging to the object. With the infant it is the impulsive act, his only means of gratification, his 'call' to the helper; but with the psychotic it is a regression to the infantile acting-out in order to resolve an unconscious conflict of the past, and is specifically oral in its nature:

> Acting-out, as opposed to other forms of behaviour, produces a specific by-passing of the ego. Since it reverts to oral activity with its rapacious, devouring disregard for objects, such reversion means further impairment of ego function. The pleasure principle supersedes all considerations of reality. [10]

More recent researches in psychoanalysis and psychotherapy have shown that acting-out is a stage of ego-development—one part of the sequence that establishes individual identity. This was first suggested by Ferenczi [104] who, in studying the development of the sense of reality, saw the following natural progression: hallucination, magic gesture, speech symbol, and the formation of objects. Later, Anna Freud postulated [119] the following stages in the developing function of the ego: denial in fantasy, in act, in work. Mark Kanzer [213] related the concepts of Ferenczi and Anna Freud; acting-out is the same as magic gesture and denial in act; sublimation is the same as speech symbolism and denial in fantasy. And so Kanzer could postulate that there is a natural growth from acting-out to sublimation: the former represents the projection and destruction of the bad parent, while the latter is the assimilation of the idealised parent. There is a sequence, therefore, to ego development: acting-out is the beginning of the process; then come dream, fantasy and play—trial actions which replace the passive perception of objects by their active motor mastery and their conscious intellectual control; and sublimation, when it comes, is the intellectualising phase which substitutes thought for action, superseding direct motor discharge for identification and symbol formation. Thus acting-out is the first stage of a growth process which leads to dramatic play which, in itself, leads to sublimation. *Dramatic play has a central position, relating the unconscious to the intellect:*

> On the borderline of motility, as it comes under the dominance of fantasy, we find such arts as singing, dancing and the drama intermediary between the magic of motor control over objects and the identifications that mark early phases of ideational control. Gesture and primitive pleasures in verbalisation reflect the infantile stages of communication from which such sublimations arise. Moreover, it is precisely these arts that are closest to the discharge of motor impulses characteristic of acting-out. Anthropologically, we find that song, dance and pantomime were definitely supposed to influence reality, as in the rituals before the hunt. [213]

Ekstein and Friedman also see acting-out as the beginning of the process of ego development, the sequence of which normally is:

1. Acting-out, where the infant's actions are for immediate gratification and are not tested against reality, and the ego organisation is symbiotic;
2. The first experimental recollections—
   (a) Play action, the slow replacement of impulsive and inappropriate action by rudimentary thought, as the ego is struggling against symbiosis:

   > Play action is orientated toward the past and represents the repetition of the unconscious conflict. It thus constitutes an attempt at recollection. [96]

   (b) Fantasy is a higher form of play action in which the need for action is given up because the gratifying object is internalised, and ego workings are autistic;
3. Dramatic play (or action fantasy) is an initial identification with a fantasied object in order to master the future experimentally; it is a preconscious trial solution (the first attempt to master the future) which is done by role taking; it is, too, the beginning of ego autonomy which is gained through identification (via imitation). In play acting, the child:

. . . tries to master the problem by cue-taking and by imitation . . . Play acting attempts to modify a past identification . . . (and to) attempt to master the future, to trial act, as it were, the future role with which he wishes to identify himself. He thus unconsciously repeats ahead of time the future rather than the past. [96]

And, from this point, the way is open for the development of the mature ego when impulse resolution is by thought.

But Ekstein and Friedman recognise that this sequence is not invariable:

Play action may become so stimulating, so powerful, that it threatens to lead to genuine acting out and impulsive action. The unconscious conflict, then, is not re-enacted via the play but tends to be re-enacted in actuality. One may liken such a child to an actor who plays a dramatic part on the stage only to find himself being driven to living out this part in actuality. [96]

But they have clearly shown in their researches, particularly with their casebook material on the subject 'Frank', that dramatic play is the link between instinctual gratification and mature thought just as Kanzer shows that useful sublimation depends on the pleasures of fantasy and successful make-believe identification in play.

SUMMARY

Dramatic play in children, like dreams with adults, is an expression of the unconscious. But the overt behaviour of play conceals its true meaning. The deep unconscious drives are the latent meanings of play which are turned into symbols and result in symbolic thought. When this symbolic thought is expressed overtly in play, it is called secondary symbolism and the child psychotherapist attempts to understand the unconscious through it and, thus, cure anxieties.

The nature of the symbols created were said by Freud to be based on the child's past—they act as a disguise for the primitive impulses of the id. Jung and others have demonstrated that symbols are also language, that they can also be based upon present experiences. Jung also considered that there was a collective symbolism common to all mankind. Certainly unconscious symbolic thought has mechanisms like primitive thought—they both work by analogy, are animistic and illogical, and consider that thought is omnipotent.

The origins of symbolic thought were considered by Freud to be within the first years of life, but Melanie Klein has demonstrated that they begin even earlier. In the first months of life, the fantasies of the 'good breast' and 'bad breast' lead to projective identification and this provides the basis for later identification and symbol formation (in a world peopled by gods and devils). Then, in the 'Depressive Position', the child has fantasies of destroying his mother; it is in the process of mourning that he gives up immediate gratification—sublimating his instincts he displaces them on substitutes—the first stage in symbol creation, symbolic thought, and the basis for linking and abstraction. It is this creation of internal symbols that allows fantasy to be developed and the process of 'as if' thinking which uses the past as an hypothesis for the future.

Modern research has shown that there is a logical progression from acting-out through fantasy to dramatic play—and it is this which allows mature thought to develop. Dramatic play is the child's method of experimenting with problems for, by acting, he can see possibilities and solutions. It is this process which, becoming internalised and thereby getting rid of associated action, becomes the adult's ability to think in abstractions.

In dramatic play, the child creates a world of his own to master reality—he attempts in an imaginary world to solve real-life experiences he has hitherto been unable to solve. While, under certain limited conditions, catharsis *may* occur, the basic play mechanism is the repetition compulsion—life experiences which have not been understood have to be re-experienced, re-enacted. In this sense, play is a projection of the child's inner world, it is the microcosm to the greater macrocosm and is the child's way of turning passivity into activity.

In the final analysis, play is based upon the child's relationship to his mother. It is this which is the basis for imitation and later socio-emotional attachments. In the same way the adult, in his unconscious, identifies all good objects with the primary good object; any loss reflects the loss of the primary object and so re-creates all the original related anxieties. Again, games like peep-bo can be seen as methods of overcoming loss. But dramatic play is not merely therapeutic, helping the past to adjust to the present. It is also the basis for all later living; by relating unconscious fantasies to the external world it is the basis of learning and understanding; through the cooperative expression in fantasy it leads to normal social development; by recreating the past and adapting it to both the present and the future, it forms the basis for the adaptive creation of the artist and the hypothetical reasoning of the scientist.

6 PSYCHODRAMA

Dr J. L. Moreno was a therapist who evolved, not only Sociometry, but a different therapeutic method from that of Freud. The method of Freud was for the patient to be alone on a couch talking to the analyst. Moreno put the patient, together with others, in the theatre. He called this Psychodrama. This was different from Sociodrama, which is a dramatic method of studying the group. In psychodrama, the analyst is concerned with an individual acting with others; in sociodrama, he is concerned with the whole group involved in the dramatic situation.

Psychodramatic acting is improvised, like the earliest and most common forms of acting—the *commedia dell'arte,* or the primitive rite and ritual where the mimesis influenced events. Where Aristotle saw drama as an imitation of life, Moreno sees it as an extension of life, or the:

> . . . recapitulation of unsolved problems within a freer, broader and more flexible setting. [265]

The therapeutic method is that of catharsis and this is achieved in four ways: somatic, in bodily release; mental, with the author (who creates it), the actor (who lives it out), and the audience (who co-experience the events); through the individual; and through the group. Therapeutic theatre is:

> . . . the spontaneous and simultaneous realisation of a poetic, dramatic work, in its process of development from its status nascendi on, from step to step. And according to this analysis catharsis takes place: not only in the audience— secondary desired effect—and not in the dramatis personae of an imaginary production, but primarily in the spontaneous actors in the drama who pro- duce the personae by liberating themselves from them at the same time. [265]

Moreno says his work is based on a 'socio-interactional' theory of personality: the self is seen as a total of social and private roles which the individual plays in his inter-action with others: and the roles of the individual, and of the individuals within his group, are measurable units of behaviour. The individual's ability to 'read' his own roles (to fully comprehend them) and produce appropriate role responses, is the skill essential to further human enterprises.

CREATIVITY & SPONTANEITY

For Moreno, creativity has five characteristics: spontaneity, a feeling of surprise, 'its unreality which is bent upon changing the reality within which it rises', acting, and one another:

> But these processes determine not merely psychic conditions; they produce mimetic effects. Parallel to the tendencies that lift certain processes into consciousness are others that lead to their mimetic embodiment. This is the fifth character of the creative act. [265]

Spontaneity is the ability of a subject to meet each new situation with adequacy. The spontaneous individual is creative in moment-to-moment adjustments, is flexible, evaluates, is aware of alternatives, and he plays his role of response resourcefully. In contrast, the stereotyped individual plays his roles conventionally, and only makes momentarily acceptable adjustments. Thirdly, there is the impulsive individual who misreads and misevaluates; his role responses are irrelevant or even irrational. 'Warming-up' is characteristic of spontaneity: genius 'warms-up' to creative deeds; and the infant 'warms-up' in miniature; in psychodrama, the process starts from the physical aspect:

> The subject may move around or begin to breathe heavily, make grimaces, clench his fists, move his lips, shout or cry—that is, he will use physical starters in order to get started, trusting that the neuro-muscular or other physical activities will eventually clinch and release more highly organised forms of expression such as role-taking and creative inspiration, bringing him to the maximum degree of warming-up to a spontaneous act in the meeting of a novel situation. [265]

In fact, the 'warming-up' process manifests itself in every expression of the living organism 'as it strives towards an act'.

We are all actors. From the moment of birth, the child is an actor. He has to improvise:

> He has to act quickly on the spur of the moment—that moment when a new breathing apparatus is put into function, or that moment when he must, for the first time, suck fluids from the breast or bottle. [265]

We know that the infant is to some extent capable of self-starting spontaneously; but the degrees of doing so vary between individuals. Acting provides the individual with a dramatic quality of response:

> It is that quality which gives newness and vivacity to feelings, actions, and verbal utterances which are nothing but repetitions of what an individual has experienced a thousand times before—that is, they do not contain anything new, original, or creative. The life of a man may be, thus, in his

expressions and social manifestations entirely uneventful but may be considered by his contemporaries and his friends as unique because of the flavour
he is able to add to the most inconspicuous daily acts . . . [265]

Moreno compares this process of living with the process undergone by
the professional actor:

> The same phenomenon can be observed in the productions of the legitimate
> actor. He takes a role, learns and rehearses it until it has become a complete
> conserve, a stereotype at his command, so that when he reproduces the role
> on the stage, no utterance or gesture is left to chance. But the great actor, like
> the idealised man . . . is able to inflate and warm up this conserve to an
> exalted expression by means of this 's' factor, that is, to add a newness,
> vivacity, and dramatic quality to the faithful literal rendering of the play-
> wright's script, which makes his performance appear undiluted even after
> repeating the same performance a thousand times—thus, drama conserves
> can be linked to the self giving them the character of true self-expression and
> to the actor's illusion of a great creator. [265]

The process of acting is really role taking and this is part of our
identity. The infant's role taking process is twofold: role giving (as
the giver) and role receiving (as the receiver). In the feeding situation,
for example, the role giving is acted out by the auxiliary ego (the
mother). The infant needs a helper to eat, sleep, to move around in
space but, from the child's point of view, these helpers appear to be
extensions of his own body; it is this extension of the ego, which is
necessary for the child's living performance and which has to be
provided for him by a substitute person, which Moreno calls an
auxiliary ego. And so:

> This process of intercommunication between infant and mother is the
> nourishing matrix of the first independent role taking of the infant. [265]

The mother and the child interact with the result that a reciprocal role
expectancy is gradually established in the partners of the role process.
It is this role expectancy which lays the ground for all future role
exchange between the infant and his auxiliary egos.

Psychodramatic Techniques

In the therapeutic technique, the individual improvises spontaneously. He does not do so in the same way as in the Stanislavsky
method, where the actor is improvising as a supplementary method

prior to playing Lear, but in the same way as in creative drama in the classroom—spontaneously, and just for that performance. And as the improvisor also creates the story, the actor is also the producer.

Before anything is begun, the subject is 'warmed-up':

> Psychodramatic Tests require that the subject be warmed-up to a *feeling level* in which he will release highly personalised affect material. Since the emphasis is deliberately on the *act and feeling* of the subject, the director is able to glimpse functional levels of intelligence and to detect behavioural efficiency in crisis situations. [161]

In the 'warming-up' process, and for the process of psychodramatic acting itself, great stress is laid upon body training. He is trained in the ability to relax, to liberate the reflex systems, in impromptu dancing and gymnastic exercises.

> The body of the player must be as free as possible, it must respond sensitively to every motive of mind and imagination. It must have the power to perform as large a number of motions as possible, and perform them easily and rapidly. These motions must, indeed, be spontaneous so that the player may not fail in a crisis. It may well happen that an idea may occur to a player unaccompanied by any hint of a suitable gesture, and if he is not resourceful the whole act may go to pieces. To eliminate this danger, (*a*) as large a supply of possible movements must be stored up in the body as the player can acquire, so that these may be called forth by the ideas as these occur. (*b*) creating of responses ('creatoflex') must be learned. [265]

The psychodramatic situation is controlled by a Director (the analyst) who is assisted by a number of trained performers who act as auxiliary egos to the subject. The director will choose the subject for the improvisation related to the subject's anxieties, and then train the performers in the roles they will be required to take as auxiliary egos; clearly these performers have to remain alive to the unique response of the subject (and to a variety of subjects if the same material is being presented to a number of subjects separately).

Del Sorto and Corneytz evolved the Projective or Expressive Action Test [84] for various subjects one after another:

> . . . a set of experimentally constructed test situations which provide a norm for interpreting the differential response of subjects as a *planned operational procedure*.

It emphasises spontaneous expression: it combines spontaneity and role concept, and explores the individual's relationship to fantasy and reality by encouraging the subject to externalise highly personalized fragments of his inner world. Thus a series of carefully planned situations are presented, designed to release specific parts of the personality. Test situations are as follows:

1. IMAGINARY PERSON SITUATION (no auxiliary ego used).
   Action: improvisation with any imaginary person (time, place, etc.) as wished.
   Aim: (a) what does social relationship mean to the subject?
        (b) how does he communicate?

2. IMAGINARY OBJECT AND REAL AUXILIARY EGO SITUATION (one auxiliary ego used).
   Action: improvisation with imaginary object (name given) and an auxiliary ego.
   Aim: (a) does subject monopolise, share or surrender objects?
        (b) what are the differences in acting with a real and an imaginary person?

3. THREE IMAGINARY OBJECTS SITUATION (no auxiliary ego used).
   Action: improvisation with 3 imaginary objects (names given).
   Aim: (a) which objects are chosen, emphasised, rejected?
        (b) does he have a need to integrate them?
        (c) is his interest in them functional or aesthetic?

4. PERIODIC STIMULATION TEST (several auxiliary egos used).
   Action: improvisation to a given situation, time and place, with several real persons (e.g. as an artist in a studio to whom several persons enter).
   Aim: (a) how expansive is the subject within the role?
        (b) what are his spontaneous adaptations to surprise elements?

5. THE HIDDEN THEME SITUATION (two auxiliary egos used).
   Action: subject enters into an existing situation being acted by 2 others, and relates himself by improvisation.
   Aim: (a) what is his perception of the theme situation?
        (b) how well does he create his role in relation to these?

6. THE MUTE SITUATION (one auxiliary ego used).
   Action: improvised mime with another person to a given situation.
   Aim: what physical resources does he use for communication and expression?

7. REVERSAL OF ROLE SITUATION (one auxiliary ego used).

Action: improvisation with one other in given roles and situation;
later, roles reversed and original improvisation replayed as
exactly as possible.

Aim: (a) what is his awareness of the content and manner of expression of both roles?

(b) what sensitivity has he to others in social situations?

8. THE TRIPLE SITUATION (auxiliary egos as required).

Action: improvisation in 3 given consecutive situations without a
break.

Aim: (a) what is his spontaneous adaptability to such shifts?

(b) what residues of role expression carry over from one
situation to another?

9. DESCRIPTIVE SITUATION (no auxiliary egos used).

Action: improvised description of any locality and action, but as
though within it.

Aim: to elicit a perceptive protocol.

Analysis of these test situations is then made as follows:

A. IMAGINAL CONTENT.

His choice of objects, definition of his own role and those of
others, and his introduction of ideas and their development.

B. METHODS OF PROJECTION.

His descriptions, and his perception in action.

C. PLASTIC INVOLVEMENT AND ORGANISATION.

His organisation of objects and involvement with the plastic field;
his organisation of themes and situations.

D. SOCIAL INTERACTION.

The channels of social interactions he uses, and his social-interaction
type (imitative, sympathetic, demonstrative, or solitary).

Clearly such a test explores and evaluates the subject's natural spontaneity level, his role performance and their relation to reality and fantasy, and his interactional capacities in a range of expressive situations and in many areas of contact.

Sociodrama

In psychodrama an individual is improvising, perhaps with others, and the attention of the director and the staff is centred on his problems. In sociodrama a group is improvising. The group can be small or large, but what is created is a real-life or life-like situation which will concern the group: a negro/white situation in an area where there are colour problems, or a Christian/Jew situation where there are religious problems.

Characterisation is usually two-dimensional, a type rather than an individual—a typical English gentleman, a moralising parson, a 'Jim Crow' negro:

> Therefore it is not an individual Negro, who is considered, but all Negroes, all Christians, all Jews, are considered. There are inter-cultural conflicts in which an individual is persecuted, not because of himself, but because of the group to which he belongs. [265]

In sociodrama, the subject is not an individual but the group and, therefore, representatives of the group are acted.

Sociodrama explores and attempts to treat group members who share similar problems. Primarily it shows the role behaviour of individuals through a planned series of real-life situations and asks: how, and how well, is the individual comprehending himself and the others who are co-actors in the life situation?

IMPLICATIONS FOR EDUCATION

Moreno himself examines some of the implications of his methods for education, particularly spontaneity. He considers that spontaneity training can help in both social and formal learning. For social learning, the children improvise a series of situations as they may occur in everyday life—in the home, at school, at work, and so on:

> (These) are at the beginning as simple as possible, and the student enacts a specific function in them. When these are well performed, the students are gradually placed or place themselves in more and more complex situations. No new step is undertaken until the preceding one is satisfactorily mastered. The students are told to throw themselves into the situations, to live them through, and to enact every detail needed in them as if it were in earnest.
> [265]

This is followed by a discussion:

> The criticisms range from consideration of the sincerity of the emotions

displayed in the situation, to the mannerisms, the knowledge of the material nature of the situation, the relationships to the persons acting opposite, the characteristics of carriage, speech, and facial expression. The social and aesthetic effects of the individual performance come to the front and are evaluated. Many traits which indicate personality difficulties are disclosed: anxieties, stagefright, stuttering, fantastic and unreasonable attitudes, and so on. [265]

Formal learning can be of various types. Training for a job can be assisted by improvisation as close to life as possible; the trainee sales-woman, for example, learns through improvisation to meet a simple situation before she is thrown into a complex one. Learning subject-matter can, in many instances, be greatly helped by spontaneous improvisation; learning a foreign language for instance:

> The training of language through spontaneity techniques requires that phrases to be learned enter the mind of the pupil when he is in the process of acting, that is, in a spontaneous state. In consequence, when the pupil at a later time is again in a process of acting, for instance, in social situations, these phrases will recur simultaneously. Since the use of them began in the course of a spontaneous activity, he is able to use them again in the manner of spontaneous expression. [265]

Spontaneity in education is play:

> The pupil 'plays' that situation, he dramatises the state, impromptu. He is disciplined in many situations varying in content but focusing upon achieve-ment of the needed condition. Thus he builds from within, through the process of imagination, or if you will, through the creative impulse, just what condition his personality lacks. [265]

The educational implications of the technique of psychodrama, rather than pure spontaneous play, are just as important. The process of 'warming-up' is a valid educational technique in many aspects of education: in Creative Dance or Physical Education it is a prere-quisite, and many other subjects would benefit by it. And his comments on preparing the body for expressive purposes have more importance as sedentary civilisation proceeds. As to specific techniques, like the Projective or Expressive Action Test, simplified educational variants are of value to the teacher of backward or retarded children. I have used many such variants with such children in Yorkshire and found them to be of great assistance in helping me to understand these children.

Sociodramatic techniques are of most value in youth or adult education, where specific social anxieties can be comprehended by the students. I have found them of considerable use in areas where there have been colour problems, and other locations where large new communities have been resettled ('new towns') within an existing community.

7 THE UNCONSCIOUS & THE THEATRE

Psychoanalysts from Freud onwards have been vitally concerned with the theatre. It is no accident that much Freudian terminology derives from the Attic theatre for analysts have always been concerned with the relationship between the unconscious and creativity in the theatre.

AESTHETICS & CREATIVITY

Freud

Freud saw conflict as the basis of both neurosis and creativity, but there is a difference: although both have withdrawn from an unsatisfying reality into the world of the imagination the artist, unlike the neurotic, can find his way back from it. There is a definite relationship between unconscious conflict and imaginative behaviour; a poet's fantasies:

> ... are also the first preliminary stage in the mind of the symptoms of illness of which our patients complain ... Many imaginative productions have travelled far from the original naive day-dreams, but I cannot suppress the surmise that even the most extreme variations could be brought into relationship with the model by an uninterrupted series of transitions. [135]

Where the normal individual might respond to tension by establishing a neurosis, the creative artist utilises it:

> As the instinctual pressure rises and a neurotic solution appears imminent, the unconscious defence against it leads to the creation of an art product. The psychic effect is the discharge of the pent-up emotion until a tolerable level is reached. [86]

Conflict produces emotional tension: with the creative person, 'freely rising' ideas come up from the unconscious and are accepted; the non-creative person, however, suppresses such ideas. To illustrate the point, Freud quotes from a letter by Schiller:

> In the case of a creative mind, it seems to me, the intellect has withdrawn its watchers from the gates, and the ideas rush in pell-mell, and only then does it review and inspect the multitude. You worthy critics, or whatever you may call yourselves, are ashamed or afraid of the momentary and passing madness which is found in all real creators, the longer or shorter duration of which distinguishes the thinking artist from the dreamer. Hence your complaints of unfruitfulness, for you reject too soon and discriminate too severely. [41]

The creative person allows for an interchange between the unconscious and the ego; unconscious processes become ego-syntonic and so arise 'achievements of special perfection'.

Freud also indicated that there is a direct relationship between creativity and humour:

> ... the denial of the claims of reality and the triumph of the pleasure principle, cause humour to approximate to the regressive or reactionary processes which engage our attention so largely in psychopathology. [134]

Freud's third main proposition was that creation is based upon childhood experiences:

> You will not forget that the stress laid on the writer's memories of his childhood, which perhaps seems so strange, is ultimately derived from the hypothesis that imaginative creation, like day-dreaming, is a continuation and substitute for the play of childhood. [135]

Thus creative behaviour is not merely an elaboration of 'freely rising' fantasies and humorous regressions, but derives from play activities and is a substitute for them.

Schneider

Daniel Schneider presents an interesting aesthetic view which is, however, questioned by classic psychoanalysts, particularly Kanzer [212]. Schneider considers the artist to be in the same position as the analyst: he translates dreams into forms which are intelligible and aesthetically pleasing to the universal consciousness of man. Pleasure derived from art is made up of dreams which the artist converts into beauty:

> ... *all art form is essentially the form of a dream* ... a dream whose form is essentially that of a sleeper's dream and made by exactly the same forces and then *turned inside out,* orientated toward external world-reality rather than to dream-world reality. [330]

And so:

> ... artistic technique is a *conscious mastery of the inherent power of the unconscious in its work of dream-formation.* [330]

Drama is seen as being synonymous with the skill in drawing a spectator into a magic circle and depicting his conflicts in such a way as to induce a dream-like cathartic effect from which he emerges refreshed. According to Schneider, dramatic art is the acting out of an analytic interpretation but, as Kanzer says, Sophocles does not interpret the Oedipus complex—he describes it.

Ehrenzweig

Ehrenzweig, who had an exceptional authority in the fine arts, evolved a curious amalgam of concepts: he used a basically Gestalt understanding of form and combined it with a Kleinian attitude to analytic material. In this way he evolved two concepts: a 'surface mind' which has well-defined configurations; and a 'depth mind' which is relatively formless. He relates this to Nietzsche's distinction between Apollonian and Dionysian art (see p. 20): the former provides dispassionate surface symbols; the latter provides pleasure from depth symbols. Thus Ehrenzweig can make such judgements as: classical art is concerned with conscious surface form; modernistic art is concerned with the less articulate elements from the preconscious—like dream, the attention shifts between background and foreground [95].

Ernst Kris

Where Freud placed the emphasis upon the unconscious, Kris considers the preconscious as the basis of art:

> . . . ego regression (primitivisation of ego functions) occurs not only when the ego is weak—in sleep, in falling asleep, in fantasy, in intoxication, and in the psychoses—but also during many types of creative processes. This suggested to me years ago that the ego may use the primary process and not be overwhelmed by it. The idea was rooted in Freud's explanation of wit according to which a preconscious thought is 'entrusted for a moment to unconscious elaboration' and it seemed to account for a variety of creative or other inventive processes. [223]

Creativity is seen as an act of regression in the service of the ego: in dreams, the ego is submerged by the id; in art, the ego dominates the id—the ego regulates its own capacity to regression. And by this striking concept, Kris explains art, wit and laughter. He disagrees with Freud that the emphasis should be on the unconscious: art is concerned with the daydream rather than the dream; the sense of beauty has an object relatedness, and the creative urge tends to establish contact with objects. Art is midway between the unconscious and reality: it draws its strength from the dream but keeps its attention clearly on the external world; preconscious artistic fantasies show greater freedom from superego control than ego reflections because they are more accessible to the id. In this way, ideas from the id reach consciousness more easily than with rational processes and the artist wards off any guilt by attributing the ideas to some outside agency, like a divinity or the Muse.

With a series of most striking photographs of the art of the insane, Kris examines the relationship of artistic style to mental processes. The schizophrenic, for example, avoids empty spaces and produces rigid shapes, stereotypes and symbolism; in particular he projects his own facial features into his figures in an effort to see and control himself (as with the typical mirror theme). Kanzer summarises:

> If style and creativity are influenced by illness as well as by attempts to communicate and achieve social approval; if, as can be demonstrated, they vary with education and tradition, then the role of the secondary processes must receive due recognition. Or, as Kris puts it, gifts have to be studied in relation to individual development and social conditioning. [212]

In fact, for Kris artistic creativity is a type of problem-solving behaviour —it integrates 'private meanings' into a product of social value. It is the artist's way of adjusting himself to society.

We should note, too, that Kris' attitude to catharsis is very similar to that of modern child psychotherapists:

> We are no longer satisfied with the notion that repressed emotions lose their hold over our mental life when an outlet for them has been found. We believe rather that what Aristotle describes as purging enables the ego to re-establish the control which is threatened by dammed-up instinctual demands. The search for outlets acts as an aid to assuring or re-establishing this control and the pleasure is a double one, in both discharge and control.
> [224]

Catharsis has its place in aesthetics because it provides both discharge *and* control. The aesthetic illusion provides both safety and freedom from guilt.

There have been two developments to Kris' preconscious theory in recent years, formulated by Martin Wangh and L. S. Kubie.

Wangh, in summarising modern psychoanalytic approaches to aesthetics, proposed that a certain condition must exist if controlled

regressions were to take place as Kris indicated: this Wangh called a
pivotal condition.

> Our ego has to be secured in a situation which is outside the creative situation
> if we are to allow ourselves the luxury of temporary regression. We establish
> a pivot, for instance, in sleep, with its peculiar inhibition of motility, and only
> then does regressive thinking get a free range . . . In the same way, the
> recreational situation in the theatre is a safe one which permits the spectator
> to have an aesthetic experience—but let there be an unruly crowd, and all
> possibility of pleasure derived from the state of controlled regression is gone.
> In the creative situation, the artist must be similarly secure in a pivotal
> situation whence he engages in the creative act. Very likely the pivot is
> provided by the artist's identification with the anticipated audience in its
> secured recreational situations. [373]

The ego controls its capacity in regression, allows the artist to dip into
the id for creative purposes; but, Wangh says, the right conditions
must obtain if this is to be done safely.

Kubie goes further than Kris: he denies the role of the unconscious in
the creative activity, even considering it harmful. He agrees that the
preconscious processes are the vital ones for they have:

> . . . the highest degree of freedom in allegory and in figurative imagination
> which is attainable by any psychological process. The contribution of
> preconscious processes to creativity depends upon their freedom in gathering,
> assembling, comparing and reshuffling of ideas. [225]

The flexibility of symbolic imagery is essential if the symbolic process
is to be creative. This flexibility is only possible through the free,
continuous and concurrent action of preconscious processes. But they
have to work against the ego and the id, against the unconscious
processes and those of reason:

> Preconscious processes are assailed from both sides. From one side they are
> nagged and prodded into rigid and distorted symbols by unconscious drives
> which are oriented away from reality and which consist of rigid compromise
> formations, lacking in fluid inventiveness. From the other side they are
> driven by literal conscious purpose, checked and corrected by conscious
> retrospective critique. The uniqueness of creativity, i.e., its capacity to find
> and put together something new, depends on the extent to which pre-
> conscious functions can operate freely between these two ubiquitous con-
> current and oppressive prison wardens. [225]

The Relationship of Play & Art

We have seen that Freud considered art as 'a continuation and substitute for the play of children', that the artist is a man who uses the world of fantasy as a child does in his play. The artist turns from reality because he cannot come to terms with the demands to renounce instinctual satisfactions; and so, in fantasy, he allows full play to his erotic and ambitious wishes. But (unlike the neurotic) he finds a way to return from the world of fantasy back into reality. With his special gifts, he moulds his fantasies into a new kind of reality—which others consider a justification as a valuable reflection of actual life. It is in this sense that art is related to play: both are attempts to relate the id to reality. Hadfield's two concepts that play and dreams each solve problems, and that identification in play (being symbolic) matures the development of ideas, can both be extended into artistic creation. Lili Peller sees art as the adult counterpart of oedipal play. Kanzer indicates that dramatic play is central to the process of growth from instinctual action to sublimation—and artistic creation is true sublimation to the classic psychoanalyst. Fenichel says:

> The psychological function of play is to get rid of . . . tensions by the active repetition or anticipation of them in a self-chosen dosage and at a self-chosen time. [102]

Art, too, is a method whereby the human being can relieve tensions and gratify wishes, albeit in a sublimated way. But:

> Fantasy, the successor to play, in some ways represents a step backward. The child ordinarily feels no need to conceal his play, and while play may be solitary, it is just as frequently social. In contrast, adults tend to hide their fantasies from others. They know, or believe, that they have no business daydreaming; they are supposed to be concerning themselves with the important things of life, such as earning a living. They are ashamed also of the subject matter of their fantasies, which nearly always revolve around the fulfilment of egoistic or erotic wishes. [234]

The artist, having a serious purpose to his fantasies (creation), can indulge them.

Yet why are there different forms of creation? Why does one artist become a dramatist, another a painter and the third a sculptor? The psychoanalyst would say that, while the process of development from play to artistic creation is similar, the actual nature of the activity varies

according to the infantile experiences of the individual child. A. A.
Brill, for instance, discusses poetry:

> Poetry is nothing but an oral outlet, an outlet through words and phrases to
> express a genuine emotion. Poetry is a sensuous or mystic outlet through
> words, or, as it were, through a chewing and sucking of nice words and
> phrases . . . The poet invariably subordinates the thought to the feeling, the
> affect always comes first, the words and thoughts later. Like a bird, suddenly
> trapped, the poet, when under stress of an emotion, finds himself compelled
> to abandon thought in favour of sound, logic in favour of rhythm, rhetorical
> law in favour of poetic license. The omnipotence of thought which originally
> received its first rude shock when the infant had to cry for the mother's
> breast, but which was finally gratified through breast sucking, still dominates
> the poet. He compulsively repeats this whole process and like the infant his
> affective state can only be pacified through a rhythmical expression of
> pleasurable sounds. [40]

Most Freudians would consider that exhibitionism is one of the
unconscious motives in artistic creation; after all, the production of a
work of art implies an audience. Not all psychoanalysts would agree.
Bergler, for instance, considers that voyeurism appears before
exhibitionism:

> . . . voyeurism is unconsciously warded off by substituting exhibitionism.
>   [28]

But, even if artistic creation is exhibitionistic in character, the individual
nature of the impulse is determined by infantile experiences.

Ernst Kris has postulated a logical development from play to artistic
creation. Play shows three phases of development: mastery of the body
and mastery of the plaything; the active dramatisation of the inner
world of the imagination in order to maintain psychic equilibrium;
and functional pleasure (following the terminology of Spencer and
Groos) which arises from a sense of mastery. But the first and last of
these clearly differ from the second:

> Pleasure in mastery *plays itself out in the present,* and is experienced as such.
> Comic pleasure . . . refers to a past achievement of the ego which has
> required long practice to bring it about. [224]

Kris can, therefore, distinguish between two types of play activity—
play *per se,* and fun:

Illusion takes the place of reality—and in this world of make-believe forbidden things are suddenly permitted. Freud admitted as much and we can
now add that all fun is directed toward a second person. Play can be solitary,
fun is sociable. By its play the child tries to dominate the outer world, and in
fun it is looking aggressively or libidinously for a companion. [224]

Having laid down his basic postulates, he can move on to show the
development from play to art. The first step is with the older child who
instead of doing what he wishes impulsively, can play at doing it, or
pretend to do it. (This relates to Ekstein and Friedman's distinction
between impulsive action, or acting-out, and play action or play
acting). At this point, the world of make-believe is thinly separated
from the real world in the view of the child. The second step is when
the belief in the 'reality of play' co-exists with the certainty that it is
only play:

Here lie the roots of aesthe ic illusion. [224]

And the third step is when the child accepts the fantasies of others as
well as his own. This is the period of fairy-tales which assume such a
vital importance in the life of the child.

Kris also points out that there is another factor which relates play
to art: the concept of magic. In all forms of early life, images give
power over what they depict. In folk-lore the image-maker is a
magician. Whether the image is realistic is of no consequence. The
shape of idols, for example, is unimportant; man projects his hallucina-
tory vision into the object. The 'omnipotence of thought' is a constant
feature of infants' play which may or may not communicate to others.
But art is a form of creation for communication and, whereas gestures
must be seen and words must be heard in order to communicate,
pictures can be read later—they can overcome time. Thus, they are
magical. The pictures of the prehistoric cave-dwellers, for example,
are magical in two senses: they both symbolise the past and are
examples of 'sympathetic magic'. It is in this way that the artist is seen
as magical: he creates the world anew—he controls the world through
his work.

It is in these ways that psychoanalysts approach creativity. Play
develops into art, though individual analysts differ in details. But those
parts of play which are dramatic have their future purposes, as we have
seen, and so the arts centred on the theatre have a particular significance.

THE ARTIST IN THE THEATRE

The Actor

The psychoanalyst considers that all artists show both a need and ability to exhibit. Exhibitionism is the result of an unconscious desire to show the body, or body parts, to onlookers and, in infants of both sexes, this is a desire to show the genitals. Later the male concentrates upon exhibiting the genitals as a reassurance against a fear of punishment; this may lead to the adult perversion of 'exhibitionism'. Female exhibitionism is displaced to the body in general and, socially encouraged, becomes the concept of female beauty. And if sublimation of exhibitionism is seen as particularly feminine, this makes it understandable that acting is often looked upon as a feminine art [381].

But the exhibitionism of the actor is specific and differs from that of other artists. Weissman indicates that it derives from a failure to develop a normal sense of body image. Melanie Klein had pointed out that important moment, towards the end of the first year, when the baby recognises his mother as a whole person; but, at the same time, he distinguishes himself from the nonself. It is this latter development that Weissman indicates that the actor has not completely achieved. Natural 'billing-and-cooing' is an essential part of mother-child unity, but:

> If the activity continues beyond the realistic affective needs of the infant, it encourages continuance of the symbolic union of the infant with the mother, and delays development of differentiation between self and nonself. [381]

Weissman stresses that not *all* actors have this characteristic: but he indicates from casebook material that some performers *do*. Also, unresolved conflicts of childhood exhibitionism may shape the direction of an actor, and so may a father or mother who had hoped to be an actor—in directing the child to continue his parent's occupation or dream of acting. He makes a further valuable distinction between *types* of actors utilising Ekstein and Friedman's terms 'play action' and 'play acting':

> . . . the actor who is limited to the play-action level of his art is usually an inferior, exhibitionistic artist and may be emotionally disturbed. The play-acting actor controls and regulates his acting technique and therefore is likely to be a competent professional. Depending on his talent and training, he may give a highly creative performance. [381]

Psychologically, acting is a twofold process: the ability to create another character, and the ability to express this to an audience. It may well be that success in transforming oneself into created characters is the result of lack of body image.

The exhibitionist nature of acting is also related to narcissism. In primary narcissism, the infant feels omnipotent; later he loses this, feeling that adults are omnipotent and seeks participation in the lost omnipotence. To seek to be reunited with powerful persons, or to obtain gratification in such a way, is to attempt narcissistic and sexual satisfaction simultaneously. Fenichel says that the sexual pleasure of the actor consists in using the spectator to satisfy his narcissistic needs:

> Actors, that is, persons who supply their dependent needs by a sublimated and desexualised exhibitionism, are persons with specific anxieties; or rather, with specific ways of handling their anxieties by influencing an audience. [103]

Fenichel also raises the relationship of the actor's exhibitionism to magic—the way to influence an audience. Display is a form of unconscious reassurance; or, as the psychoanalyst might say, the man shows his penis as a weapon to frighten away demons, and the woman shows her genitals as a threat of castration to frighten away demons. The origin of the theatre was, in this sense, exhibitionism: a display or 'show' to influence the gods and spectators—in all periods, the influencing of the audience magically has played a part in the unconscious of performers. If, as Hanns Sachs said [326], the artist unconsciously expresses instinctual wishes and induces the public to share in these wishes through praise (as well as participating in his guilt) this is especially true of the actor. The performer's unconscious aim is to make the audience feel the same emotion he is displaying; spectators tacitly acknowledge that they identify themselves with the characters:

> In a good theatrical performance (as in ancient worship) actor and audience feel, 'We do it together'. The audience, knowing it is 'only a play', loses its fear of the deed, and the actor (likewise the author), secure in the same knowledge, loses his feeling of guilt through the approval of the brothers (audience) which releases him, the hero, of his loneliness. [103]

Yet the actor is in a key state of balance: unconsciously he wishes to seduce, charm, intimidate or even destroy the audience; yet he must not do so or he would turn the audience against him. Pity and fear have to be evoked:

. . . the fear of God who was imitated by the acting priests—was certainly one of the main aims of the primeval theatre . . . (Also the) combination of seduction and intimidation is the essential content of all totem festivals, initiation rites, religious rites, and theatrical performances. [103]

The actor shows in his choice of career that he has sublimated the wish of his childhood—exhibitionism—achieving this by constantly testing the possibilities of his self. He tests his emotions, part by part; playing a part is making a test-identification. The actor displays his physical self to the audience but conceals his real self within the character: yet, as no good actor can create an emotion he has not experienced to some extent, in a sense he is playing himself. Fenichel says everyone has his fantasies about what he would like to be, but the actor's special quality is that he has a high number of fantasy-selves. And it is only through acting a part that the actor can sublimate his anxieties: he displaces tensions onto imaginary persons and sublimates 'unmastered' tensions by identifying with them.

So we can see that acting in a very real sense is an extension of dramatic play. Play, acting and thought are inter-related: they are mechanisms by which the individual tests reality, gets rid of his anxieties, and masters his environment.

The Dramatist

Weissman sees the dramatist dealing in the art of conflict and action like the actor, but without the latter's specific problems of exhibitionism and identity. Some dramatists may have tendencies towards acting-out but this is not the source of their creative talent.

The dramatist must be dissociated enough to transform unconscious enactments into creative enactments, and this dissociation is a function of the ego; but when personal enactments cannot be controlled the artist has a noncreative phase, thus relating to Kris' concept that creation is self-regulated regression in the service of the ego. Delayed re-enactment is inherent in the creation of a dramatist. He creates action on all levels or, more accurately, thoughts or verbal representations of actions. Thus:

What is significant is that the dramatist must contain his personal tendencies toward action—be they impulsive, direct, delayed, or acting out—and must redirect this tendency into his creations. A playwright on political, religious, romantic, or psychological drama cannot be a ruler, a priest, a lover, or a psychiatrist. Hence, whatever his personal traits, habits, and drives may be, in his artistic life the direct expression of his personal actions must be transmuted into his dramatic actions. [381]

The relationship between the dramatist's conscious and unconscious is specific: consciously he resolves the world as it matters to him, and he designs his characters as he fantasies them to be. Shaw, for example, created the *ménage à trois* of Eliza, Higgins and Pickering in *Pygmalion* from his own childhood experiences. Although consciously the dramatist attempts to portray his own special views and feelings:

> . . . he is *unconsciously* driven by revived, forgotten, unresolved, traumatic, and unpleasant childhood experiences to re-create new solutions that aspire to restore an integrated equilibrium to the disturbing effects of these long, lingering incidents and fantasies. [381]

Possibly the dramatist creates infantile situations by the repetition compulsion: certainly he has been mainly concerned with the family situation from the time of Aeschylus and the oedipal theme has been the basic dramatic subject for centuries—though central to Sophocles, Shakespeare, Sartre, O'Neill and Pirandello, it has been an inescapable element of many more. So:

> The dramatist's script is much like the manifest dream. The produced play can be compared to the latent content and secondary elaboration of the dream. [381]

The actor and the dramatist have a different unconscious relationship with the audience. The actor anthropormorphises them into a single person (they are 'cold' or 'warm') while the dramatist writes for 'everyone' and, so, for society as a whole.

The Producer & Artistic Director

One aspect of the oedipal situation is the wish to become the parent—usually the mother but occasionally the father—and this is sublimated by the stage producer into directing stage performers. As Weissman puts it:

> Maternal or paternal in origin, the identification is transformed and expressed

in the sublimated wish to be an artistic parent to his artistic children, the performers. [381]

Gordon Craig's identification with his mother, Ellen Terry, was specific: from his youthful wish to resolve his mother's financial embarrassment, he came to identify himself with the paternalist figure of Irving (who did solve 'E.T.''s money problems); his long ambition to establish a permanent theatre of his own can be seen by Weissman as a displacement of his wish to provide for and protect his mother's children; and from his fear of the dark (when 'E.T.' had to leave him to go to the theatre) came the wish for a strong father—reversing the role, his self-identification came to 'the man who could save the theatre'.

Weissman indicates that the artistic director also identifies with the ego-ideals derived from the parents' ideals, as well as his own sublimation of rivalry with the father, and this reinforces the child's artistic endowment:

> ... and drives toward a paternally influenced directorial career in a maternally influenced artistic world. [381]

Thus he 'brings up' the work of the dramatist as if it were his own child. Just as parents are inclined to bring up their children according to the principles of their own parents, so artistic directors are likely to treat a dramatic text in a cavalier fashion or with devotion.

The director identifies himself with the contents of the drama concerned but in many famous instances (the Greek tragedians, Shakespeare, Molière) the director may also be the playwright; in other instances (Irving, Stanislavsky, Gielgud), the director may also be the leading player. The dramatist-director may well fail when he fails to identify with his own works as well as those of others because (once it has been written) it is no longer part of himself. The director-actor may fail when the necessary self-exhibitionism of the actor conflicts with his parental identification.

THE AUDIENCE

What is it, in a great play, that makes us respond? Thinkers over the centuries have been occupied with this question* and psychoanalysts are no exception.

* For philosophic views, see my 'Drama & Aesthetics', *Brit. J. Aesth.*, April 1968.

Freud

Freud says that the hero's:

> . . . repressed desire is one of those that are similarly repressed in all of us, the repression of which belongs to an early stage of our individual development, while the situation of the play shatters precisely this repression. Because of these two features it is easy for us to recognise ourselves in the hero. [133]

In other words, there is a mutual identification between the artist and the audience: the creating artist identifies with his audience, and the audience identifies with what the artist communicates. For Freud the drama is concerned with:

> . . . suffering and misfortune, whether as in the play mere apprehension is aroused and then allayed or as in tragedy actual suffering is brought into being. [133]

Drama, of all the arts, has the deepest emotional possibilities and:

> . . . is supposed to manage to transform even the forebodings of doom into something enjoyable and it therefore depicts the embattled hero rather with a masochistic satisfaction in succumbing. [133]

As to the audience's reaction to this:

> It appears to be one of the prerequisites of this art form (psychopathological drama) that the struggle of the repressed impulse to become conscious, recognisable though it is, is so little given to a definite name that the process of reaching consciousness goes on in turn within the spectator while his attention is distracted and he is in the grip of his emotion, rather than capable of rational judgements. [133]

Although the audience identifies with the dramatist's creation, it is the unconscious of the audience which reacts to the unconscious content of the drama.

Thus it is logical for Fenichel to say, as we have already seen, that the actor and audience both need each other and both feel 'We do it together' [103]. It also follows that Kanzer's view of the theatre audience as engaging in group sublimations is strictly in line with Freud's thinking:

> The isolation, the privacy of the proceedings, the resentment and tension of being interrupted, the recurrent and ritualistic need for renewed participation —all testify to the basic drive that is being discharged. [213]

5

Schneider

Schneider parallels the identification in the theatre with infantile identification. In normal development, the male child makes a 'good identification' with the father, as a result of the Oedipus complex, and also relinquishes his infantile drives towards the mother. In the theatre:

> We *identify* ourselves with the created protagonists and react to their antagonists as though *we* were alive upon the stage. We *identify* ourselves, in our very bowels, with the protagonist; we *project* ourselves onto the setting and own the furniture, *feel* the dialogue as though it came off our own tongues, know the ambivalence (conflicting virtue) of love and hate, work up to the self-same pitch of crisis and climax, and 'let go' only slowly as the resolution of conflict permits us to recover ourselves as audience rather than as participant. *That* is theatre! [330]

But there is a difference between infantile identification and identification with the protagonist:

> ... when we *identify,* we do not 'pattern ourselves after' a model; we *become* him ... Not only do we identify with the character's person—with his *Ego;* we identify with his *traditions and ideals*—his Super Ego; in his portrayed time and place—with his history; for an evening in the theatre, we even take over some portion of his Id: his repressions, organised as they are with his primitive, archaic and elemental impulses, and held back by his traditions and ideals. We see him—his Ego borrowed by us for a few hours— struggle between tradition, convention, morality (Super Ego forces) on the one hand and his repressions and elemental savagery (Id) on the other. [330]

Ernst Kris

Kris' emphasis on the preconscious enables him to see the audience as having three basic relationships with a work of art: first, recognition— the subject matter is found familiar and is brought into relation with some memory trace (though, with abstract art, this is repressed); second, some experience of the character becomes part of the spectator; and third, there is identification with the character (in fine art, this is with the artist).

Kris makes a major contribution to the theory of comedy and, in particular, its effect upon an audience. Comedy helps to overcome the strange and terrifying, but not just by itself: it presupposes control over emotion before it becomes effective; once the control comes into being, comedy combines mastery and pleasure. The comic mask conceals something sinister which was once feared and dreaded—satyrs were once goat demons and the fools owe their origins to devils. The development of masks and grotesques can be seen in the Gothic gargoyles: in the thirteenth century they were terrifying figures of apotropaic magic; in the fourteenth century they were merely intended to amuse.

> When we laugh at the fool, we never forget that in his comic fancy dress, with bladder and cap, he still carries crown and sceptre, symbols of kingship.
> [224]

The fool is man, good and bad, foolish and omnipotent; but the omnipotence of the fool is inherited from the omnipotence of the demon. The uncanny and the comic are similar, as we may see in the derivation of many European words which can mean both (as *drôle* in French and *komisch* in German). Comedy is double-edged for, at its height, its effect is near pain—indeed, sometimes it produces pain rather than pleasure. Kris also defines the grotesque as:

> . . . sudden and surprising relief from anxiety which leads to laughter. [224]

Further, he makes a connection between the comic and exhibitionism: the comic is a mechanism of defence, a testing of reality, one form of which can be exhibitionistic.

Kris also raises the whole problem of ambiguity. William Empson [97] had stated that there were seven main types of ambiguity to which an audience responds. The effect of a symbol upon an audience is far from clear-cut; in any group of people there is a range of responses to a particular word or action, and these responses are grouped in clusters. Kris revalues the effect of ambiguity upon an audience but multiple meanings in art of all types are not necessarily distinctly present in the minds of the artist or the audience. Mostly they remain preconscious— in 'the back of the mind'.

Consideration of ambiguity led Kris to analyse an audience's standards of interpretation. He says there are three: (1) correspondence with the content of the work—for example, knowledge of myth is necessary for the understanding of T. S. Eliot; (2) intent, implying knowledge of the artist in terms of his society; and (3) coherence, for the interpretation of the part must cohere with the whole. All three must be complete for, to achieve the utmost effect, an audience's interpretation must supply a synthesis.

Kris goes even further and examines ambiguity in the sociology of art. The degree to which an audience interprets a drama varies according to the period. Ambiguity varies: in a period of low ambiguity, stringencies (standards) are high, and this approximates to ritualistic or academic drama; in a period of high ambiguity, ideals and social value are in doubt. To a certain extent this affects the survival of a play through history: if it is written in a period with a high level of ambiguity many interpretations can be placed upon it, and so it can have an effect in many periods. Looked at in this light, it is understandable that the plays of the Colmans are virtually unknown today, whereas dramas of the Renascence or the early twentieth century are immensely popular.

Response to a Play

To the psychoanalyst a drama reflects universal themes from man's unconscious. The greater the play, the more universal the theme. The audience identifies itself with the protagonist: the greater the identification, the more 'important' will the play appear to be. Thus the psychoanalyst fully accepts the origins of the theatre as being religious, for religion represents the conscience and morality inherent in man's psychic structure (the superego) without which no conflict can ever be fully portrayed or resolved.

From Freud on, psychoanalysts have discovered the universal themes of incest, guilt and aggression within plays from the Athens of the fifth century B.C. to the present day. Perhaps the most famous example is Ernest Jones' *Hamlet and Oedipus* [198] where Hamlet is examined as though on the analyst's couch. Jones sees the character of Hamlet fixated within the Oedipus complex. When the guilt of Claudius is revealed to him, Hamlet exclaims:

O my prophetic soul! My uncle?

Hamlet's uncle had fulfilled Hamlet's own guilty and unconscious wish—to kill his father, and marry his mother. As a result he is stunned by the internal conflict which has been re-awakened—and it is this which accounts for his supposed irresolution.

In the same line of strictly Freudian interpretation, is Franz Alexander's essay, 'A Note on Falstaff' [6]. The unconscious of a member of the audience identifies with a character or an aspect within the play, and can participate in a guilty action because he is not responsible for what he feels.

Alexander sees *Henry IV* as the study of Hal:

> The bad boy, after he has thoroughly destroyed hopes in his future, turns out against all expectations to be good. [6]

Hal has to overcome two problems which face all of us in infancy: simple childish hedonism (represented by Falstaff), and male destruction (symbolised by Hotspur). Aggression is overcome in *Part I* and hedonism in *Part II*:

> When he kills Hotspur on the battlefield, he overcomes symbolically his own destructive tendency. In killing Hotspur, the arch-enemy of his father, he overcomes his own aggressions against his parent. But he must overcome also the Falstaff in himself if he is to become a fully balanced adult. [6]

It is in this context that Alexander can answer the eternal question, 'What is the great appeal of Falstaff to audiences of all periods?':

> He represents the deep infantile layers of the personality, the simple innocent wish to live and enjoy life. He has no taste for abstract values like honour or duty and no ambition . . .
> The indestructible narcissism of Falstaff which cannot be shaken by anything is the strongest factor in its effect upon us . . . He is childish and sincere; there is no psychological situation, no matter how degrading it may be for Falstaff, from which he cannot extricate himself, from which he cannot escape with unimpaired self-appreciation . . . (His) primitive mode of lying and the indiscriminate use of any method to save his face, this mentality of a three or four year old child in the body of the fat old man, this unperturbed confidence in his own perfection, has something extremely refreshing in it . . . The child in us applauds, the child who knows only one principle and that is to live, and does not want to recognise any external obstacle. [6]

Although classic psychoanalytic treatments of great dramas are of considerable value, modern approaches are more inclusive. In a dramatist's theme, a universally shared unconscious wish is seen as varied according to the artist's psychic structure, socio-economic changes and scientific discoveries. It is possible to see this in the varying treatments of the Orestes–Electra legend. The three major Greek tragic writers all deal with this theme, but in different ways:

> Aeschylus' ability to assuage Orestes' guilt and Euripides' final condemnation of Orestes' deed are indications of the varying severity of the religiously influenced superegos of the two dramatists.
>
> Sophocles, drawing on the same legend, did not utilise the Furies and passed no judgement. He neither approved or condemned; rather, he portrayed the psychological make-up of Electra and Orestes. As a dramatist, Sophocles' superego did not stand in his way. [381]

Sartre produces an existentialist solution to the same problem in *The Flies,* while Eugene O'Neill's *Mourning Becomes Electra* and Jack Richardson's *The Prodigal* show two different solutions, based on modern psychology, to this ancient legendary conflict.

Apart from the audience's direct interpretation of a play, psychoanalysis has also had a further effect: it has produced the dramatist who, as Kris puts it:

> . . . borders on pathology and conquers it in his work. [224]

One thinks immediately of Strindberg, O'Neill, Pirandello and Genet. This imposes a further role upon the spectator: with dramatists of this type we are more consciously aware of the unconscious of the creator.

Weissman also brings his survey right up to date by considering the Theatre of the Absurd. By intentionally abandoning reality in plot and character, and ignoring logical communication in dialogue and convention in literary style, this form of drama makes the audience:

> . . . approach its language with an immediate regression identical with the author's departure from logical and reality-oriented thought processes. The author's communication and own responses are more totally in the realm of the preconscious and unconscious world. [381]

The Popular Theatre

Each member of the audience identifies in his unconscious with some person or aspect within the drama. The original ritual and religious theatre, according to Fenichel, intended to frighten and impress the audience by their experience [103] through which they attempted trial identifications with the imagined god already feared just as the original actor (the primitive priest) made a trial identification with the god.

Thus the primitive man worked through his anxieties in both an active and a passive way: he could identify with the god as well as work through his fear of the god.

The theatrical experience in all ages is similar. And this applies to the 'popular' theatre of the fair, the circus, the side-show and the variety 'entertainment' just as much as the 'serious' theatre and drama. As Tarachow says of the circus:

> The circus is the degraded pregenital arm of the theatre, but it is theatre nevertheless. It is the child's theatre, dramatising the child's fantasies, conscious and unconscious, his daydreams, his games, his nightmares, his anxieties, his wildest dreams. There is little concern for reality . . . The child is presented not only with victory over space and gravity, magic and illusion, as well as triumphs over ferocious animals; he also is presented with an opportunity to work through specific anxieties and fantasies, mostly of a pregenital nature.
> [352]

This type of entertainment offers child-like opportunities to work through disconnected problems as one act follows another in rapid succession. Nothing is resolved: there may be reassurance against certain terrors (such as the infantile problem of maintaining an erect posture, as with tight-rope walkers, or defying death with animal tamers), but no mature personal relationships are dramatised. Clowns display in their disfigurement a kind of castration as well as a form of exhibitionism:

> The circus is occupied with the same problems Lewis Carroll was as well as the problems which occupy fetishists and transvestites. [352]

The clown mask is related to masochistic aggressions:

> Certain patients, especially obsessive-compulsives and deeply masochistic ones, express many of their aggressions through facial grimacing. The clown mask may be considered a fixed, stylised grimace . . . There is a strong similarity between the clown act and spontaneous children's games, particularly in respect of simplicity and repetitiveness. [352]

The strong appeal of the clown is that he helps the child to remember that he has overcome certain childish limitations and, at the same time, offers the child a fantasy of unlimited childish gratifications. In this sense, perhaps the appeal of Harlequin and Pantaloon through the ages may be similar. Tarachow also emphasises the anal aggression of the clown, from the obvious anal slapstick of the Renascence Arlecchino

illustrations to the custard-pie slapstick of modern broad farce. There
may be some relation here to the medieval devil with his awful stink,
who was capable of producing thunder by expelling flatus. Tarachow
summarises:

> Circuses and clowns are descendants of the wandering entertainers and court
> fools of the medieval period. Just as does the conventional theatre, the circus
> traces its origin to primitive religious festivals. The circus is the degraded,
> pregenital theatre: it deals with childlike problems, avoiding problems of
> sexual maturity and sexual differentiation. It is suited for the mentality and
> grasp of the child. [352]

Puppetry, too, had its origins in the dramas of religious rituals. The
puppet stage may have originated about 5000 B.C. with the shadow
stage of East India where the main character was the comic servant
always getting a rich master into compromising situations. This form
evolved through the Greek and Roman periods, to the Italian Harlequin, the English Punch and Judy, the French Guignol, the Russian
Petrushka, the German Hanswurst (later Kasper), and the Turkish
Karagoz. Universally, the central character was the 'average man':
earthy, material, brave and cowardly, talkative, physically able, clever
and naive; he is full of both hope and despair; he trusts and is trusted,
rejects and is rejected. In fact, he provides a picture of 'Everyman's' life
as he thinks it is.

Today the type remains although the original archetype may have
disappeared. One of the most interesting modern versions, as described
by Woltman [392] was the therapeutic puppet shows at Bellevue
Hospital, New York, which had as their hero the boy Caspar. Deliberately, the puppet figures were made to parallel with what were thought
to be the child audience's desires and wishes, and as a result there was
strong identification with the puppets. Caspar, whose appearance was
ageless, expressed strong infantile desires which demanded satisfaction,
yet he knew he must adapt these to reality; here was the Freudian
'idealised ego' reaching out for reality without conflicting with the id.
Another puppet was the crocodile expressing two types of oral
aggression: his own oral aggression, and oral counteraggression (fear
of punishment). Various sides of the total psychic structure were
reflected differently.

Thus we come full circle. The psychoanalyst can see in the theatre
man's reflection of his unconscious self. The audience in the theatre

identify themselves with what takes place on the stage and the analyst can use this both for understanding what constitutes a great play (by containing the most universal unconscious themes) and also for therapeutic purposes in providing entertainment which can help his patients.

PLAY, DRAMA & SOCIETY

8 DRAMA & SOCIAL ANTHROPOLOGY

Drama is a *social* phenomenon. Based on identification with the mother it becomes impersonation—always, be it noted, the individual is relating himself to someone else. The 9-year-old playing 'Cowboys and Indians' is essentially playing with others, in groups large or small; he is impersonating as a method of adjusting to his society. So too, the theatre is a social institution. Wagner said theatre was inconceivable except as an activity of the community.

Being a social activity, drama is inextricably linked with the origins of society itself. The full range of dramatic play (from play to theatre) is observed in each civilised society, but varying according to the development of the civilisation. In one sense, the origins of society are the origins of drama because it is by impersonation and identification that man, in all history, has related himself to others.

PSYCHOLOGICAL VIEWS

Freud

It was through his study of the individual's unconscious that Freud came to see the need to explain society and its origins. In *Totem and Taboo* he developed the current anthropological views of his time (from Darwin, Frazer and Robertson Smith) and postulated his own theory as to the origins of society [120]. His thesis was that the first society was 'the primal horde', as originally described by Charles Darwin. In the original horde there was a powerful male who was the absolute ruler over the younger males and who kept all the women for his own use. The young males, kept in abstinence, revolted and killed the 'father' and ate his body. But the males' hatred for the father included affection and so there was a need for atonement and reparation. Thus arises the totem, a sacred animal (or plant) which it is forbidden to kill; this represents the 'father' and (as all the other males were his sons and the women his wives) the group as a whole. The only exception is in rituals, the sacred re-enactment of the original crime, when the members of the totem clan eat the totem father—a symbolic representation of the original parricide. Further, because competition for the father's women might repeat the original killing, the males must marry outside the group (exogamy); and, also, as the women were the father's wives, incest is prohibited. Because the father was killed, eaten and introjected his will became the law and order of the society (or the superego). The purpose of society's origins, therefore, was the need to curb man's sexual and aggressive drives—society's function is mainly suppressive. As Brown says:

> In a single hypothesis, he explains the origin of society, of religion and law, of totemism, of the incest taboo and exogamy, and of ritual and myths. Law curbs the sexual and aggressive drives, religion, myth, and ritual commemorate the crime and assuage guilt, and society is the overall mechanism of control. In the course of time the myths relating to the ritual (the ceremonial representation of the original act) led to the drama of Sophocles and Aeschylus which still makes use of the material supplied by myths, and at a further remove the modern theatre. Surely no theory has ever explained, or attempted to explain, so much. [42]

Although far from central to his main psychoanalytic theory, Freud makes use of Jung's collective unconscious to explain man's experiences of the primal horde and, more important, the occurrence of fixed symbols in dreams and myths [206]. While most modern Freudians reject the collective unconscious, Freud saw the symbols of myths and dreams as 'thinly-disguised representations of certain fundamental unconscious fantasies common to all mankind'. Society finds it necessary to disguise forbidden wishes—the sexual, the aggressive and the incestuous—and this disguise is the manifest content of symbols. But the latent content shows fixed symbols from man's archaic heritage within dreams, primitive myths, classical mythology and Greek drama, folk-tales, fairy-tales, art, religion and many other fields. Contained within them all are parricide, incest, castration, punishment and reparation, devouring monsters, matricide, cannibalism and dismemberment. Clearly there is a relationship with infantile thought. Freud shows that, in the phase of the Oedipus complex, the child wishes to kill the father, commit incest with the mother and, as a result, fears castration from the father. Melanie Klein shows that the infant projects aggression on to the mother who, introjected, becomes a devouring witch who eats little children (which relates to cannibalism and dismemberment). If, as Freud shows, both dreams and play are ego attempts to relate the id to reality, it is no surprise to discover that dramatic play has the same content as myths, rituals, folk-lore and the like.

Jung

Where Durkheim [91] had said that the individual could only be understood in relation to society, Jung said that 'collective representations' are the basic beliefs and assumptions held by a group, and these are transmitted from generation to generation. Jung also developed the 'participation mystique' concept of Lévy-Bruhl: that the non-logical mentality of primitive tribes saw relationships between things that civilised man does not—a failure to differentiate, a fusion of subject and object; thus the savage saw himself as a bird, or blamed his hunting failure upon the chance meeting with a neighbour. Jung said that the unconscious fuses things together, like society, while differentiation belongs to consciousness and individuality.

In distinguishing the personal unconscious (memories varying from individual to individual) from the collective unconscious (collective memories common to everyone), Jung infers not only the inheritance of acquired characteristics but considers that the archetypes are the symbols of society:

> The crux of the matter is that the archetypes of the collective experience, which are the symbols of the society, must be expressed through individuals; on the other hand, individuals must rely on collective material for the basic content of their personalities. [299]

The symbol itself is concerned with something that understanding does not encompass; it cannot be a means of communication as it does not refer to any known thing. The symbol does not come from experience but from the depths of the unconscious, and it emerges as an intuition. But when it has emerged from the unconscious it is 'alive' for the individual, it is a 'living thing' for him and is 'pregnant with meaning' [205].

Essentially, his view of the collective unconscious is a mystical concept:

> . . . as the body is a sort of museum of its phylogenetic history, so is the mind. There is no reason for believing that the psyche, with its peculiar structure, is the only thing in the world that has no history beyond its individual manifestation. Even the conscious mind cannot be denied a history extending over at least five thousand years. But the unconscious psyche is not only immensely old, it is also able to grow increasingly into an equally remote future. [205]

Organised religion attempts through dogma and ritual (the crystal-
lisation of original religious experience) to express:

> ... the living process of the unconscious in the form of the drama of
> repentance, sacrifice and redemption. [207]

This view is clearly sociologically based and contrasts with Freud's
definition of religion as the externalisation of man's unconscious
conflicts and their raising to the cosmic level [129]. To Freud, religion
is 'the universal obsessional neurosis of humanity' for it postulates a
loving heavenly Father who promises happiness in the hereafter in
return for the renunciation of instinctual desires on earth. Modern
society, he considered [130], was increasing its suppression; man was
becoming even more unhappy as a result and substitute gratifications
(drink, tobacco, drugs, religion, love) were increasing; sublimation
was the only answer. But for Jung, the symbols of the collective
unconscious are symbols of mankind itself, of society, and their
religious function can influence man as powerfully as can sexuality and
aggression.

However, it must be noted that, apart from direct followers of Jung,
most modern social psychologists, psychoanalysts and anthropologists
reject the hypothesis of the collective unconscious.

Otto Rank

Otto Rank follows Freud on the basic origin of society, but deviates
from classic psychoanalytic theory. The 'father' was insignificant and
the primal horde was based on group marriage where the children
belonged to the group of mothers. The trauma of birth created the
desire to return to the womb and the father was murdered trying to
prevent the sons from achieving this. Only the youngest son:

> ... remains as it were permanently attached to her, because no one after him
> has occupied the place in the mother ... [304]

and he becomes the 'Hero'. After the matriarchy (rule of mother)
comes the rule by the 'Hero' who represents both mother and father
and must:

> ... again be set up as the 'barrier to incest' against the desire to return to the
> mother ... Anxiety of the mother is then transferred as respect to the King

and to the inhibiting Ego (ideal) motives which he represents (justice, state, etc.). [304]

Society shows an increasing masculine domination in the desire to exclude women and so keep the memory of the birth trauma repressed. Crucifixion represents punishment for rebellion against the father, and resurrection the birth. Mary is the sublimated mother.

The development of society has been the gradual withdrawal from the primal birth trauma into sublimated forms as a substitution for the primal state. Primitive art created vessels as maternal symbols, and the most primitive societies were maternal. Ancient Egyptian culture was a mother type and contained three dominant trends: the religious, in the peculiar cult of the dead which emphasised, in the preservation of the body, the idea of a further life in the womb; the artistic, in an exaggerated esteem of the animal body (animal cult); and the social, in the high valuation of woman within the society. But maternal societies became modified and the developing cult of the sun-father indicates that father elements became predominant:

> The development of sun worship always goes hand in hand with a decisive turning from mother-culture to father-culture, as is shown in the final identification of the new born king *(infant)* with the sun. This opposition to the dominance of the woman both in the social sphere (right of the father) and in the religious, continues . . . to Greece, where it leads by means of the entire repression of woman even from the erotic life, to the richest blossoming of the masculine civilisation and to the artistic idealisation corresponding to it. [304]

Art itself is based on:

> . . . imitation of one's own growing and origin from the maternal vessel . . .
> [304]

and the creative artist is:

> . . . a newly created whole, the strong personality with its autonomous will, which represents the highest creation of the integration of will and spirit.
> [304]

Freud, whose theory of instincts is basically deterministic, rejected Rank's speculative system because the latter's concept of man as 'creator of himself' through 'creative will' is not in accord with Freud's ideas of the nature of empirical science.

Culture Personality Theories

Wilhelm Reich began the sociological deviation from classical psychoanalytic theory. He considered that the development of personality types was brought about by the socioeconomic system:

> ... every social order creates those character forms which it needs for its preservation. In class society, the ruling class secures its position with the aid of education and the institution of the family, by making its ideologies the ruling ideologies of all members of the society. [309]

But the man who took the final step of subordinating personality to the socioeconomic system was Abraham Kardiner, who used psychoanalytic technique to understand the formation of the personality by the environment. Child-rearing patterns produce a Basic Personality Structure, and within this structure exists the individual's character, which is:

> ... the special variation in each individual to this cultural norm. [214]

Food anxiety, for example, can in some cultures materially affect the behaviour of individuals and, thus, the formation of character. Ralph Linton showed that the Marquesans develop a specific character because they are subject to serious crop failures from time to time. Both cannibalism and the fear of being eaten arises. There is a ritual of sanctifying the hands when the child is 10 years old; after that he can prepare food for others. Food is cooked differently when being prepared for men or women, and there are whole series of taboos on food depending upon occupations. Food is one of the few things subject to theft, even in families. And so the scarcity of food has resulted in hypochondriacal characteristics within the personality structures of that culture. Linton himself says that the Basic Personality Type:

> ... provides the members of the society with common understandings and values and makes possible the unified emotional response of the society's members to situations in which their common values are involved. [240]

But this itself has its own sub-classes. Societies divide their membership into status groups: according to age and sex differences; on the basis of specialised occupations; into both family groups and association groups—based on congeniality and/or common interest; and in prestige series. Thus:

It will also be found that in every society there are additional configurations of responses which are linked with certain socially delimited groups within the society. Thus, in practically all cases, different response configurations are characteristic for men and for women, for adolescents and for adults, and so on. In a stratified society similar differences may be observed between the responses characteristic of individuals from different social levels, as nobles, commoners and slaves. These status-linked configurations may be termed *Status Personalities* . . . The status personalities recognised by any society are super-imposed upon its basic personality type and are thoroughly integrated with the latter. [240]

Culture affects the behaviour of the child as follows: first, the behaviour of other individuals *towards* him; second, the child's observation of, and instruction in, the patterns of behaviour characteristic of his society. Thus his response to a new situation:

. . . may be developed primarily through imitation, through logical processes, or through trial and error. [240]

Essentially the Basic Personality theorists see the individual as the combination of early childhood techniques and society's institutions, and that from this inter-action arise art, drama, folk-lore, mythology and religion.

Neo-Freudians

Kardiner and Linton retained the Freudian personality structure of unconscious, conscious and preconscious, and related this to the formation of the individual by the culture. But the Neo-Freudians reject the theories of instinct and libido. They consider that social and cultural factors are basic to human nature and that biological factors are not.

Horney, like Adler, is an optimist. She says that child development is not through automatic oral, anal and genital stages; rather, it all depends on how the child is treated:

. . . if others do not love and respect (him) for what he is they should at least pay attention to him and admire him. The obtainment of admiration is substituted for love—a consequential step. [177]

Being 'normal' is a term related to culture:

With us a person would be neurotic or psychotic who talked by the hour with his deceased grandfather, whereas such communication with ancestors is a recognised pattern in some Indian tribes. [179]

And anxiety, and its resultant neurosis, is a feeling of being:

> . . . small, insignificant, helpless, endangered, in a world that is out to abuse, attack, humiliate, betray, envy. [178]

Then, in an Adlerian manner, she attempts to show three human attitudes—a moving towards, a moving against, and a moving away—which, with neurotics, become helplessness, hostility and isolation.

Erich Fromm attempts to show:

> . . . not only how passions, desires, anxieties, change and develop as a *result* of the social process, but also how man's energies thus shaped into specific forms in their turn become *productive forces, moulding the social process.* [141]

Through his culture man learns to relate himself to society and, by storing up past knowledge in symbolic form, he can visualise future possibilities and consciously adapt himself through reason. Man emerged from primitive animism to being only vaguely aware of his separate existence. He grew to a state of cosmic unity where his relationship with the world and society both protected him from loneliness and prevented the full development of his individuality. In the Middle Ages, he was conscious of himself only as a member of a race, a people, a family or a corporation (as Burckhardt had pointed out); he had lost his unity with nature and, in retaining his social solidarity, was tied to the role and status determined by his birth. But in modern industrial society man has no relationship with the universe or his fellows; he belongs nowhere and is alone and insecure. Fromm sees that basic character types change as society itself changes—as did David Reisman in *The Lonely Crowd* [312]. No wonder, says Fromm, that man is willing to give up his freedom to gain security—as with totalitarianism. Both society and individuals develop four escape mechanisms—masochism, sadism, destructiveness and automaton conformity—while the 'normal' method of relating oneself to others is through love (which bears relationship to the ideas of Suttie and Theodor Reik [310, 311, 351]).

Harry S. Sullivan sees two main purposes in human activity: satisfaction and security—or the fulfilment of physical and cultural needs [350]. Anxiety, he says, occurs when biological drives cannot be satisfied according to culturally approved patterns. This is related to

J. F. Brown's concept [43] that Freud's superego, being culturally determined, is his version of the influence of culture. But perhaps Sullivan's most valuable contribution is the concept of empathy between the young child (6—27 months) and the mother. This is a non-verbal method of communication and the mother's approval or disapproval produces two opposite states (euphoria or anxiety, comfort or discomfort) and this gives rise to one of three possible views that the infant has of himself: the 'good-me' when praised, the 'bad-me' when blamed, and the 'not-me' under conditions of horror or shock.

Although called Neo-Freudians, Horney, Fromm and Sullivan are serious rebels from the psychoanalytic position. In many ways they are nearer to Adler in approach and Sullivan, with his emphasis upon field concepts, comes close to Kurt Lewin.

ANTHROPOLOGICAL VIEWS

Anthropology demonstrates the definite relationship, in origins, between society and the drama. The individual's relationship to others as expressed in dramatic play is largely determined by the nature of the society itself; and, *vice versa,* the basic thought of a community finds its complete expression in its drama.

Yet, at the same time, theories of personality directly impinge upon anthropological views of society and drama, and many of the socially oriented theories of personality came about because anthropology provided new facts which appeared to question some of Freud's findings. Freud had stated that the Oedipus complex was common to all men. Yet the anthropologist Malinowski showed that some Polynesian islanders were brought up by the mother's brother and not by the father, and that the boy repressed his wish to marry his sister because he was jealous of his maternal uncle [248]. The question was raised as to whether Freud was merely studying Central European trends. Freudians attempted to disprove Malinowski's interpretation by doing their own field researches and throwing doubt on Malinowski's psychoanalytic experience [319], but the fact remained that psychologists like Kardiner and Linton, Horney, Fromm and Sullivan felt free to develop theories of the personality based upon the socio-economic system.

Anthropologists themselves have not remained unaffected by

'depth' psychology, though it is fair to say that the vast majority have
made no use of Freud's concepts. But Géza Róheim, the distinguished
Hungarian anthropologist, interprets his evidence in classic psychoanalytic terms and rejects Jung's concept of the collective unconscious
(which is, however, accepted by Zimmer). In addition, there are
anthropologists concerned with cross-cultural studies: the comparison
of differing cultures and how these patterns affect thought processes,
perception, personality development and the like. These include Ruth
Benedict and Margaret Mead, Sapir and Whorf in linguistic studies,
Kluckhorn, Hallowell, Campbell and others who, generally speaking,
accept Freud's concepts of the personality but reject his social theories.

Cross-Cultural Studies

Just how far personality is determined by society was examined in
specific areas by Margaret Mead [255]. She concluded that differences
in character between male and female were not due to innate biological
factors for, in New Guinea, tribes show variations in the male and
female roles; and some reverse the roles as we know them. She studied
the effects on the personality of social institutions and concluded that
cultural differences produce differing personalities: where the Arapesh
are cooperative, unaggressive, gentle to children and disapprove of
self-assertion, the Mundugumor are uncooperative, aggressive, harsh
to children, and have a natural hostility between all members of the
same sex. Essentially Mead studied the sets of values dominant in a
society and concluded that these produced the 'balance' characteristic
of the specific culture. Mead recognised that there was a correlation
between early events in childhood and adult practices (like Freud).
Dramatic patterns in initiation rites, for example, have been seen as an
attempt to overcome childhood influences in varying ways: to acclaim
the youngster in his own right as an adult; to break an over-dependence
upon the mother; or to break an identification with the mother. So,
too, there appears to be a connection between child-rearing habits and
attitudes towards the supernatural: children treated kindly consider the
gods kind, while those brought up strictly consider the gods are harsh.
Benedict [27] examined the Zuni Indians, in New Mexico, and found
the same characteristics as Mead found with the Arapesh, but the Zuni
were so different in behaviour from Western European peoples that
they actually tried to lose a race rather than win it; also they were

extremely bad at assuming all types of authority and, indeed, had no wish for it. She also contrasted the Dobu, who had a permanent persecution suspicion, with the Eskimos, where war is unknown. She postulates a Configurational Personality which reflects the dominant ethos of the culture and is determined by the differing value patterns.

Modern cross-cultural studies, summarised by Price-Williams [298], have discovered many items in other cultures which differ from our own. Perception, for example, can be affected by environment and culture. A common illusion is that when two lines of equal length are placed end to end at right-angles to each other, the vertical line appears longer. But in certain African tribes the results vary: those who live in high open country (Batoro and Bayankole) are less prone to the illusion than those who live in the jungle (Bete). The ecology of peoples is probably vital. There appears to be an interaction of the perceiver and his environment—differences in habitats appear to produce functional differences in visual habits. Campbell points out that we in Western European culture live in a 'carpentered world':

> We live in a culture in which straight lines abound and in which perhaps ninety per cent of the acute and obtuse angles formed on our retina by the straight lines of our visual field are realistically interpretable as right angles suspended in space. [55]

Because we live in a single culture this sometimes blinds us to the fact that apparently basic frameworks are, in fact, created by the culture in which we live. (Cross-cultural studies of language and cognition will be considered on pp. 243–6).

Anthropologists normally study cultures either through individuals or through the collective society: sometimes they use both techniques. But, as factors outside the specific personality enter into the inferences made about the personality assessments of individuals, the collective study is normally considered more scientific. With this latter technique, the anthropologist not only studies child-rearing patterns but, particularly, collective adult phenomena—folk-tales, mythology, and the dramatic themes of rituals. In this way value patterns are traced from infancy to adulthood, spreading from individuals to society (or *vice versa*). The classic study of this type is that by Bateson and Mead concerning Bali.

Gregory Bateson and Margaret Mead's *Balinese Character* [23], attempted to show that a situation in early childhood is reflected in

both the adult character and the drama performed within the culture.
A Balinese mother stimulates her child as much as possible and then
'breaks off the climax' and appears to be indifferent to the child's
resulting emotion. Sometimes the mother even borrows other babies
in order to increase her child's emotion. The infant, as a result, is the
centre of an intense internal drama which is:

> . . . centred about the mother's breast and a Balinese baby habitually nurses
> at one breast and grasps firmly at the other nipple especially when there are
> any other children about. [23]

It follows that male adults have specific emotions in relation to women,
determined by their traumatic experiences in childhood:

> There is a conflict which recurs in each generation in which parents try to
> force the children of brothers to marry each other; to stay within the family
> line and to worship the same ancestral gods while the young people them-
> selves rebel and if possible marry strangers. Fathers and brothers may help a
> boy to carry off a girl who is not kin but no male relative of a girl nor the
> girl herself can admit complicity in any such schemes. An abduction-
> elopement is staged, but the boy fears that he will not succeed and this is
> dramatised in the theatre in a frequent plot; that of the prince who attempts
> to abduct a beautiful girl but through accident gets instead the ugly sister;
> the 'Beast' princess who is always dressed in the distinctive costume worn by
> mothers and mothers-in-law. [23]

The schizophrenic nature of the adults is reflected in a popular courtship dance:

> Little skilled girls especially decked out and trained are taken from village to
> village by an accompanying orchestra and dance in the street; sometimes
> with partners who have come with them but more excitingly with members
> of the crowd. The little *djoget* coquettes and flirts, follows faithfully in
> pattern and rhythm the leads given by the villager who dances with her, but
> always fends him off with her fan, always eludes him, approaches, retreats,
> denies in a fitful unrewarding sequence, tantalizing and remote. Sometimes
> in the very midst of such a scene the tune played by the orchestra changes to
> the music of Tjalonarang (the Witch play), a cloth or a doll appears as if by
> magic, and the little dancer, still looking her part as the cynosure of all male
> eyes, suddenly becomes the Witch. She strikes the characteristic atitudes,
> waves her cloth and dances, balanced on one foot, tentatively threatening to
> step on the baby doll which she has just flung upon the ground—a panto-
> mimic statement that witches feed on newborn babies. And after the Witch

scene, the *djoget* will again return to the role of the desirable and remotely lovely girl. The dance sums up the besetting fear, the final knowledge of each Balinese male that he will, after all, no matter how hard he seeks to find the lovely and unknown beyond the confines of his familiar village, marry the Witch, marry a woman whose attitude toward human relations will be exactly that of his own mother. [23]

In the Bali Witch Play (the play of the Tjalon Arang) the performance begins in the normal theatrical manner and ends in a series of violent trances. Performed by masked dancers, the plot is an exorcism against witches; in dramatising the Rangda's triumphs, the people aim to obtain her good will. The Witch is angry with the King because he (or his son) has rejected her (or her daughter) and, as a result, she spreads a plague and disaster over the land. The masked figure of the Witch is clearly supernatural, with tusk-like teeth and a flaming tongue, long nails and breasts that are both hairy and pendulous. The King is represented by a dragon (the Barong) who is friendly. Barongs vary according to the district, but most commonly, they have: swags of hair of cut strips of material on the sides; plates of cut leather on the back; a magnificent arched tail; an elaborate carved mask with leather surroundings; and two operators (like the men in the pantomime horse) whose bare feet and striped trousers appear below. The most common play structure is: a fight between the Rangda-witch and the Barong-dragon; the defeat of the Barong; an attack upon the Rangda by villagers with daggers; the trance of the villagers; the revival of the villagers, through magic, by the Barong; the villagers stab themselves.

Followers of the dragon armed with krisses enter and approach the witch, ready to attack her. But she waves her magic cloth—(the baby sling)—and after each attack they crouch down before her, magically cowed. Finally, they rush upon her in pairs, stabbing ineffectually at the Witch who has become a half-limp bundle in their tense arms. She is uninvolved and offers no resistance but one by one they fall to the ground, in deep trance, some limp, some rigid! From this trance they are aroused by the Dragon who claps his jaws over them or by his priest sprinkling holy water. Now able to move again—in a somnambulist state, they turn their daggers which were powerless against the witch against their own breasts, fixing them against a spot which is said to itch unbearably. [23]

This play is similar to many other 'resurrection' dramas (as in Kathakali and the Mummers' Play) but there is a difference: in dramas from

elsewhere, evil is eventually defeated, ostracised, thrown out. The Bali
Witch Play, on the other hand, has no such thing. Like the childhood
trauma, the actors approach the mother-figure, are rejected, and turn
in upon themselves.

In such ways, anthropologists have demonstrated the inter-relationship of the society, drama and personality.

Róheim & Others

While the majority of scholars studying anthropology and folk-lore
have ignored the finding of 'depth' psychologists, some have not.
Most influential in this field has been Freud and, to a certain extent,
Otto Rank.

Within Jung's own works there have been some anthropological
contributions from Carl Kerényi, mainly concerning Greek mythology,
while Heinrich Zimmer has discussed the collective unconscious in
Hindu, Buddhist and Celtic myths. He sees the archetype of the Wise
Old Man as the voice of the age-old past in man as expressed in the deep
unconscious. Thus the symbol appears as the Chinese aged sage, 'The
Old One', Lao Tse of Taoism, as well as the Guru of Hinduism:

> . . . the archetype of the Wise Old Man, the personification of the intuitive
> wisdom of the unconscious. By his inspiration and secret advice he guides
> the conscious personality, which is represented by the knights and the king.
> The figure of Merlin is descended, through the Celtic Druids, from the
> ancient tribal priest and medicine man, supernaturally endowed with cosmic
> wisdom and the power of witchcraft, the poet and divine who can conjure
> invisible presences with the magic of his songs. Like Orpheus, the singer and
> master of the mysteries and initiations of Ancient Greece, whose harmonies
> tamed the wild animals and moved the mute stones to arrange themselves
> into walls and buildings, Merlin can command the stones. [397]

The myth serves as the medium for the thought of an underlying
stratum of a population, for it contains esoteric wisdom of deep
traditions in a form the common people can understand; in other
words, it expresses in non-literal forms the symbolic figures and actions
of the collective unconscious. Indian and Celtic mythology is part of
'the soul's most ancient dreams' and it has no explicit meaning; as it
goes straight to the listener's intuition, or creative imagination,
intellectual interpretation of the myth should be resisted.

The distinguished Hungarian anthropologist, Géza Róheim, takes up a classic psychoanalytic position:

I still believe Freud was right in his assumption and that human beings probably lived in groups like the Primal Horde of Freud's *Totem and Taboo*. But what I find unnecessary is the daring hypothesis of a racial unconscious and instead I attempt to base our understanding of human nature on *man's delayed infancy*. [320]

His analysis of society is that there are universal trends common to all cultures, but that specific societies have their own particular orientations:

We can explain any specific ritual or custom on the basis of trends that are universally human and of such specific ones that occur in a given area. [319]

All men in all societies have certain things in common: sacred and accursed are both taboo since we desire what we pretend to abhor; the universal incest prohibition is a protection against the gratification of this desire; survivors of the horde punish themselves, through mourning, for their evil wishes against the dead—thus primitive kings are at first exalted and then later killed; all human relationships are ambivalent; and, lastly, the primitive 'omnipotence of thought' produces magic whereby a wish, an incantation, or the acting out of a certain situation, brings about the desired result. But, at the same time that there are universal trends in all cultures, individual societies have certain orientations of their own:

Specific forms of culture must, of course, develop after the period in which the superego has evolved for it is only with the superego that human beings, properly so called, begin. We may say, then, that every culture takes its specific colour from a compromise arrived at between the superego, as a more or less constant unit, on the one side, and the governing trauma on the other. This compromise is embodied in a group ideal. The strongest impression which the Australian native retains from his childhood is his love for the 'phallic' mother. Accordingly, a society develops whose group ideal is a father endowed with a vagina (i.e. the chief with the subincised penis; penis churunga covered with concentric circles symbolising the vagina). The group idea of Papuan society is the mother's brother (i.e. mother plus father) who is portioned out and eaten up at the feast; behind this figure, however, lurks the devouring father. Amongst the Yuma, the child is allowed to witness his parents' coitus. As a result of a systematic building up of the superego this memory is powerfully repressed and in group idea there appears the shaman who dares to dream of the primal scene and to reproduce this dream in real life. [319]

Thus it is that Róheim sees the Bali Witch Play as merely one version (but a very particular one) of a universal theme. He shows that the play bears remarkable resemblances to similar activities in Tibet and Northern India, to the wild-eyed, fanged demon amongst the Tantric Buddhists, and the long-haired devil *lakahe* of Nepal who dances like the Rangda with a white cloth used as a weapon. But when the play was introduced into Bali the ending was changed because of the inhabitants' frustrating infantile experiences. From the psychoanalytic point of view, the Balinese males are unconsciously looking for those qualities in their wives that they condemn in their own mothers. That the plot of the Witch Play has no real 'resurrection' element is no accident: in Bali a man gets what he unconsciously desires—his mother. Bali provides a specific version of a universal theme, and Róheim compares the Witch play with dramatised plots of European folk and marriage customs, drawing on material throughout the continent, and can say:

> The two dramas have a different ending; in the theatre at Bali it is regressive (the hero receives the mother). In the marriage rite of European folk-lore it is progressive (from mother to wife). [319]

Central to Róheim's work is a basic thesis: the cultural patterns of a society are directly related to the play of children. In primitive societies he discerns three types of play:

> One group in which they exercise motor skills; that is the functional pleasure of the skills mastered by the developing ego. The second group, the forma-lised games, are abreactions of the trauma of separation. The third group, also practically universal, is 'playing grown up'. Little boys call each other 'men' and they call the little girls they play with 'women'. The range of these imitative activities may vary from actual attempts at coitus to play-imitations of useful or ritual activities. [322]

While all three groups inter-relate, play as a whole provides intro-jection:

> The young of our species grow up by a partial identification with adults which gradually becomes a complete identification. [322]

Universally girls pattern themselves on their unconscious mother-figure and boys on the father-figure: it makes no difference whether the child is brought up by its real mother or father (thus answering Malinowski). He takes up Groos' point of the relationship between play and the long infancy of the human race and allows, therefore, that 'pre-exercise' exists in the play of children:

> Our delayed infancy is caused by certain biological factors. In the psyche it manifests itself in the make-believe or play phase of our life which is the human way of preparing for adult adjustment to reality. Karl Groos in his two volumes on play writes about the imitative and preparatory function of playing. In this sense we can clearly see the inevitable teleological function of the oedipus complex: in the mother we have the forerunner of all the goals we wish to achieve, in the father the prototype of all the opponents that will face us in adult life. [322]

It is only with the more developed mammals that infantile memories are repressed and that play, as we know it, is needed: as a defence against separation anxiety.

The unconscious defences characterised by play activities in childhood grow into adult life. Culture is, as Suttie saw it, a development of play:

> Our specific ways of adapting to reality are based on inventions and these inventions are sublimations of infantile conflict situations. Culture itself is the creation of a substitute object; the substitute object partakes both of narcissistic and object erotic qualities, represents both the mother and the child. In this respect it is identical with the mechanism of play: a defence against separation anxiety based on the transition from the passive to the active position. [320]

Like Suttie, Róheim relates play to culture but in a much more specific way. Drama, ritual and similar patterns are the civilised version of the mechanism inherent in play:

> The imitative or play-element in ritual is indeed very conspicuous . . . It is in play that young animals or human beings learn to substitute a dead mouse or a ball for a live one, a few twigs for a child, a piece of bark for a kangaroo. Lafcadio Hearn describes this principle in Japanese religion: 'Now there are queer old Japanese beliefs in the magical efficacy of a certain mental operation, implied, though not described by the word *nazoraeru*. The word itself cannot be adequately rendered by any English word for it is used in relation to many kinds of mimetic acts of faith. Common meanings of *nazoraeru* according to dictionaries are 'to imitate', 'to compare', 'to liken', but the esoteric meaning is to substitute in imagination one action for another so as

to bring about some magical or miraculous result. If somebody desires to erect a temple of Buddha but lacks the necessary means, it is just the same thing if he deposits a pebble before the image of Buddha, or instead of reading the 6771 works of Buddhist literature he may turn a reading-mill. A doll into which he sticks pins is equivalent to the enemy whom he wishes to injure'. A Vogul widow kisses and embraces a doll as a representative of her dead husband. The Chippewa make an image of a dead child and pretend that it is alive, the widow carries her husband's bones in a bundle and calls the bundle 'husband', and the Chinese believe that grave puppets and straw 'souls' are living beings or may become so at any moment.

The make-believe of young animals becomes a life-long, socialised, and serious attitude of primitive man, and finally in its endless ramifications gives rise to our own civilisation. [318]

Thus, for Róheim, the child's dramatic play and the theatre of the adult serve the same purpose, and society originates in:

. . . delayed infancy and its function is security. It is a huge network of more or less successful attempts to protect mankind against the danger of object loss, the colossal efforts made by a baby who is afraid of being left alone in the dark. [321]

The Thinking of the Child & Primitive Man

Róheim and other Freudians consider there is a relationship between the thought of primitive man and that of civilised children. Not that there is a direct connection; rather, both individuals have certain patterns of thinking in common. And these patterns of thought are reflected in their dramatic activity. The Balinese play is an example (whether we consider, like Margaret Mead, that the drama reflects external childhood patterns or, like Róheim, that it reflects an unconscious defence against separation from the mother) and it is remarkably like other, older dramatic rituals and performances. In fact, there is a far-reaching parallelism between survivals of primitive life and survivals from the individual past. There are striking similarities in the dramatic patterns and religious beliefs of folk-lore, mythology, present-day savages and civilised children.

Animism is characteristic of primitive and infantile minds. The child considers that objects have emotions and experience like his own (the psychoanalyst would say that he thus can eliminate some of his own

tensions and so master anxiety). But, related to animism, is the 'omnipotence of thought', or magic. Where the infant can release his
aggression against a model, the primitive sticks pins in an effigy of his
enemy:

> It is true that the child's thinking has largely a magical quality. He can
> master his environment by magically controlling the world through his own
> actions in the play situation, thereby counteracting to some extent the
> magical powers that caused his tension in the first place. In the case of
> primitive people, however, it is not enough merely to feel better in this
> magical way; there is an actual carrying out of the complete disintegration
> of the hated person . . . The feelings of hostility are sometimes fortified by
> ceremonial dances and chants that have the added quality of releasing guilt
> by sharing the aggressive impulses with the medicine man and with the
> members of the tribe. To some extent this happens in the therapeutic
> situation between the child and the therapist and in the normal situation of
> group play of children. [344]

To the infant and the primitive there is little difference between the
intention and the act, and if an action is reprehensible then the punishment is already felt. In folk-lore we see that every custom, ritual or
formula which was designed to bring about results in the outer world
(like preservation from sickness or the improvement of the crops) was
based on the belief that the human mind had, in some way, the power
to influence natural events. The psychoanalyst would say that the young
child's 'omnipotence of thought' is his unconscious belief that wishes
possess a magical power of reaching fruition in the outer world.
Ernest Jones puts it that:

> One result of this unconscious over-estimation of the power of thought is a
> tendency to ascribe external happenings to spiritual forces and to depreciate
> the significance of physical factors, just as a truly religious man must logically
> ascribe everything to God's will and has only a limited interest in the rest of
> the causative chain. Its consummation is a perfectly animistic state of mind,
> of which we see plain traces in our children when they get angry with the
> table for being so wicked as to injure them. [199]

In similar ways primitive man and the young child both consider that
unconscious thoughts influence reality but, as man is an imaginative
being, this accounts for the apparent disregard of logical connections.
Both the savage and the infant might appear, at first sight, to make
irrational connections. The savage who beats a saucepan during an

eclipse has (like the child who blames the table for being wicked) his own imaginative logic: he is attempting to frighten off the wolf who is trying to devour the hero.

But how does such seeming irrationality come about? Ernest Jones says that savage judgements are often psychologically accurate when objectively inaccurate. Dreams, for example, are considered by infant and savage to be a part of reality, and dreams are one of the bases for magic (which is 'omnipotence of thought' par excellence). Savages are preoccupied with wizardry, witchcraft and evil spirits, and infants (according to Melanie Klein) conjure up a witch-like figure of the phallic mother; and both can be seen as projections from the unconscious—unconscious hostility projected into the outside world to become an external, hostile, purposive agent. But if witches and giants are the projection of infantile thoughts about parents, so are animals. Animal symbolism exists in games and folk-tales, ritual dramas and legends, in dreams, fantasies, myths, religions, fairy-tales and simple customs. Almost universally they are projections of some aspect of the family situation—most often as father, but often as mother, siblings and children. Tribes saw themselves as descended from animals (like the English from horses) and analysts see ancestor worship as the displacement of similar attitudes to the father; heraldry and imaginative animals (unicorns, dragons, etc.) are merely a further stage of a disguise. Ernest Jones gives evidence from anthropology [199] as to how primitive symbolism can work in many ways. A cowry shell is seen by primitive man as a symbol of female pudenda but: first, the cowry became identified with life-giving powers; yet, second, the part was used as the whole and the whole as a part—the cowry is the mother of the human family, is the Great Mother Goddess who is nothing more than a cowry shell; and third, the unconscious association is really an actual identification—the cowry is also seen as the actual creator of all living things. Psychoanalysis, although recognising that there are countless symbols, considers that the number of ideas symbolised is about half a dozen; these centre on blood relatives, body parts, and the phenomena of birth, love and death. Yet the symbols considered by analysts, anthropologists and ethnologists are all concrete, albeit that they are looked at with different emphases. To the ethnologist, confetti represents rice which, itself, represents the wish for fertility to the bridal couple. The psychoanalyst, on the other hand, sees rice as the *emblem* of fertility and the *symbol* of the seed from which all the other acts and thoughts proceeded [131]. Primitive minds, in other words, use projective magic for positive action:

> The throwing of rice at weddings is symbolic: it represents an old custom among primitive people of inducing fertility. Children in playing also use symbols and dances to help approach the real world of adults. [340]

It is logical for strict Freudians to see a basic sexual element in both culture patterns and folk-lore material. For them, the simple unconscious idea of throwing an old shoe after the departing bridal pair and saying, 'May you fit her as well as my foot fits this shoe', is sexually symbolic, and female representations are found in the cowry shell, the crescent moon, goblets, cauldrons, caskets—in fact any object with an opening—throughout folk-lore.

Another important concept of classic psychoanalysis which relates to primitive thinking is that of bisexuality. Freud said that unconscious thoughts are only positive and their opposites are seen as identical: thus, in the unconscious, big/little, strong/weak, and so on, are seen as interchangeable identities. Anthropology has shown that exactly the same condition existed in the earliest languages (Egyptian, Aramaic, and Indo-Germanic) and that all present differentiations come from an original identity of opposite ideas. Melanie Klein, as we have seen, considers that the thinking of infants is similar. The thinking of early man, modern savages, and civilised infants, therefore, is inclined to be more inclusive and less prone to classification than that of modern civilised adults. Thus animism and magic are more likely to occur.

These characteristics of infantile and primitive minds are important both for dramatic play and for drama within the theatre. But not only these. A similar example is in the phenomenon of the fairy-tale.

Essentially the fairy-tale is didactic; its content is the process of growing up. It is only real in the primitive and child-like imaginative sense: the hero is often a human being involved in magic and even his birth is strange; he may be suckled or reared by an animal, and can develop superhuman characteristics or incredible cleverness; he can change his form to a bird or a tree, even in death. Marriage is the most common fairy-tale subject, but the actors are projected symbols of the unconscious—the bad Stepmother, sorcerer, spirits of natural things (like winds and the moon), the little people, or dangerous figures like man-eating giants. Apart from having characteristics applicable to all men, each fairy-tale reflects the culture from which it arises: those from

6

Germany, for example, give a high regard to children and a low value to women, provide heroes from only two strata (the high and the low), and being a soldier is seen as the hero's calling.

The fairy-tale can reflect specific primitive beliefs: Rumpelstiltskin shows that power over a man's name brings power over the man who becomes impotent once his name is uttered (derived from the belief that the gods had their own language); it can reflect totemism—the Bear-Son who is born to a bear and his human wife—or even cannibalism, as in 'The Robber Bridegroom'; and, particularly, that special people have magic powers based on specific secret information. Magic is:

> . . . very closely related to omnipotence feelings of childhood and plays a great part in the child's struggle to cope with his environment, to understand and control sources of security and gratification.
>
> Magic is used by the child not only in relation to parents, to gain their love or to secure a love object, but also in relation to siblings . . . Sometimes it is a factor in deciding the mother-daughter struggle, where the mother (or her surrogate) is seen in the framework of the Electra complex as the person who thwarts the daughter from achieving her love object ('Snow White'). [332]

Even without the psychoanalytic interpretation, it is quite clear that magic (or 'omnipotence of thought') as characterised by the primitive and infantile mind is present. Tolkein says:

> The mind that thought of *light, heavy, grey, yellow, still, swift,* also conceived of magic that would make heavy things light and able to fly, turn grey lead into yellow gold, and the still rock into swift water. If it could do the one, it could do the other; it inevitably did both . . .
>
> An essential power of Faërie is thus the power of making immediately effective by the will the visions of 'fantasy'. [359]

The hero's fortune might be made by his own actions but, more certainly, by skill or magic deriving from without. This is the 'luck' which is a constant factor in folk-lore, seen by Ernest Jones as a desire to be free from unconscious punishment. There is a child-like attitude to size: the body and its parts are emotionally important for size is part of our unconscious reality and of our understanding of the external world; even Alice alters size alarmingly, and Snow White meets with little people. She has been born of a magical wish of her mother, who died at her birth; her growing sexuality (beauty) brings a struggle with the phallic stepmother who will eat the girl's heart; from the seven dwarfs she learns house-keeping, animism, magic:

> The stepmother in disguise laces her bodice up till she's breathless (swaddling? suppression? the breasts?); combs her hair with poison (seduction? false love?) to no avail. The third time, Snow White shares the poisonous apple (sexual knowledge? the mouth?). She succumbs (enters latency?) and is put under glass until the prince comes along and awakens her (arouses her sexually?); at last they marry. So the story ends, but not without first telling about the stepmother's punishment. [332]

There is a basic primitive wish to overcome death—to ward off death and perpetuate life beyond the grave (which is seen in the rituals of rebirth). The unconscious itself, of course, cannot realise death as itself; rather it sees death as punishment (castration to the psychoanalyst) or as a reversal of the birth act (return to the womb); and endless myths and folk beliefs are based on this, either partially (as coitus) or wholly (as a birth). Of course, Freudians would say that the unconscious would see these as the same thing. The rebirth rituals present symbols of female pudenda to the dead body and this has a dual symbolism: as a promise of rebirth and continued existence, as well as a giving to the dead person their mother's womb. In Ancient Egypt, male symbols (both phallic and seminal) were also used in such rituals; sexual union and rebirth were seen as the same and thus phallic symbols helped to restore life; while magical fluids of all types from divine nectar to ambrosia were symbols for the seminal fluid, or the magical elixir of life which prolonged life and brought good luck.

But, as Frankfort tells us [114], true myth must be distinguished from legend, saga, fable and fairy-tale. Although the latter may contain the elements of myth, they have been elaborated until they are mere stories. True myth presents its images and its imaginary actors, not with the playfulness of fantasy, but with a compelling authority. It perpetuates the revelation of a living, animistic, natural world.

The importance of the myth, and its distinction from the fairy-tale, brings us to the drama.

9 SOCIAL ORIGINS OF THE DRAMA

Drama is one aspect of a society, but a vital one. By its very nature, drama presupposes communication—and this is the primary social process. A play (by Shakespeare or Sophocles, Hauptmann or Hroswitha) is an attempt at communication of a particularly important kind within a society. For primitive man it was an attempt at communication with a god, or spirit, and was an indissoluble part of communal life. In the modern world it is an attempt to communicate between man and man, between the dramatist and the community or, as the psychoanalyst would put it, between the unconscious of the artist and that of the audience. Dramatic patterns, whether in the early mimetic dances of the savage or in the intellectual poetry of T. S. Eliot, reflect in a detailed and emotionally important way the thought and life of the community. The history of the drama is the history of the human race. But, instead of being told in actual events, it is the story of man's developing mind. In this way sociologists consider the development of intelligence is related to the changes in language, myths, dramatic rituals and the social life as a whole.

THE SOCIOLOGICAL APPROACH

The sociological study of the drama considers how the culture pattern and the dramatic enactment inter-relate. That the dramatic expression of a community and its social structure and beliefs are intertwined is an unquestioned fact. How they do so, however, is a question of relating evidence from history and philosophy, anthropology and ethnology, psychology and sociology. Or, to put it another way, we are concerned with cross-cultural dramatic studies and how they relate to the development (particularly in childhood) of modern man.

Although many scholars in the last century examined sociological facets of particular periods of the drama, it was not until recent years that detailed sociological approaches could be related over the full range of drama and theatre.★ Thus it is possible for Burton to postulate [51] an all-inclusive sociology of drama.

★ Since this was written, Professor Zevedei Barbu's article, *The Sociology of Drama* has appeared (in *New Society*, 2.2.67; pp. 161–3). He considers the periods when drama reached its peak as a form (in Greece in the 5th century B.C., in China between A.D. 1279 and 1368, in India in the 5th century A.D., and in 17th century Japan, England, France and Spain) and notes that they were all periods of great social tension creating 'in many

(1) The Origins & Development of Dramatic Play

The study of dramatic play involves consideration of the tribal, racial and cultural needs and patterns with which early dramatic practice is associated. Drama in the primitive community has sociological, psychological and religious (magical) functions. Man as a hunter has a specific need of the drama.

This relates to children's play (where evidence is provided by both philosophers and psychoanalysts) and also their traditional games—the 'ring' games and 'arch' games, with their associated speech and movement patterns.

(2) The Temple & the Beginnings of Theatre

From dramatic play we move to the origins and development of drama and theatre. The settled tribal group were farmers or nomadic herdsmen, and a more stable civilisation led to physical and religious developments. Their religion had its social expression in the growth of communal enactments within the intellectual framework of the ritual myth. This led to the establishment of the sanctuary or temple—the model of the higher life and the divinity. The stylisation of ritual became liturgy.

(3) The Emergence of Theatre

Although there are still surviving temple-theatres (the Kathakali, on the Indo-Tibetan borders, etc.), in many cultural areas the theatre

---

individuals and groups powerful non-conformist, deviant and even anarchic tendencies'. He indicates that the 17th century Kabuki plays of Chikamatsu are 'expressions of a critical state either in the structure of society—conflicts of loyalty, for instance—or in the relationship between the individual and his society, between the individual's inner life and the norms and values of society'. In relating the beginning of European drama to the Reformation, and Calvinism in particular, he states that 'drama is the literary expression of the first stage in the conflict between traditional society and the rising spirit of individualism'.

Clearly this approach has much support from incidental material within previous studies of specific dramatic forms: M. C. Bradbrook's *The Rise of the Common Player* for 17th century England, Bonamy Dobrée's *Restoration Comedy,* and Allardyce Nicoll's *History of English Drama,* are merely examples. What is interesting, however, in Professor Barbu's viewpoint is that it would account sociologically for the perennial appeal of such figures as Oedipus and Harlequin, Hamlet and Falstaff—just as the concept of 'infantile drives' would account for their appeal in psychoanalytic approaches.

emerged from the temple—in Athens during the fifth century B.C., in China, and in medieval Europe with the later development of the Mystery cycles. The bonds of rituals and liturgy having been loosened, theatre became more secular and drama developed in a number of ways. The method varied according to the existing structure of the culture. All used the elements of 'total' theatre—acting and identification, dance, dialogue, the mask, music, spectacle, costume, fantasy, improvisation and stylisation—but each society placed its own emphases upon these elements according to its own social and historical patterns. From within the division of priests and celebrants of the temple, the theatre evolved the division of actors and audience. The ritual myth, however, persisted within the drama as the basis for plot within two forms: in comedy as communal adjustment, and in tragedy as ultimate experience.

Subsequent studies consider the relationship of social patterns to the theatre of the specific period.

(4) *The Communal Dramatic Inheritance*

Each society possesses inherent dramatic patterns. Within our own society, despite the breakdown of forces which weld communities together (largely due to increasing means of transport and communication), certain such patterns still exist: folk-plays and ballads, festivals and folk-dances. Variety entertainment (with its tribal and communal origins in prowess and expertise based on primitive funeral games), fairs and circuses, carnivals and fancy-dress dances are all part of our dramatic inheritance.

Other social facets are related. The therapeutic use of drama in psychotherapy or psychodrama, the educational use of drama for personal and social development and as a method for intellectual awareness—these are merely some.

(5) *Dramatic Theory*

Related to all dramatic studies are the concepts and notions of theatre which have varied through the centuries as they have been affected by human activities. Theatre has an artistic centrality in relation to all other art forms: it is the source of music, dance, the visual arts and literature. Thus the sociological approach to drama is concerned with the great critics (from Aristotle in Greece to Bharata in India). It sees in dramatic forms the relationship of man's beliefs to the theories and approach of developed culture—examples are the tragic, comic and satyric forms in Greece (and how they affected the Renascence), the Balinese drama from the Witch Play to the village dance, Sanskrit drama and the Japanese *No* plays. It also considers the nature of the audience from period to period as a sociological study.

We shall now consider aspects of this sociological approach in some detail.

THE DRAMA OF THE SAVAGE—(1)

Drama is the oldest of the arts—drama as a danced movement impersonating a spirit, an animal or a man. From it comes the dance (the movement when acting), music (the accompaniment to acting), and art (the illustration of acting). At least, this is how artistic activities were regarded by the most primitive man. Dramatic origins, however, are intricately linked with religion and belief, with the magic and magical rites which gave dramatic activities their purpose.

Man the Hunter

It was the hunter who created rites. He hoped that their magic would help him in the chase. The performer half-danced and half-acted in mimesis (the simple imitation of real action) and he dressed in masks and skins, mainly of the animals concerned in the hunt. In this way, man attempted to create the magic which he believed would control events. By acting a hunt, and his success in it, he tried to make it come true. We can see this quite clearly in the wall paintings at Lascaux where, as well as drawings of real animals and real men hunting them, there are also drawings of men dressed in animal skins acting out their parts in the rites.

The most primitive rites were simple ceremonies by the folk. They showed their cooperation with the gods, for the advantage of themselves or for both.

Although we call these rites religious, we do not use this term in the way it is used of modern religion. For primitive man adoration, as we know it, was absent. Living was an immediate question of survival, and the rites that man used were based on fear and the concentration of power. Man tried, through rites, to assume the fertility of the animals and plants, the power of the thunder and of the mountains. Mania was an essential part of the process: in a wild, frantic dance man felt himself actually become a 'spirit' with all the power that this involved. The process was helped by the primitive percussion instruments, the meaningless chants, the hypnotic rhythm of the movement, and the mask. The more fantastic was the mask, the more the other dancers felt there was an identification between the wearer and the power concerned; and this, in turn, would work upon the wearer until he felt union with the power. It is no wonder that the mask has played such a significant part in the whole history of man, particularly in the Drama. At first, the whole tribe would join in during the rite. After a while, only the males would dance while the women would stand around chanting (possibly the origin of the chorus). Later still, only the 'wise ones' and those initiated would perform while their leader commented.

Mimesis & Dramatic Dance

Man the hunter impersonated himself and the animals within the hunt in the dramatic action known as mimesis. This was a simple imitation of real actions and events. But it was not acting as it is known today: rather, it was a mixture of impersonation and dramatic movement and dance—with 'large' bodily movements, jumps and leaps as well as the wearing of animal skins and foliage to identify with the 'spirit'.

Many of the dramatic dances in existing savage tribes are intended to arouse religious excitement. The shamans of Siberia and Mongolia dance wildly to frighten away devils [362]. Many African witch-doctors do the same. The Bogomiles of pre-Soviet Russia and the Alfurus of the Celebes dance frenziedly to work up religious fervour. Even this simple type of dancing, however, is a social activity. Radcliffe Brown tells us that the dancing of the Andaman Islanders makes the individual submit his whole personality to the action forced upon him by the community; he is constrained by the effect of the rhythm, as well as by the custom to take part in the collective activity, and he is required to conform his action to its needs [44]. Evans-Pritchard makes the same point about the Zande beer dance in the Sudan [100]. But perhaps the most vivid of dramatic dances extant amongst savage tribes today is the war dance. Loomis Havemeyer describes a war dance of the Naga tribes in North-east India as follows:

It commences with a review of the warriors who later advance and retreat, parrying blows, and throwing spears as though in a real fight. They creep along in battle array, keeping as near the ground as possible so that nothing shows but a line of shields. When they are near enough to the imaginary enemy they spring up and attack. After they have killed the opposing party they grab tufts of grass, which represent the heads, and these they sever with their battle axes. Returning home they carry the clods over their shoulders as they would the heads of real men. At the village they are met by the women who join in a triumphant song and dance. [167]

That this simple imitative and danced activity could lead to a more dramatic form is seen in the description by Roth of a Dyak native play:

One warrior is engaged in picking a thorn out of his foot, but is ever on the alert for the lurking enemy, with his arms ready at hand. This enemy is at length suddenly discovered, and after some rapid attack and defence, a sudden lunge is made at him and he is dead on the ground. The taking of his head follows in pantomime . . . The story then concludes with the startling discovery that the slain man is not an enemy at all but the brother of the warrior who has slain him. At this point the dance gives way to what was perhaps the least pleasing part of the performance—a man in a fit, writhing in frightful convulsions, being charmed into life and sanity by a necromantic physician. [323]

The Dyak play is clearly one step on from the Naga dance; with its resurrection element and its emphasis, not on the sacrifice, but on the victim we are verging on the ritual myth.

PRIMITIVE MAN & THE BEGINNINGS OF THEATRE—(2)

Man the hunter began to settle in regular communities, possibly first as a nomadic herdsman and later relying upon agriculture. A more regular existence and a communal pattern led to a formalisation of his religious observances (ritual) and the concept that there was a continuing pattern in life (explained by the myth). This led to a temple drama, more clearly observable as 'religious' to modern eyes.

Man the Farmer

When man came to live by agriculture, he was completely dependent upon the seasons. His greatest terror was a ruined harvest and a bitter winter. His whole consciousness centred on the terror of winter (death) and the hope of spring (life), the sowing of seeds (burial) and the reaping of the harvest (resurrection).

There were other changes, too. The simple rite grew and developed into a ritual, a much more formalised type of worship. And the early mimesis developed more into mime as we know it—a more formalised movement which became, to a certain extent, more secret.

To primitive man, the order of ritual had a magical significance:

> The time-honoured orderly sequence itself was endowed with such magical significance that any infringement of the customary order of enactment was prohibited at the peril of life, lest the dis-order of the smallest particular invite chaos and disaster. Although modern man has arrived at a weaker belief in magic, the tendency of his religions is to continue to enact ritual in its ancient forms, and with scrupulous observation of its ancient order, even though we are less consciously aware of the magical motive. For example, the Mass has undergone no important changes in thirteen hundred years. [230]

But civilised children, too, consider that there is magic in order. Infants constantly demand that what is to be read or enacted should be in the strictest sequence.

It was natural for the association of the seasons and the life/death concept to become related to a particular man. In these early rituals, the figure of a year-king (or year-priest) overcame death (winter) to bring life (spring). Often, the old year-king turned into the daemon of death and was overcome by the new year-king. Sometimes there was a substitute year-king, or mock-king, who was fêted for a short period and then put to death so that the true year-king could emerge. And so a whole series of rituals developed at specific periods of the year: death was driven out at the winter solstice and purification followed; and at the vernal equinox the tribes celebrated with a spring ritual.

The Ritual Myth

From within the ritual grew the myth. Previously, the ritual seasonal dance-dream had been essentially simple. Now the interchange of life and death was replaced by the deeds of a particular priest, or king or, finally, god. The central figure of the seasonal drama was given individuality. With time, more deeds and actions were told and the myth developed. Instead of seeking a 'rain-spirit' or a 'spring-spirit', man sought a Tammuz or a Dionysos. The old seasonal pattern of life and death was now interpreted as the story of a Tammuz, or a Dionysos or other god, who died and was resurrected.

The ritual itself became more formalised, even liturgical [49]. A difference grew up between the celebrants (the actors) and the congregation (the audience who actively participated). The mask was still worn and it had the same power that it had in the earlier rites, but now it was also an essential part of the performer's characterisation of the god. It was at this point in time, when priests began to withdraw from the ceremony and impersonations of gods and heroes were required, that acting, as such, began. The myths told stories; so plot developed. Thus, although the rituals are still seasonal with their struggle between winter/spring, death/birth and dark/light, we are almost at the beginning of theatre.

Near-Eastern Ritual Myths

The first western developments were seen in the Middle East and around the Aegean. In these dramas, action came first, accompanied by chanted words. Elsewhere in the world, the developments had different emphases: some peoples developed mime and rhythmic movement to dance proper; in Java, the words and actions developed equally; in China, all the elements developed together into a form which included stylised diction, dance and intricate mime, a symbolic ritual and animal disguises.

From the Near East we have the Egyptian king-drama, in variants of about 3000 B.C., which is probably the oldest written drama in existence, as Gaster shows [143]. Like many others from the same area, its purpose was to keep alive and vivid the memory of the god. The basic plot is of the wise king Osiris, treacherously murdered by his brother Set who was himself defeated by Osiris' son, Horus—the new year-king succeeds the old year-king. When he was killed, Osiris' wife, Isis, went on a pilgrimage to collect for her son the pieces of her husband's body (a paraphrase of the sacramental meal) which, as relics, became the foundation for the worship of Osiris.

This relates to the psychoanalytic concept that man needs:

. . . to liquidate guilt over destructive impulses by celebrating the renewal of an identification with the ideal aims of conscience. [230]

Whereas today this may lead to the creation of art (the magical regeneration of the destroyed object in a symbolic substitute), early man found his restitution for guilt in myths celebrated collectively:

> For example, the myth concerning Osiris: when Horus, son of Osiris, felt compelled to seek revenge for his father's death, the collective conscience imposed upon him the duties of putting together the fragments of the body of Osiris, of making a mummy of his remains, and of performing the necessary ceremonies to reanimate the mummy, all in order to secure the continuation of his own existence . . . [230]

For primitive man, the very order of the ritual had a magical significance.

The Egyptian ritual myth is similar to Hittite, Canaanite and Hebrew semi-dramas which were still fertility rituals containing the death of the old king, the resurrection of the new, ritual combats and communal feasts and fertility rites. The Hittite *Purili Play* has a direct invocation for fertility while the Canaanite *Drama of the Gracious Gods* has a sacred marriage and divine offspring who have gargantuan appetites (which still survive in Macedonian and Thracian folk-plays). And the ritual combats come down to the duel between St George and the Turkish Knight (or Bold Slasher) in the English Mummers' Play. (For details, see Gaster [143].)

The content is always basically the same: off with the old and on with the new. As Cornford and Gaster have shown [71] this can be in a number of ways. Often there is expulsion of the old (king, 'death') and induction of the new (king, spirit of fertility, maypole); and there is a combat between the old year and the new, summer/winter, rain/drought, often followed by a sacred marriage of the new king to ensure fertility; or by a mock death and burial, followed by a resurrection.

It is interesting to note the growth made in dramatic structure. The Egyptian *Ramesseum Drama,* in the original, contains a great deal of repetition and no regular sequence; it was performed at successive stations along the processional route. The Canaanite *Gracious Gods,* however, is a much later and more popular drama. It begins with an introduction, which is a fertility invocation (in later drama, this becomes the prologue). Then the episodes of the myth are separated by songs, processions or dances which celebrate the god. Clearly this structure directly relates to that of Aristophanes and Euripides.

The Dramatic Dance

The savage dance was in mimesis—simple dramatic imitation. The ritual dramatic dance, on the other hand, is religious in the sense that it directly associates the actor with the concept of fertility and increase. In ancient Egypt there were at least three types of dramatic dance associated with the Osirian drama: the dance of lamentation by performers of both sexes imitated the movements and gestures of Isis and Nephthys in their sorrow over the death of Osiris; the protective dance performed by armed men miming as defenders of the god, and in the immediate proximity of the king-god or the actor representing him; and a fertility dance performed by both men and women, which attempted, through vigour and strength, to resurrect the god and thus give vitality to the crops and herds. Associated with the Egyptian funeral dances were the *Nemou:* these appear to have been African dwarfs or pigmies, who skipped and balanced, but also represented burlesque 'kings' within the ritual dance. Spence points out [346] that the same figure can be seen in the wall paintings of Aurignacian Man; and his descendants go down to the medieval 'mock-King', the physically malformed clown, Dossennus and Punch.

In Egypt and the Near East, as in many nomadic and farming tribes and civilisations, the dance was an inherent part of the religion. Its mimetic quality related the actor to the concept of fertility. The ritual myth is still alive and believed amongst such peoples as Mandan Indians in Dakota, with their Buffalo Dance, the Pawnees in Nebraska and North Dakota with their Bear Dance, the Zuni of New Mexico, the Hopi folk, and the Yukon Esquimaux. The men of the Torres Straits mime the actions of pigeons in the fertility dance, and the actions of the dead in funeral dance-dramas. Similar dramatic dances are found amongst many African tribes—the Yorubas and the Quallos in West Africa, the Nkimba in the Lower Congo, the Bagesu of Mount Elgon, to name but a few.

The Temple

The formalisation of simple religion into the ritual myth, and the more settled communal civilisation, the patterning of seasonal life and the growth from mimesis to a more formal dramatic dance, led to the establishment of a physical focus for spiritual life. Thus the sanctuary or temple occurs as the model of the higher life and the physical representation of the concept of the divinity.

Where the ritual combat, or mimetic battle between life and death, was enacted within the temple by performers, the building itself had to be purged and cleansed at the beginning of the new lease of life. In Egypt, sacred buildings were ritually cleansed during the annual celebrations of the mysteries of Osiris. The Hittites ceremoniously destroyed and replaced the furniture and vessels of the holy place. That this practice continued long after the ritual myth had lost its power is not merely attested by examples from Rome, the Hebrews and the Incas, but also amongst modern cultures: in Siam, Eastern Russia, Togoland, South-east New Guinea, India, Cambodia, and elsewhere (as Frazer shows [115]). It was also associated with removing from the temple the boughs and twigs from the previous year's celebration, and replacing them with new ones—degenerating into the common European practice of introducing new maypoles each spring.

It follows that, within such a holy place, worship became more formal. The ritual became a form of liturgy which, even in Christian forms, is a dramatic method of demonstrating the life of the divinity. But it also implies 'explanation' for when the ritual had become so detailed, so mysterious, even so secret, a form of words and actions had to be so designed that it would communicate its message to the 'people'.

THE EMERGENCE OF THEATRE: GREECE—(3)

Of the many variations of the emergence of theatre from the temple, probably the most famous is the development of the classic drama. Greek religion was very similar to that of the Near East and, to a certain extent, developed from it. While in the villages it centred on the small public sanctuary, larger communities had their temples. But, within a comparatively short period of time, dramatic activity had grown from an entirely religious enactment to a communal expression of religious material which is 'theatre' in its complete form.

There are, of course, many direct relationships between the Ritual Dramas and the world of Greece and Rome. The Syrian and Babylonian ritual myths celebrated Tammuz Adon (or Adonis) who was also a powerful god in the Greece of the seventh century B.C. As late as 499 B.C. Herodotus reported two surviving Egyptian resurrection plays and noted their influence on Greek mystery cults. All these dramas had the strong tension and emotion of bloody deeds and merciless acts: we should remember that the highly emotional rites of Attis, which spread throughout Asia Minor at this period, even caused a sensation in the Rome of the third century A.D.

But possibly the most important ritual influence upon subsequent drama (particularly the great Attic plays of the fifth century B.C.) is to be seen in the figure of Dionysos. Probably originating in Assyria or Thrace, the worship of Dionysos was similar to many other worships throughout the Near East. Homer mentions the Maenads, the wild women raging through the Thracian mountains, frantically dancing in circles, wearing flowing garments of animal-skins with horns, and carrying sacred snakes. At the height of their frenzy they tore the sacrificial bull (Dionysos was often symbolised as a bull) to pieces, limb by limb, and devoured it raw (*omophagia*) thereby spreading the god's power over the world. The frenzy was deliberately sought (the convulsive attempts at union with the god led directly to *omophagia* in many similar religions) because, through this ecstasy, man's soul could force its way into the god. (When man can do this, says Plato in *Ion*, the streams will run with milk and honey and life will be eternal bliss.) When the Dionysian cult reached Greece it was remarkably popular. His myth grew quickly, taking over attributes of other gods and associating with the whole background of fertility ritual. This frenzied worship saw Dionysos as the god of fertility, spring and growth, then of wine and the worship of the dead; and his mania was particularly associated with the phallus attribute. The great dramas of Aeschylus, Sophocles and Euripides were in honour of Dionysos and the place where they were performed was The Great Dionysia in Athens, still standing today.

So, from the king drama of the Egypt of 3000 B.C. to Euripides' *Bacchae* (c. 408—406 B.C.) we are concerned with the same type of material: the ritual myths, set within a liturgical framework and telling of the most elementary and vital problems of living and dying. But, in the Attic theatre, there is a different emphasis: the bonds of ritual and liturgy have been released: although still performed within a religious building it is a theatre *and* a temple; and there is a gradual development from Aeschylus to Euripides, from acceptance to questioning of the gods. Further, there is a development from the ritual as such to the dramatic forms of tragedy, comedy and satyric drama.

Greek Drama

We have seen how the Attic drama grew out of Dionysian worship. In its greatest days in the fifth century B.C., it was an act of worship in the Theatre of Dionysos in Athens. Yet (according to Aristotle) it:

> ... began with improvisations; (tragedy) from the leaders of the dithyramb, (comedy) from those who led off the phallic songs which still exist as institutions in some of our cities. [14]

The dithyramb was a poetic song for Dionysos about the springtime lust for life. Originally improvised and rhapsodical, it became more literary although still passionate and accompanied by the Phrygian flute.

In Greece, the change from ritual to drama came quickly. Originally, we assume the chanting of a worshipping chorus with a leader (*exarchon*). Later, the leader (now styled *coryphaeus*) turned into a commentator (*hypokrites*) and so, by progression, into a certain character whose words were answered by a chanting chorus. The development from this initial stage is assigned by tradition to the legendary Thespis of Icara (about 535 B.C.): perhaps it was Thespis who introduced an actor to talk to the leader of the chorus (which is the essence of Western drama) and who put a table or a cart in the middle of the circle where the chorus danced (the cart and circle being the origin of the stage and *orchestra*). By the fifth century, out of the six days given up to Dionysian celebrations, three were for dramatic performances. Three tragedies (by one poet) and a comedy were given on one day and were written for one performance only. And to win the dramatic contest brought great religious honour and glory to all who had taken part. The development from magic ritual to dramatic art in Greek civilisation has many analogies in other culture areas and the common element, as Kris tells us [224], is the reduction of action and its replacement by other (substitute) elements.

The socio-religious origins of tragedy are clearly seen in the figure of Dionysos who, like so many other figures in the Near East, is symbolic of seasonal change and includes within himself the concepts of fertility and the worship of the dead. Although this 'Year Demon' theory has been admirably propounded by Jane E. Harrison [166], Gilbert Murray [272, 274], and Gaster [143], there is one factor unaccounted for: *omophagia*. The word 'tragedy' may have come from the prize (a goat, *tragos*) awarded to the first winner of the contests for tragedy (supposedly Thespis). Or it may have come from 'the song of the *tragoi*', the followers of Dionysos (possibly the original chorus) who slaughtered the god in his incarnation as a goat and ate him in a sacrificial meal. Although *omophagia* is a convulsive attempt at union with the god and the spreading of his power over the land, it has also been suggested that:

Tragedy arose out of human sacrifice; it is still a substitute for it. [5]

Human sacrifice was still practised by fifth-century Greeks, though degenerating. The substitution of an animal victim had probably been the first development, accompanied by songs and mimetic dances. Then there came a shift of interest from the *act* of sacrifice to its *victim*. Thus ritual and heroic myth are combined and there results the fusion of dance, instrumental music, acting and majestic hieratic language which is Attic tragedy.

Attic comedy had a lower social origin [71]. It grew out of the ribald and noisy Dionysian street procession which ended in a phallic song. Whereas tragedy had one chorus, comedy had two: the satiric shouts of the onlookers in the streets became incorporated into the drama. In existing Attic comedies (all by Aristophanes) the Dionysian elements are clearly seen in the obscenities, the animal choruses, and the aggression in the *parabasis* (the oldest element in the play). But in these plays, too, we can also see the farce influence of the Dorians of Megara. Aristotle said they claimed the first comedy, naming it after one of their villages (the *comai*), and the Dorian mime certainly existed in the Peloponnesus from the sixth century B.C. Its style is seen from period vases (illustrated in Nicoll's *Masks, Mimes and Miracles* [276]: pairs of masked figures are dancing in grossly-padded tight-fitting costumes; vases (illustrated in Nicoll's *Masks, Mimes and Miracles* [276]): pairs of orgy and theft. There was a buffoonish Heracles, animal masks and various *moros*—the generic name for the mimic fool, a slapstick clown-dancer-juggler whose descendants perform right down to the present day. Aristophanes inherited both the Dionysian and Dorian traditions.

Greek Dramatic Dance

In no civilisation did the dramatic dance reach such a ritualistic and religious height as in Greece. 'Its main aim was to make gesture represent feeling, passion and action', and all parts of the body were used. Chiefly associated with the cults of Apollo and Dionysos, these choral dances were so mimetic that Gilbert Murray [166] saw the origin of tragedy in the ritual dance for Dionysos. The *Geranos,* or Crane Dance, was supposed to have been performed by Theseus on his return from the Labyrinth at Crete, and represented the windings of the maze at Knossos in its three parts: the strophe, with movements from right to left (the ominous régime of the Minotaur); and anti-strophe, where the movement was reversed (the release from the Minotaur); and the stationary, slow and grave (thanksgiving). The performers danced in line, like cranes, as though following the clue by which Theseus solved the Labyrinth. The Phaiakian Dance was performed by young men circulating around a singer—like the Egyptian protective dance. At Dionysian festivals three dances were performed—the *Eucmeleia,* the *Kordax* and the *Sikinnis* (tragic, comic and satyric)— which tradition said had been introduced from Egypt and originated in the ritual dramas of Osiris. The *Hyporchema* Dance, sacred to Apollo, was sometimes danced for Dionysos and Pallas Athene, while the *Pyrrhic* Dance was imitative of battle and was said to have originated in Doria. The importance of the dramatic dance in Greece cannot be over-estimated. Spence says:

> . . . ritual is the mimetic magic by virtue of which religious acts for the behoof of the community are performed; myth is the account of those acts in words, while the dance actually brings them to view. It is thus a living frieze of ritual action from which the myth emanates in the choral song which frequently accompanied the sacred dance. Yet all three—ritual, dance, and myth—are really one; they were originally indivisible parts of a single thought-process . . . [346]

Thus, in the Attic drama, dance reached its ultimate form in theatrical expression.

DRAMA WITHIN A SPECIFIC CULTURE: MEDIEVAL EUROPE

The sociological approach considers the inter-relationship of all cultural factors and their specific relationship to the dramatic activity of the society. While it is possible to do this within any specific culture, perhaps medieval Europe can provide us with the simplest example. After the fall of the Roman Empire, Europe rebuilt its dramatic traditions from its original bases—from remembrances of rites and rituals, folk beliefs and customs. Then, from the tenth century, a new temple drama began to evolve, developing into theatre proper with the Mystery cycles in the thirteenth or fourteenth centuries.

(1) *Origins & Development of Dramatic Play*

(a) FOLK BELIEFS & THEIR DRAMATIC CONTENT

Pagan rites and rituals were a vital part of medieval man's consciousness. The Germanic tribes of Europe were not easily made Christian [153] and much of folk-lore goes back to the pagan days—some modern customs are residues without the participants realising the origins [282]. So strong were the traditions that, although the Church opposed them rigorously, it was only Gregory the Great's policy of assimilation, whereby pagan celebrations were used by the Church in its missionary policy, that the Church achieved its final victory.

Throughout Europe there are semi-dramatic activities associated with dances, games, and seasonal activities. English examples are paralleled in folk activities from Scandinavia to Thrace [292] and they all bear resemblances to Dionysian celebrations. The purpose of the dancers and the mummers was always to make the crops grow and showed the eternal struggle: sun/moon, winter/summer, darkness/light, death/life. The old year-king dies that the new year-king may live— like Osiris and Horus.

The periodic death of the year-king, and its association with sacrifice, was essential to the well-being of the community. It occurred in the Feast of Fools [59], and in the revival carried out by the 'Doctor' in *St George* plays. In other ceremonies a mock Death (a doll, some twigs or some straw) might be carried round the village and finally expelled; sometimes the pagan folk brought back with them the summer tree. Sometimes a real man was expelled: the Pfingstl in Bavaria, a 'wild man' in Thuringia, and 'Jack o'Lent' in England; a 'scapegoat' was expelled from Athens in May, and Frazer [115] provides examples from the Incas, Siam, Eastern Russia, Togoland, New Guinea, throughout India, Cambodia, the Esquimaux and elsewhere.

The medieval folk lived in an animistic world: when both trees and animals were worshipped, the mummers dressed themselves in leaves as well as horns and skins. Also, they honoured and feared the dead:

they asked for their help in war and the agricultural struggle, and they
were kept in good humour by food—often beans and peas (even in late
Tudor times they chose a King of the Bean and Queen of the Pea on
Twelfth Night) or at a banquet when 'The Table of Fortune' was laid
out [188] for the ghostly 'Wild Hunt' from the spirit world. But the
mummers also had expulsory rites for the dead: shouting, ringing bells
and brandishing swords; or sweeping the dead out of the house with a
broom. Where ancient Babylon purged death by fire, the medieval
folk expelled the dead with bonfires or by running round the fields
with flaming torches [382].

Primitive rites and rituals, being seasonally based, were usually
performed at 'critical' times of the year. But medieval Europe had to
absorb all the Celto-Teutonic, Roman and Christian calendars within a
comparatively short space of time; as a result, there was much con-
fusion and overlapping of the rites to be celebrated at particular
festivals, and mummings of similar types could be performed at
Christmas, Shrove Tuesday, Easter or May Day.

The mid-winter celebrations combined the Celtic Yule, the Roman
Kalends and Saturnalia, and the Christian Christmas [382]. Yule
attempted to create magic for the future prosperity, was a festival for
the dead (surviving in All Saints' Day and All Souls' Day), and was a
time of sacrifice—November was Bede's 'Blot-Monath' when animals
that could not be fed during the winter were slaughtered sacrificially.
The Kalends relaxed rules of conduct and inverted social status:
masters and slaves changed places, acted each other's roles, feasted and
played at dice together. (This inversion of civilisation is central, in a
different way, to psychoanalysis). The Church denounced it (and its
survival, the Feast of Fools) as it recognised the pagan element in the
dramatic procession of mummers in animal-skins, masks and women's
clothes, and in the *cervulus*—the hobby-horse that was the survival of
the sacrificial victim [59]. The Twelve Days of Christmas was an
intercalary, or epagomenal, period: the gap between the lunar and
calendar years and inserted by civilisations as far apart as India and the
Aztecs, Ethiopia and the Mayas. The Twelve Days were 'outside time',
of suspended animation, and so superstitions clung to it and, although
officially ending on the first Monday after Twelfth Night (Epiphany or
Plough Monday), it was eventually extended to Shrovetide, or
Carnival. Carnival was a relic of the Roman Saturnalia when there
were rites of sowing and ploughing, waiving social rules like the

Kalends, making a mock-monarch to preside over the revels, and proto-dramatic activities like masquerades, broom-sweepings, the burial of the fool, and so on [382]. Shared between a number of the Twelve Days is the Perchta myth, and the *Perchtenlauf* still takes place today in the Tyrol [190]: terrifying figures in masks, black sheepskins and hoods of badger-skins, run, leap, crack whips, blow ash in people's faces and create general uproar with their 'grotesques'—the Fool and his girl, the drummer, the man in woman's clothes, and the 'Doctor'; suddenly the Wild Perchta leaps in amongst them, they dance ecstatically, leap higher and higher over a well and then, either flee to safety in a nearby house, or chase the man in the Perchta mask—isolated stone crosses indicate the result.

Medieval spring and summer festivals were similarly confused. The Roman summer festival was May Day when precautions were taken against the dead (like spitting out black beans), but May Day in Europe, particularly England, was merry. It celebrated the rite of the sacred tree (maypole), an ancient cult associated with the mysteries of Osiris, Attis, Adonis, Persephone and others. In England it was simple fertility magic and was associated with two dances: the 'round', or dance about the maypole; and the danced procession about the village boundaries (surviving in 'beating the bounds' of the English parish). The May spirit, or soul of the tree, may have been a doll, puppet, twigs, or in human form: 'Jack-in-the-Green' in England was a village lad in green leaves, or a town lad blackened (like one of the mumming chimney sweeps, for magic was created by reversal of natural body colour).

(*b*) RITUAL GAMES

The dramatic element in ritual myths affected every part of com-munal life, even games. Roman games were supervised by priests as well as magistrates, and the Greek games included not only all the physical achievements like races and musical turns by the bards but, also, dramatic scenes and interludes concerning the lives of the gods. Essentially the sacred games *represented* the lives of gods, the ideal of existence, although the myths concerned were not of the primary sort but rather extensions into the gods' adventures—the Nemean games, for instance, celebrated the killing of the Nemean lion by Heracles. At the same time, the games were intended both to placate the ghost of the deceased god and ask his help in fertility. Such games are universal from the Olympian to the Irish Tailltenn games.

Spence shows [346] that the Mexican game of *tlachtli* was similar: played on an enormous court, the object was to drive a rubber ball through rings in the walls; a successful player had the privilege of stripping the onlookers of their clothes and ornaments. In Mexican secondary myths the demi-gods play the same game and the motions symbolise the movements of the sun and moon—the god Xolotl plays ball ('olin' means 'shadow' or 'ball') with the sun and moon and, like the Hindu Rahu, is a sun-swallowing monster. In the ancient Persian, Ormuzd fights evil and darkness in a symbolic game of ball. Thus games were related to growth: they strengthened the dead by a reinvigoration through human blood and force, and the mimetic element allowed this process to take place.

And drama was an inherent part of medieval games: the dances were mimetic and, although the plays were rustic, they were still drama. They took place at propitious festivals: the sword and *St George* plays at Christmas, the Pace-Egg plays at Christmas or Easter, and the Robin Hood plays on May Day—hard-boiled eggs are still rolled down hills at Selby today while Pace-Egg plays take place at Halifax.

May Day increased in popularity in medieval times, with its songs, dances and games round the maypole. From the thirteenth century they elected a May 'king' and 'queen' and, by the fifteenth century, they were known as 'Robin' and 'Marion'. Quickly, the 'king' became associated with Robin Hood as the result of three traditions: the historical outlaw Robin Hood, first mentioned in *Piers Plowman* (*c.* 1377) and, from about 1500, celebrated in many popular ballads; the tradition of the travelling French minstrels who sang of the shepherd Robin, in love with the shepherdess Marion (Adam de la Hale of Arras even wrote his play, *Jeu de Robin et Marion,* in the late thirteenth century); and the probability, as Lord Raglan suggested [303], that Robin became associated with the vegetation deity of old England who had to fight for his title annually (but now with bow or quarter-stave):

> By this time—the early part of the sixteenth century—the original fabric of the old rite as practised centuries before seems to have degenerated into a species of folk-play . . . the games of Robin Hood represented the last shadow of an enacted rite which narrated the life and adventures of a god or wood-spirit, and ended with the sacrifice of his human representative, who was

despatched with a flight of arrows . . . The flight of arrows symbolised the rain-shower, for in all parts of the world the flint arrow-head is the emblem of rain . . .

Robin Hood, we are told, was slowly bled to death in the Abbey of Kirklies by the Abbess, which, I take it, is merely a more modern rendering of the myth of his death by gradual bleeding at the sacrificial stake in order that his blood might enrich the forest environment. That trees, and more especially the oak, were anciently regarded as food-bearers which gave sustenance to both man and beast in 'mast', or acorn, is now a recognised fact, and that victims were annually sacrificed to them by the Celts is quite as certain. [346]

By medieval times, dramatic dance had become folk dance. Normally there is also an intermediate stage when the form remains but the religious significance is forgotten (as with the *nautch* girls of India), but there is little trace of this in medieval Europe. The vestiges of the original dramatic dance come from the ancient sword dances, first performed by the early dancing smiths of the Aegean and, later, by the Salian priests (the Roman dancing brotherhoods) who performed at 'stations' along the route, banging swords on their shields, while magical words were said by a Soothsayer [65]. Their folk dance descendants appeared in the fifteenth century: the sword dance and the Morris dance. The sword dance [8] was accompanied by a presenter who introduced each character, and the rough dialogue and the ritual combat associate it with folk dramas [282]. The Morris was a village activity with a mock combat, bells on ankles and knees, faces masked or blackened, and much clashing of sticks and waving of handkerchieves. Thus, with the Morris and sword dances, as well as the 'round' and the processional, medieval dances were inherently dramatic.

In England the sword dance mingled with the Plough Play performed on Plough Monday (January 6th, the old New Year's Day). Ploughmen took a holiday, harnessed themselves to a plough and dragged it round the village accompanied by sword dancers and performers. The ceremonies had existed since the Anglo-Saxons had enforced Plough alms (indeed the plough-car may be associated with the Egyptian ship-car) and the ceremonial plough was kept in the church (like the horns of the Abbots Bromley dancers today). The plays were agricultural and pagan: the 'Tommy' or 'Fool' wore an animal's skin and tail; the 'Bessy' was usually a man dressed as a woman; there was a death and resurrection—at Revesby, the old year (father) is ritually killed by the new (sons); and there were bawdy love scenes, like the wooing of Cicely in the Revesby play, which are essentially 'Fescinnine'. The Revesby play [59] includes a hobby-horse and a dragon, common in many medieval folk dramas from Robin Hood to the mummers and associated with the 'Furry Day' festival at Padstow and the horned performers at Abbots Bromley. We have already seen that Mead and Róheim relate the European figures to that in Bali, but it is conjecture that they originate in horse-sacrifice, known to be a venerable rite to promote fertility and increase. Certainly the plough was one with the sword or Harlequin's slapstick—a fertility symbol; and it is in this sense that Shakespeare uses it of Cleopatra:

> Royal wench!
> She made great Caesar lay his sword to bed:
> He ploughed her, and she cropped.

The Mummers' Plays of St George [60, 282, 356] are a curious mixture of the pagan Plough plays and the Christian element possibly from Richard Johnson's romance *Seven Champions of Christendom* (1595) or, more likely, John Kirke's seventeenth-century play of the same name (printed in 1638, and later sent about the country as a puppet play). Certainly the Mummers' Plays contain Christian morality within a pagan framework. Their origins are in the seasonal ritual: the life/death battle becomes a comic joust between the 'gallant Christian knight' and an evil enemy, and there is a comic 'Doctor' on hand with his huge pair of pliers to stage a 'resurrection'; each character introduces himself by the Vaunt ('I am . . .', and so 'I am St George', etc.) which is a common feature in ritual dramas from the Cornish cycles to the Japanese *No* plays—and, as Richard Southern has pointed out [345], let two players vaunt in opposition before others and we have *agon* and *antagonist* before a chorus. The processional is fundamental: they march from house to house, or to each 'station' along a street, where each character gives his sing-song chant, obscure because by medieval times magic itself had become obscure.

Essentially all these dramatic forms—of Robin Hood, the sword and Morris dances, and the Plough and Mummers' plays—took place when games of all sorts abounded. On Midsummer Day, Celts lit bonfires for pagan purposes; at Whiteborough in Cornwall a fire with a great pole at the centre was lit, and wrestlers contended for prizes at a tumulus where giants were supposed to be buried. On the same day, images of a dragon and a giant were carried through the streets of Burford in Oxfordshire as remembrances of the god's victory over an evil figure (much as the Indian god Vittra and the Persian god Titra were represented as victorious). Throughout the world, secondary myths of gods bring forth ritual games and their associated dramas—fertility activities attempting to placate and invigorate the dead for the well-being of the community.

(2) The Development of Church Drama

(a) THE BEGINNINGS

Two pagan influences bear on the growth of Church drama: heathen rituals and the travelling players. As we have seen, pagan rites were part of medieval man's consciousness and, for the growth of the religious drama, the vernal equinox (March 25th) was particularly important. The primitive mysteries of Tammuz, Attis and many others culminated at this time and the Church had been forced to associate the birth of Mithra (a sun-god) at the vernal equinox with that of Christ. No doubt the recently converted pagans confused the reasons for the celebrations. Certainly Christmas and Easter saw the most frequent dance processions in and around the medieval church. (On Christmas night in 1020 as Mass was about to be celebrated at the church at Kolbigk, Anhalt, it was invaded by wild men and women who danced with primitive fury [190].)

And the travelling players, descendants of the irreligious mimes, still performed at wayside fairs and within the ritual games of the villages. Although the Church fathers constantly pronounced against such things, the lesser clergy certainly joined in the dances. As early as 911 these *tripudia* (dances in three-step) were being performed at the monastery of St Gall. In the Feast of Fools, too, clergy danced in the choir dressed as women, pandars or minstrels, and wore masks. Like all such dances, they were free and mimetic, and were a rigorous basis upon which the Church drama could grow [276].

(b) MEDIEVAL CHURCH (TEMPLE) DRAMA

Despite the dramatic seasonal rituals, and the influence of the travelling players, it was from within the Church itself that the true drama grew. The Mass itself, of course has the seeds of drama—chanted dialogue and a theme of action—but not the essential quality of impersonation.

Impersonation began with the *trope* sung during the night before Easter. A *trope* was an extra chant written to accompany Church music on special occasions. The earliest of these was the tenth-century *Quem quaeritis trope* of the Benedictine Abbey of St Gall in Switzerland:

> *Quem quaeritis in sepulchre, o Christicolae?*
> (The Angel asks, 'Who do you seek in the sepulchre, O followers of Christ?')
> *Jesum Nazarenum crucifixum, o coelicolae.*
> ('Jesus of Nazareth, the crucified, O heavenly one', say the Marys.)
> *Non est hic: Surrexit sicut praedixerat.*
> *Ite, nuniate quia surrexit de sepulchre.*
> (Angel: 'He is not here, He is risen as he foretold. Go and announce that He is risen from the dead'.)

Originally this *trope* was sung by the two halves of the choir within the Mass; later it was moved to the Matins (the prayers which precede daybreak) and placed between the Last Response and the concluding *Te Deum* so that it had time and place to develop. At the same time, a book of *tropes* (illustrated in Hunninger's *The Origin of the Theatre* [190]) is illuminated by figures of mimes, the old professional performers. So it is possible that the professional performers were used by the Church to introduce the element of impersonation. It is also possible that the *trope* was moved to the Matins so that it could coincide with the pagan festivals at the spring equinox—an attempt to Christianise the heathen vigils. In the Mass, the *trope* had been sung by the choir. When repositioned, it became a separate little scene performed at Matins on Easter morning; much like a tiny opera, three people impersonated the Marys and one the angel before an improvised sepulchre.

About A.D., 970 St Ethelwold, Bishop of Winchester, described how the *trope* had become a real little drama involving impersonation and action:

> While the third lesson of the matins is being chanted, let four monks dress themselves. Let one of these, wearing an alb, enter as though to take part in the service, and let him approach the sepulchre without attracting attention and sit there quietly with a palm in his hand. While the third respond is being chanted, let the remaining three monks follow, all of them wearing copes and carrying censers filled with incense. Slowly, as if they were looking for something, let them approach the sepulchre.

All these things must be performed in imitation of the angel seated in the tomb, and of the women coming with spices to anoint the body of Jesus.

When the seated Angel sees the three women approach him like people who are looking for something, he must sing in a dulcet voice of medium pitch:

'Whom seek ye in the sepulchre, O Christian women?' And when he has sung this to the end, let the three women reply in unison:

'Jesus of Nazareth, the crucified, O heavenly one'.

He must then reply:

'He is not here. He is risen as He foretold.

Go and announce that He is risen from the dead'.

At the word of his command, let the three women turn to the choir and say:

'Alleluia! The Lord is risen!'

The seated Angel, as if recalling them, then sings the anthem:

'*Venite, et Videte locum* (Come, and see the place where the Lord was laid)'. And saying this, let him rise, and let him lift the veil to show them the place bare of the cross, but only the cloths laid there in which the cross was wrapped. When they have seen this, let the women put down the censers which they carried into the sepulchre, and let them take up the cloth and hold it up before the eyes of the clergy; and, as if to demonstrate that the Lord has risen and is no longer wrapped in the linen, let them sing this anthem:

'*Surrexit Dominus de sepulchre* (The Lord is risen from the sepulchre)'.

And let them lay the cloth upon the altar. When the anthem is done, let the prior, rejoicing with them at the triumph of our King, in that, having vanquished death, He rose again, begin the hymn:

'*Te deum laudamus* (We praise Thee, O God)'.

And this begun, all the bells chime out together. [59]

St Ethelwold's description much resembles a prompt book being full of directions for the production of the *trope*.

The little drama was gradually added to. In the eleventh century, the apostles Peter and John raced through the church to the sepulchre; later, Christ appeared and Mary took him for the gardener. Processionals occurred: characters marched up one aisle and down the other. An early development, too, was the introduction of a comic character: the unguent merchant who bargained with the Holy Women. In the Christmas plays that developed slightly later, the comic character was the Herod who roared and raged. These comic characters may well have been the invention of the professional players—the merchant (*mercator*) was sometimes called *medicus*, or 'Doctor'.

This type of development continued until *c*. 1250. Latin gave way to

vernacular, and chanting to speech, and the single incident to a full
sequence of Biblical stories. The performances moved from the choir
to the nave and, then, the church exterior—already the marriage
ceremony (but not the Nuptial Mass) took place in the porch, so there
was nothing strange in this development—but the exodus of the plays
was not uniform, and it merely took place when the size of the dramas
demanded it. Yet the people's enthusiasm for the plays gave the Church
second thoughts and, by the time they were performed outside the
church (at the west door, in the churchyard, or by procession through
the town), priests were forbidden to perform in plays outside their own
walls.

(3) *The Emergence of Theatre*

Although in secular hands, everyone concerned was still a member of
the Church and there was little lessening within the plays of the
religious motive. Nor is it certain whether the lay clergy took a more
important part in the Mystery Cycles than has hitherto been thought.
So, too, there was little separation in medieval life between the sacred
and the profane. But the control of the Cycles passed into the hands of
the quasi-religious trade guilds and became organised into complete
Cycles (from the Creation to the Last Judgement) grouped as a whole
which, although based on the Bible, had additional matter thrown in
for good measure.

Being religious, the Cycles were performed on a festival, particularly
Corpus Christi (Thursday after Trinity) which had been inaugurated in
1311 on one of the longest days of the year. The most characteristic
Corpus Christi celebration was the procession of the guilds, carrying
banners denoting their craft—and it is one step from a banner to a stage
on wheels (pageant-waggon). Yet cost prohibited all but the large
towns from staging a Cycle; villagers had to be content with their
mummings and dramatic games.

The influence of the professional players continued, mainly in the
comic scenes which were as broad and farcical as the Roman mime [276].
Comic servants and shrewish wives, and particularly the rustic shep-
herds were treated in this way. But humour can be akin to horror: the
medieval fool and devil traditions often mingled—hairy creatures with
terrifying masks (much like the bird-like figures of the ancient rituals)
were also comic, and taken to be so by the audience. There were also

stock figures which are common to the Roman mime and the Renascence *commedia dell'arte*: in the York *Joseph and Mary* play, there is a row between Joseph and Mary concerning the Conception that is much like the adultery mimes; and the mimic braggart—the *miles gloriosus* of Rome and the Capitano of the *commedia*—is the Herod who rants and raves, like his mimic relations, in a variety of languages; and the ritual 'Doctor' who becomes Il Dottore of the *commedia* occurs in medieval Church plays throughout Europe.

Medieval post-Church drama is a curious mixture: based on the Christian belief, it includes elements of the irreligious mime, heathen dances and pagan customs. Despite isolated dramatic heights (the rough comedy in *The Second Shepherd's Play* and the beauty of the verse in the Brome *Abraham and Isaac*) society did not allow tragedy to flower completely. As Fromm has said [141] medieval man was a corporate animal, only conscious of himself as a member of a community, a guild or a family. In fifth-century Athens, man was at the centre of suffering; he was Dionysos, just as the Egyptian was Osiris. But medieval man knew his place. Society was stratified to such an extent that tragedy belonged only to Christ—divine suffering was greater than human suffering. To Euripides, divine suffering was like human suffering. Thus the Greeks produce 'sacrificial' plays while the medieval period (like the Japanese with the *No* dramas) creates dramas where the sacrifice is reflected upon—the real struggle is over and victory is won—all that is needed is care in order to prevent evil from conquering again.

SOCIAL ORIGINS OF DRAMA IN OTHER CULTURES

The relationship between the dramatic enactment and the culture pattern can be examined in many social areas and in various periods, as Burton has shown [49]. Major examples are the following.

China

About 3–2000 B.C. semi-nomadic tribes began to settle in the valleys of the Yangtse-kiang and the Hoang-ho and, from their original mimesis and dramatic play, more formal elements began to develop. By the Shang dynasty (1766–1122 B.C.) ceremonial dance dramas with flute and percussion had developed, and there were seasonal activities where a boys' choir and a girls' choir would engage in antiphonal singing, answering each other in gesture as well as with voice. Clearly the elements of drama, like that in the Near East, concerned fertility and increase. Although we lack evidence for the Chou dynasty (1050–255 B.C.) we do know that this was the height of ancient Chinese civilisation—including the philosophers Lao Tse and Confucius—and the dramatic dances of the agricultural festivals became more formalised and developed into a temple drama.

Political chaos halted dramatic evolution for a time. Then, with the Han dynasty (206 B.C.–A.D. 220), it began again and a further dramatic impulse was gained when the first Buddhist monks reached China. By the late fifth century A.D. a temple drama was fully active, based on a highly stylised dramatic dance established in Confucian centres. The dramatic elements, however, had a different emphasis from the Near-Eastern and European pattern; by the sixth century, music, ritual drama, story and masks were combined in a specific convention.

The classic Chinese theatre emerged about the eighth century, coinciding with the arrival of many influences to the now prosperous China—from Persia, India and the Middle East generally. The theatre had a variety of forms—within the Court, with marionettes, and in various popular styles. Although the later Mongol invasions disturbed the dramatic development, the Yuan dynasty re-encouraged growth so that, by the Ming dynasty, both Chinese rule and the theatre itself were firmly established.

The last dynasty of Imperial China saw Western influences affecting the theatre, and the present Communist rule, although removing existing religious elements, encourages dramatic expression to a high degree [15, 61, 211, 333, 398, 399].

Japan

The exceptionally disturbed social history of Japan has, of necessity, affected the development of drama. Dramatic rituals concerning rice exist even today—there is much clashing of sticks, and they are concerned with the ideas of fertility, placating the dead, and the death of the 'Year Demon', much like Dionysian rituals and the English folk dance. But, because of the disturbed history, dramatic developments have only occurred in periods of social stability: the No theatre in the comparative stability of the Shogunate rule in the fourteenth and fifteenth centuries—an upper-class theatre (though its origins were in folk dances), it retains today the dialogue and form of its original creation; the *Kabuki* developed in the stable seventeenth century as a popular form of the *No* drama for ordinary people, but slowly it evolved into a middle-class theatre. Thus the ordinary populace are left with marionettes, and general 'variety' entertainments [36, 94, 196, 209, 216, 241, 261, 300, 334, 371].

India

The sub-continent of India contains many cultures which vary considerably one from another. The earliest civilisation was centred on the Indus (much as the early Near-East cultures were based on the Tigris, Euphrates and the Nile) and had its own rituals and primitive dramatic celebrations, some of which are described by Frazer [115]. Similar dramatic activities continue today amongst the Tamil speakers in the south.

The Indo-Germanic invaders brought not only Sanskrit and the caste system, but also the beginnings of a temple drama. But as the invasion of such a vast area was piecemeal, and with great differences from area to area, the dramatic evolution was uneven. For example, the ritual myths of 400 B.C. are still performed in the dance dramas of the Kathakali of Kerala, while the earliest fragments of a written drama (by Asvaghosa) occur about A.D. 100.

One development needs special mention: the classical Sanskrit theatre of the fourth and fifth centuries A.D. This was in many ways comparable with the Attic theatre: the Aristotelian figure, Bharata, established dramatic canons for later theatre; and amongst the group of first-rate dramatists was Kalidasa, whose *Sakuntala* is comparable with the *Oresteia* as a major statement of dramatic vitality. Centred on the city of Ujjain, the classical Sanskrit theatre grew out of dramatic enactments for specific religious festivals and only later was performed in a temple or the royal palace. Unlike Athens, there was no physical theatre; rather, like the Stuart Masque, everything was arranged in a special setting for a specific performance. Later, theatrical companies evolved on a touring basis—much like the European Interlude players [11, 149, 152, 157, 196, 210, 215, 331, 395].

South-East Asia

Burmese culture varies from the pagan hill tribes to the Buddhist cities, and dramatic trends show the same variety. The Shans in Upper Burma, less under Indian influence than the cities, have dances deriving from primitive times. But most Buddhist centres have ritual dance dramas more like 'entertainments' than plays—highly stylised dancing, rich costumes and songs, all accompanied by large orchestras. The basic forms are: large-scale entertainments lasting through the night, and based on classical and Buddhist stories; extracts from these, arranged as separate shows, and basically clown-like performances; processional pageants based on allegories; puppet shows; plays of the dead with full audience participation; and general interest stories set within the usual framework of song, dance and spectacle.

Dramatic forms in Thailand vary from danced mimesis to theatrical presentation while Cambodia, like many South-East Asian cultures, bases its dramatic forms on a chanting chorus accompanied by an orchestra, with mythological themes, gorgeous costumes and highly stylised dancing. Thai, Cambodian and Laotian theatres are centred on the dramatic dance, a form similar to the related shadow theatre.

Malayan culture is basically Indian with a strong Chinese influence but, away from the population centres, ancient fertility forms still exist. In various areas, professional troupes tour to play in front of palm-tree huts with the audience gathered round on three sides; stories from old romances are broken by interludes of dances, while there are farcical elements and masks reminiscent of the European mimes. Urban groups are also amused by danced musical satires of their own communities.

In Indonesia, Bali is renowned for its many dramatic forms. We have already examined the Witch Play and its related village dance (see pp. 135–8, 140) but there is a full range of dramatic forms from simple ritual dances of fertility to temple plays, and a number of varieties of the theatre evolution [23, 37, 227, 325].

Central & Southern America

The initial Indian population had dramatic traditions which were based on pagan religions and, upon these, influences from across the Atlantic were built. In many areas Spanish priests (Portuguese in Brazil) changed the dramatic ritual to that demanded by Catholicism (with greater or lesser success) while, in Brazil and Cuba, negro influence also became dominant. Primitive traditions still continue, of course, though heavily overladen with outside influences. This is the case, too, in Mexico with its ceremonial religious pageants; but there also exist *carpa*—small improvised comedies in the mime tradition with both primitive and sophisticated clowns. The great urban centres have strong theatrical traditions in the Western manner, many of which are developing interesting features of their own [30, 364, 366].

Yiddish Theatre

Although all branches of European and North American drama can be approached sociologically, perhaps none is so rewarding (or so obvious) as Yiddish drama.

In 1876, Abraham Goldfadden moulded the Jewish variety entertainments held in Roumanian wine-taverns into a plot which was improvised in a *commedia dell'arte* manner; a little later, Jacob Gordin in America came to write the first actual plays in Yiddish. From these two inauspicious events, Yiddish drama grew. Slowly the Jewish communities, responding to the relaxation of prohibitions in Slav Europe, began to build their own dramatic traditions: in 1908 the Hirschbein Troupe was created in the comparatively free atmosphere of Odessa, and later toured Russia with Yiddish plays; in 1916 the Vilna Troupe was formed, later to create the première of *The Dybbuk* in 1920; and Yiddish companies in Poland after the First World War experimented with a variety of acting shapes. The Soviet government, in its early days, actively encouraged Yiddish culture in many ways and specifically the theatre; one result was the famous Habima company, later to emigrate to Israel. Unfortunately, Yiddish cultural life was virtually eliminated from Poland after the Second World War, and from Russia from 1952. However, the general Jewish exodus from Europe as the result of the pogroms meant that Yiddish theatre increasingly flourished in America so that, where earlier in the century Yiddish drama was clearly related to one or more Eastern European cultures, today there is a whole body of newer American-Yiddish dramatic literature. Clearly social conditions have had a direct and immediate bearing upon the development of Yiddish theatre [288].

7

OTHER ASPECTS OF THE SOCIOLOGICAL APPROACH

If the drama is intertwined with man's basic beliefs in such a way as the sociological approach would imply, it clearly impinges on a whole host of related fields of study: how man has viewed himself in relation to the universe (philosophy and religion); the various understandings he has had of his world from time to time (history) and how this has related to his understanding of drama and dramatic form (theatrical criticism); how man has viewed the workings of his own mental processes (psychology) and the relationship of these to artistic creation (aesthetics).

There are, in addition, other fields of dramatic study which are specifically related to the sociological approach. The shape of the acting-area and the relationship of the audience to it, is one. The earliest dramatic dances were performed in a circle (theatre-in-the-round in modern terminology) and this slowly evolved to the 'open' shape: actors in a semi-circle backing on to a wall or curtain, with the audience arranged in 180° around it [77]. Further evolutions varied upon the culture concerned: Western traditions evolved the end-stage and, thereafter, the proscenium form; but other cultures (Bali and Japan, for example) developed other shapes. But just how far does the shape of the temple or theatre determine the nature of the drama created for it? Or does the nature of the drama determine the shape of the acting-area? This problem can be most clearly seen in a highly dramatic culture with its vital theatrical form—as in the case of Kalidasa, Aeschylus or Shakespeare. For example, the kaleidoscopic effect of the last half of Act V of *Troilus and Cressida* could only have been created in a theatre where there was an unlocalised stage, various side doors, a separate central acting-area, and an upper level—certainly in a modern proscenium presentation it can appear anachronistic. But did Shakespeare write the play in this way *because* the playhouse needed a play of this dramatic shape, or were theatres created in this manner because this was the most expressive dramatic form for the culture in this period?

A second major problem is the relationship of the drama and the audience it is created for. Bonamy Dobrée implies [89] that Restoration comedy has its particular flavour because society was 'like that'. But just how far does the nature of the society and its needs determine the drama, and the particular emphases of the playwright determine the interests of society? The nature of an audience certainly has a consider-able bearing upon the nature of the performance. Nicoll tells us that an audience is a unit yet remains diverse, has a lower intellect than the individual members, is both gripped by the make-believe and yet stands apart from it, and (this being the difference between an audience and a mob) has no desire or call for action [279]. With this specific problem, however, we impinge directly upon another field of study: that of the group.

Education & Dramatic Residues

Each society possesses inherent dramatic patterns and these are passed on from generation to generation. A vital education is one that utilises these patterns.

Folk traditions are handed down today in the dramatic elements of games and rhymes. The very ancient labyrinth game (like the medieval 'Troy Town' or the maze) is played in many modern ways: 'hop-scotch' is one example, where the early Christians replaced the original shape with that of the Basilica, or early English Church. Although most modern games have not so direct a ritual origin, Lady Gomme's authoritative *Traditional Games* [147] clearly shows the underlying bases. Most remnants of traditional games are associated with courtship, love and marriage: 'The Mulberry Bush' is the remnant of a marriage dance around a sacred bush or tree; 'Nuts in May' is related to marriage-by-capture and exogamy; 'Oats and beans and barley' originally depicted the farmer sowing the seed and waiting for a marriage partner; and there are hosts of others. Not quite so numerous are games deriving from contests, or the taking of prisoners and territory; there are also games associated with funerals, harvest customs, divina-tion, the belief in ghosts, charms, well-worship, tree-worship—in fact, the whole range of pagan life.

Many modern sports are related to ritual ball-games, like the Mexican *tlachtli*. The Irish shinty was supposed to be a favourite game of 'the little people'. The original football was a contest between towns when the ball was kicked in one direction only—the one favourable to the sun's course—and was probably mimetic of the action of the gods. The rolling of a sphere was connected with ancient pagan rites in Britain: this developed not only to Pace-Egging but also to cricket of which the first known version was 'stool-ball'—eleven men and

women a side on Easter Eve used a dairymaid's stool as a wicket, and
the winners received kisses and tanzy cakes as prizes.

Children's popular rhymes are full of pagan remains. The cow that
'jumped over the moon' may not have a direct connection with the
Egyptian goddess, Nut, as was once thought; but gods and goddesses
were pictured alongside animals and ritual dishes and ampullas in the
calendars and almanacs that spread from Rome to Gaul and throughout
the Empire: and sacred dogs, cats and cows are found throughout
British folk-lore. While 'Old King Cole' was probably the pagan
British king Coel, 'Little Jack Horner' is no more than a bowdlerised
version from *Robin Goodfellow, his mad pranks and merry jests,* published
in London in 1628. From Britain to China, there is a rhyme asking a
snail to put out its horn and, in all countries, the snail is both significant
of birth and is a smaller (magical?) member of the dragon family.
'Ride a cock horse' was probably a hobby-horse; but a white horse was
also a most ancient figure in British pagan traditions, and there were
almost certainly rites where nude women rode on horses (but not beheld
by men)—and so the rhyme may relate to the same pagan traditions as
the story of Godiva, particularly as one version omits Banbury and
inserts Coventry. The invocation to the ladybird to fly home as her
house is on fire and her children are in danger is precisely how peasants
got rid of evil spirits. And the wassail rhymes, performed on Twelfth
Night in Cornwall, Devon and Suffolk today, are invocations to the
spirits of the trees. The lion and the unicorn represent the ritual combat
between sun and moon, light and dark—they are even pictured in
conjunction in Assyrian sculpture and on a coin of Akanthos [346].

We have seen that many thinkers consider that there is a similarity
between primitive thinking and the thought of childhood. Dramatic
patterns in games and rhymes make a direct appeal to the thought of
the child because they evoke the elements of human nature—the primal
opposition of light and dark, life and death; magic and the omnipotence
of thought; animism and irrational connections and the identification
of opposites. The residues of primitive rituals have compelling force
within the mind of the modern child simply because they relate to the
inherent dramatic patterns within all human beings.

10 THE GROUP & DRAMA

Dramatic Education is concerned with the study of groups in two ways. First, dramatic play is continued in groups, large or small, for it is a social activity—the child is always acting in a group of his own or another's choosing. Second, the theatre itself concerns the interaction of two groups (actors and audience), and specifically with the audience as a collection of individuals within a group.

THE GROUP & DRAMATIC PLAY

In the classroom situation, much of the children's work is in groups and it is obviously important that Dramatic Education should take full account of modern research into the characteristics of groups.

As with so many intellectual fields within the social sciences, group study originated with Freud. In 1922 he said [124] that social groups were based on the pattern of the family, and that this has a certain biological unity. The basic model of group formations is, however, not quite the family as it really is, but the family as it appears to the child's imagination. Perhaps, says Money-Kyrle, most of society's troubles result from the fact that the two are by no means the same: the real family contains two parents—but the imaginary one contains at least four—two good ones and two bad ones—who are the prototypes not only of divinities and devils but of the abstract ideas of good and evil. Thus:

> When a number of individuals find common symbols for the elements in this unconscious pattern they form a group. They have common values to defend, a common enemy, a common leader and a common standard of behaviour. [262]

Contrasting with this, modern social psychologists start with the group rather than the individual—the group is studied as a group. Freud considered the individuals within the group. But social psychologists are more likely to study work-groups, or groups that are doing some specific task and they look for the causes of behaviour within the social environment.

Basic Characteristics of Groups

It is fair to say that social psychologists consider that the ability to

participate in groups is conditioned by the experience of the first group
of two (mother and child) and later extensions of this (the family).
Thus, the individuals within a group preparing an improvisation will
react (in general terms) to other members of the group in similar
patterns to the way they react to their family group. Sprott defines the
group as:

> . . . a plurality of persons who interact with one another in a given context
> more than they interact with anyone else. [348]

Interaction is basic to groups, and they all have a moral element in that
the standards obeyed by the groups are collectively pursued. They may
vary in the standards of tightness in which their customs are kept but
there is always a consciousness of membership of a group.

Sprott further distinguishes primary and secondary groups. Primary
groups meet in intimate face-to-face situations for association and
cooperation—as with a group improvising. Secondary groups (nation,
city, trade union, etc.) only achieve unity through symbolic means—
language, social interaction by transport, or administrative methods.

Basic to the approach of the social psychologist is that members
of the group are not regarded as individuals but as a social
entity:

> The self, as that which can be object to itself, is essentially a social structure,
> and it arises from social experience. [253]

Sprott says:

> The concept of 'human nature' has dwindled to a few basic biological needs
> and a large range of potentialities one selection of which is cultivated by one
> society, another by another.
> This should make us pause to reflect when the educationalists speak about
> the 'full development of the personality' as being the aim of education, more
> especially when some of them advocate extreme permissiveness. They speak
> as though there were in each of us a little seed called the 'personality' which
> must be carefully tended and allowed the maximum freedom for it to grow.
> Nothing could be more mistaken. A permissive social environment shapes
> and produces one sort of personality, an authoritarian one produces another.
> Permission is not the *removal* of social influence so that the 'natural' person-
> ality can have a chance to develop; it merely replaces one kind of social
> influence for another. [348]

In other words, when we are setting up a group organisation for improvisation, movement drama, and the like, we are providing children with a specifically structured group environment which influences the personality in a specific way.

Perhaps the main group pressure on the individual is towards conformity. Children receive these pressures in two main ways: from parents and other adults, and from other children—and both ways use the methods of reward and punishment. But clearly there are other group pressures: the class, the school, and aspects of society as a whole (as with the mass media). The group improvising is a transitory group though, when choice of group is free (as it normally is), particular individuals tend to stay in the same group formation. And modern research has shown that people in general, and specifically children in dramatic groups, tend to conform: they like to be with those like themselves, to stick to the familiar, and friends even tend to become like each other. Abercrombie gives research illustrations [1] to show that an individual's judgement on matters of fact—like the size and weight of objects—also tend to become influenced by others within a group. In general terms, when we say that the child 'is working well within the group' we mean that he is attempting to reduce his dissonance with other people in order that he may fit better into the group. But a warning note is sounded when modern research shows that adults who do not conform are more effective intellectually, more mature in social relationships, more confident, less rigid, less authoritarian, more objective and realistic about their parents, and more permissive in their attitudes to child-rearing practices [78].

There has been a whole series of modern studies on communication within groups [105]. Different patterns of communication are better for different purposes: thus, if five people in a group are attempting to solve a problem, it is better if one person is at the centre to organise solutions as they occur. Spatial relationships affect communication: when two people sit at a table, it is best for communication if they each sit on one side of a corner and not opposite each other. There are immediate relevances here for dramatic education: what is the best spatial relationship for groups engaging in one type of dramatic activity as compared with another? and what is the best physical position for a teacher in relation to a class when one dramatic activity is compared with another?

The Group & Dramatic Education

In improvisation, dramatic movement and many aspects of Dramatic Education the children work in a variety of group structures: as a class, in large groups, small groups and pairs. Progress is made by a slow development towards increasing responsibility for organisation and increasing freedom for preparation and performance. To begin with, much of the work is on a class basis; and, often with the older child too, the first minutes of a lesson period are taken on a class basis. In both instances, the class is trained in spontaneous groupings of varying numbers but with nonpermanent membership and structures. Steadily, however, more independence is provided until responsibility is made that of the group.

Adolescent boys working in groups dramatically can successfully overcome the difficulties that arise in discussion and organisation provided that: the group is bound together by friendship; the Leader is approved by the members and the members are liked by the Leader; the Leader has the approval of an authority delegated by the class teacher; the group task is within the understanding and capability of the group and offers the opportunity for success; the group meets regularly for the purpose for which the group was formed; there is a suitably permissive attitude adopted by the teacher which encourages group responsibility and initiative. In dramatic work the most effective size of a group depends on the nature of the group task. In the secondary school it has been suggested that five be taken as a basic unit and varied according to the task in hand [3].

Quite clearly, such practical considerations raise a whole host of problems and we naturally turn to modern group studies for assistance. These have ranged over a very wide field, and some have more relevance to Dramatic Education than others. Some of the more important are considered below.

Sociometry

This was first developed by Dr Jacob Moreno [264] who said there were, in any group, complicated patterns of attraction, repulsion and neutrality; thus groups contain large reservoirs of feeling. He developed The Sociometric Test whereby group members express their preferences for each other in terms of companionship or working partnership. All the participants in a group situation are asked specific questions:

who would they like to sit next to? who would they best like to work with? spend leisure time with? share a room with? and so on. Socio-metry insists that the questioning is specific. It is not, 'Whom do you like best?' but a specific question as to preference in a situation. Preferences can then be correlated and charts and diagrams prepared (See *Fig.* 2) which show such phenomena as: pairs chosen by no one

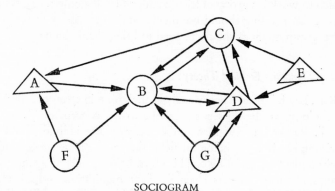

SOCIOGRAM

Triangle=a boy.   Circle=a girl.
Arrows =how each child chooses friends.
Thus: C, B, & D=popular children;
　　　E, F　　　=children no one chooses for a companion.
　　　[Note: information gained from individual sociograms must be used with great care because the social interrelations indicated are relative only to the group in which they were obtained; one of the above children, placed in another social group, may choose—(and be chosen)—more or less frequently.]

Fig. 2

but each other; cliques; chains of friendship; popular stars; unchosen isolates. The teacher can discover a great deal about the social structure in the classroom—particularly about the less popular and isolates—and can provide a factual basis upon which to build a policy for grouping children within a class, invaluable in creative education.

Sociometry has many uses: therapeutic, as with people who are frustrated when others reject them; in work processes, as with those who like or dislike one another in a factory or school; and to measure the cohesion of any group in any situation. Taking our examples from education, it was found by Richardson [314] that an experimental group learning English composition by group methods showed significant gains over a control group conventionally taught. My own

findings support those of Richardson. Experimental groups learning
History, Geography and English showed gains over conventionally
taught groups; but, further, that groups formed through sociometric
testing and then working dramatically in these subjects made significant
gains over those taught conventionally *and* over groups not working
dramatically. Generally it is found that the most satisfying group in
which to work is a group of friends and, when Sociometric Tests show
these exist, teaching should use them; when Tests show these do not
exist, group methods should be used to bring them about.

Group Dynamics & Field Theory

Kurt Lewin's Field Theory analyses the group in terms of individual
psychology, yet he does not subscribe to the concept of 'the group
mind'. Rather, he says that as the study of the individual and his
environment is a psychological field, the study of the group and its
environment is a social field. This social field consists of groups, sub-
groups, members, barriers, channels of communication, and so on; and
these entities have relative positions within a field according to the
group concerned. The balance of the field, and the distribution of the
forces within it, determine group behaviour. Each group, therefore, is
made up of a field of forces [237].

He considers the personality within the group. The individual is
exposed to pressures from external forces and inner tensions resulting
from the disequilibrium between himself and the environment.
Different cultures activate different kinds of pressures and so a personality type depends on a culture (linking with Kardiner and Linton).
Child-rearing practices are social forces moulding personality, and each
stage of childhood is a restructuring of the 'life-space'. Within each
individual, certain tensions demand release and so the 'life-space' is
dynamic—forces push the individual towards goals, or erect barriers to
prevent him reaching them.

Group dynamics, therefore, show how the behaviour in a group is
affected by the personal characteristics of its members, by different
forms of leadership, by different structures and institutionalised settings,
and by different tasks and purposes. In *Resolving Social Conflicts* (1948),
Lewin discussed the functions and modes of leadership, and the basic
behaviour patterns in the interaction of group members. White and
Lippit [385] showed that children behaved differently according to

social 'climate': they showed more solidarity, learning and productivity in a democratic 'climate' than in autocratic and laissez-faire 'climates'. At the same time, French has shown [117] that the necessary interdependence includes an identification with the group.

Lewin raises a whole series of questions concerning the effective life of a group, and these affect our knowledge of children in dramatic play. It is quite clear that appropriate leadership produces satisfactory drama, and that the differing structures and 'climates' of groups produce more or less effective dramatic play. Autocracy or laissez-faire, for example, produces stilted or formless group play, while democracy (choice of leadership with relative freedom of action) is conducive to good creative group work. But we must be careful of overstatement in this area: despite Cohen [68], it is clear that, although the influence of the group is large, individuality is still an important factor in behaviour; what has happened to a child in the past is not irrelevant to his dramatic play—and certainly cannot be ignored as Lewin [236] would have us believe.

Group Purpose

Homans' work contains many relevances to Dramatic Education. He states that groups are purposive:

> Groups do not just get together; they get together for a purpose. [175]

This group purpose he calls the 'external system'. Every group tends to throw up a leader (thus developing a pyramidal structure) and is also made up of three factors: sentiment (including the original motives and those which grow out of group motives), activity and interaction. But interaction leads to mutual liking:

> If the interactions between the members of a group are frequent in the external system, sentiments of liking will grow up between them, and these sentiments will lead in turn to further interactions over and above the interaction of the external system. [175]

The initial interaction will lead to further interaction, which he calls the 'internal system'.

From this structure he can examine behaviours within a group. The external system, for example, provides the norms of conduct for doing a job:

The higher a rank of a person within a group, the more nearly his activities conform to the norms of the group. [175]

Interaction between individuals of different rank produce variant behaviours:

A person of higher social rank than another originates interaction for the latter more often than the latter originates interaction for him . . .

When two persons interact with one another, the more frequently one of the two originates interaction for the other, the stronger will be the latter's sentiment of respect (or hostility) towards him . . . [175]

It follows that dramatic groupings must always be for a purpose which is clearly seen and felt and that, should specific groups be maintained for any length of time the interaction within the 'internal system' must be carefully developed. The whole question of rank does not normally affect the group in the classroom situation, but it does affect dramatic groupings in other situations—particularly with older adolescents and adults.

Group Psychotherapy

Psychoanalysts have also contributed recent research to group study under the title of Group Psychotherapy. Many fields have been examined, even the theatre. Friedman and Gassel [139] returned, like Freud, to Sophocles whose *Oedipus Tyrannus* contains the prototype of the social group:

The tragedy presents a conflict of wishes in the mind of the audience, the wish to commit Oedipus' crime and the wish to escape its consequences. The character of Oedipus stands for one wish and the chorus for the other, and the tragedy is played out between them. [112]

The leader of the group has violated the social taboos and the negative attitudes of the chorus do not represent open hostility to the hero:

. . . they are nevertheless as clearly expressed by the tendency of the chorus to remain objective. The chorus does not become actively involved in Oedipus's travails, nor does it exert itself to prevent him from going to his doom. By remaining detached, it absolves itself from responsibility . . . actually the chorus maintains a driving demand upon the hero to fulfil what the community expects. [139]

The community is eager for the leader to assume responsibility (which Oedipus does) like any other helpless community. Once he is out of the way, however, the chorus (community) can evaluate its feelings—view life from a new perspective and move to higher standards. The play demonstrates:

> ... so many of the mechanisms we see at work in the therapeutic group: the inescapable emotional tie uniting actors and audience, between members who are active in the group at any moment, and those who are passive; how the conflicting tendencies in the group find their spokesmen who voice feelings common to all; the group defensive mechanisms, which operate to preserve its ignorance of its own wishes, and to project them on to an individual scapegoat, very often the conductor, who is the person called upon to 'know' the things which the group does not yet dare to know; how the re-enactment of the drama of a conflict under the guidance of the conductor can lead to a re-evaluation and re-integration of feelings which finally make his presence unnecessary; how the chorus as opposed to the hero, the group as opposed to the conductor or any one member, becomes the field in which the basic conflict is located. [112]

Therapy within existing groups has also been considered by Freudians. Bion's *Experiences in Groups* (1963) shows how a group under observation by a psychoanalyst studied its own processes of member interaction and how it gradually learned to recognise and deal with the latent bonds of hostility and affection that existed within it. Originally conceived as a therapeutic technique, other workers have developed the concept in factories (Jacques [195]), hospitals (Menzies [257]), teacher-training (Herbert [171]), and tutorial groups (Richardson [314]).

It is in this context that Ben Morris examines the implications for education. He considers that human beings develop by means of relationships with one another but their initial reactions to these relationships are guided by the past: patterns of feelings in childhood affect adult conduct:

> At any stage we can best take advantage of opportunities for learning when these make use of patterns of relationships which recapitulate the patterns established as favourable to learning in the past. [267]

But our behaviour and learning is affected by the search for an image of what we wish to become—for a personal identity.

To be favourable, learning experiences should therefore connect easily with
our aspirations and should provide us with roles which enable us to develop
the kinds of relationships in terms of which our ideal self image is cast.
[267]

But our ideal self image is influenced by our paternal figures as we have
internalised them, and by our relationships with other adults: Freud's
superego, in fact.

In a successful group, the common task forms the focus of endeavour,
but only if the goal is clear and close to the interests of the members:

> ... (if it) offers them roles sufficiently in conformity with their past ex-
> perience and with aspects of their self image. [267]

A successful group: is dependent upon whether it can allow individuals
to abandon their private objectives; is often focused on the leader's
personality but, to grow, intrinsic interests must emerge; is often
incompletely formulated at the start, for there must be adequate
opportunities for the participation of the members; is often best at
functioning when opposing something (as in war). In many ways, this
could be a model for the successful group in dramatic play and in
general creative work with children [183]. Morris has a further
comment which has importance for the teacher with children in
Dramatic Education:

> There has to be a common task to the formulation of which members have
> themselves contributed. On the part of the leader there has to be a readiness
> to accept contributions from whatever source and to encourage all to make
> what contributions they can. He must display an evident and felt concern for
> all members of the group equally and for the progress of the group as a
> whole ... Above all he must be a good listener and observer. While
> recognising the importance of language he must learn to detect 'the music
> behind the words', i.e. the latent dimension of feeling entering into all
> behaviour. [267]

Certainly the effectiveness of a teacher within any classroom
situation is enhanced by knowledge of the general characteristics of
groups, as Fleming has shown:

> Change in response to teachers' wishes appears to occur only when the
> prestige of the teacher is high, when the purposes displayed in the class-room

are in line with those already accepted, and when modification of procedure can occur without undue forfeiture of the esteem of others whose good opinion is of importance for other reasons. The effect of one pupil upon another is governed by quite similar laws . . .

Perception, learning, character formation, personality development . . . can now be seen to be a product of group pressures and to be modifiable by group experiences. [109]

THE AUDIENCE

The audience is a collection of individuals; each member of the audience responds both as an individual and as a member of the group.

Psychoanalysis tells us that the individual's unconscious reacts to the unconscious level of the drama so that the audience and actor both feel 'we do it together'. Kris tells us of two other processes: the audience relates itself to three levels within the theatre experience—the subject matter, the experience of the action, and the character; and also that the audience synthesises the content, the intent, and the coherence of the play.

In one sense, the presence of a group of spectators (the audience) is the characteristic difference between the Drama and any other art form. Painting, sculpture and the like demand only one person to be an auditor and, while we can listen to a symphony concert as part of a large audience, it is equally possible to appreciate the art form if we are the single listener. But, in the theatre, the presence of an audience is a prerequisite. The audience actually participates in the creation of the final art form: the playwright creates the words, the actor performs, the director assembles the parts together, and the audience reacts. Without the audience's reaction, the art form hardly exists—as any actor knows who has performed to an empty house. The actor even personifies the audience as 'warm' or 'unresponsive'. Thus the art form of the Drama has an immediacy lacking in any other form.

The group formation which is an audience has a number of particular characteristics. Allardyce Nicoll has already told (see p. 179) that an audience is a unit made up of diverse elements, generally has a lower intellect than the individual members, cannot follow a logical argument but is emotionally acute, can be gripped by the make-believe and at the same time stand apart from it, but does not seek (like a crowd or mob) to make this make-believe a motive for action.

As with all primary groups, within an audience there is a pressure towards conformity. We have all had the experience of finding the beginning of a comedy distinctly unfunny yet, slowly, we catch the amused reactions of the rest of the audience until, eventually, we are enjoying the whole performance. Yet it is characteristic of the art form that the conformity, in many instances, is not permanent: another common experience as a member of the audience is to be 'carried away' by the play and the production within the theatre building yet, later, to reflect that 'perhaps it wasn't so good after all'. The individual within the group audience, therefore, not only has a detachment at the same time as being affected by the group experience, but can also reconsider and re-evaluate at a later time. The degree to which an audience conforms varies with the sophistication of its members: the Edwardian music-hall, with its communal songs and 'elementary' jokes, required more conformity from its individual members than the programme at The Royal Court Theatre in Sloane Square under the Vedrenne-Barker management. So, too, sophistication (and, thus, conformity) varies between periods: the mid-twentieth-century audience rarely finds a mid-nineteenth-century melodrama acceptable.

The structure of the audience affects the nature of the art form. The social patterns and behaviours of the community can materially alter playwriting, production and acting. In the early nineteenth century, with the evening meal early, plays were written in five acts, contained many raw scenic splendours, and the evening contained various other entertainments apart from the play. During the century, society moved its evening meal later: as plays started later they became shorter and were written in the three-act structure; and as the growth of the public transport system in London meant that more middle-class people could attend theatres, meal habits became even more important as the century wore on. The arrival of the middle-class at the theatre meant a more discriminating taste: thus acting, production and décor became less extravagant and more sophisticated in their approach.

The physical nature of the playhouse influences the inter-relationship of audience and performance—and thus the nature of the dramatic art form. In the late medieval period and the Renascence theatrical performances were in the open air, with the audience mostly on three sides: even in the Elizabethan theatre the actor was performing within the spectators. Thus there is a natural growth from the Mystery Cycle to *Faustus,* tempered only by the interior form of the same shape by the

Interlude performers in the great halls. But with the rise of Inigo Jones, the picture-frame stage with its scenic splendour and its audience inside a building created a different actor-audience relationship. Now the actor was performing towards one end of a hall (not completely at the end) and against painted scenery, whereas Burbage had been backed by Elizabethan architecture and surrounded by the audience. The third great change in the actor-audience relationship came in the nineteenth century with the introduction, first, of gas-lighting and, later, of electricity. Now the auditorium could be darkened, and the audience look into a window where the lives of others were acted out. No longer were they actually *sharing* a relationship with the actors—they were watchers, voyeurs. Thus it was that the nature of the plays themselves changed, as the relationship between the actors and the audience was altered by the physical theatre.

Today, the structure of our society materially affects the nature of the audience and, thus, the plays and performances within our theatres. The large community theatre of the late nineteenth century is no longer built; community theatres—like those at Leicester, Nottingham and Guildford—are smaller and more intimate. The Englishman or American, with his television for the evening and his car to run him wherever he requires at weekends, asks much of his local theatre if he is going to be bothered to come. Quality has to be high: acting and production standards must not seem false to a member of the audience who has witnessed thousands of hours on television; naturalistic plays of domestic life can appear more naturalistic on the box in his living-room than from the twentieth row of the stalls; and, when paperback criticism is available at a few shillings, the quality of dramatic writing must be high for the audience to be satisfied. Of course, the standards in the West End and on Broadway are rather different: they are the artistic centres for millions of people. But in the normal large city—Birmingham or Montreal, Nottingham or Chicago—the theatre is still supported (or not) by the community, and the patterns of society materially affect the nature of the theatrical entertainment.

Essentially, the Drama is an art form seen in the process of formation. Three elements—the play, the players and the audience—create it, and without any one of these three the art form cannot exist.

11 SOCIAL PSYCHOLOGY & GENERAL THEORIES OF PLAY

We have already examined a number of explanations of play: as surplus energy (Schiller and Spencer), as instinct (Groos and others), as a physiological mechanism (Recreation, Relaxation, Recapitulation, and others), as catharsis and repetition (Freud), and as a projection of a child's inner world in order to master external reality (child psychotherapy). But all these concepts start from the individual in an evolutionary situation and, while environmentary factors have importance, heredity is the basis. But, as we have already seen in connection with group studies, social psychologists reverse the emphasis: man is a social animal, determined by the forces in his environment, while many consider that heredity has only a small part (some think none) to play in the creation of character. And whereas the social psychologist studying the group looks at each group as having its own identity, the social psychologist considering the individual sees him as the result of environmental forces.

Early American behaviourism affected this type of thinking. Thorndike had said that all learning involves reacting and, without reaction, nothing is learned.

Play offers the individual opportunities to react and, therefore, to learn. J. B. Watson considered play to be a mechanism of individual adjustment: a boy is 'straightened out' by the knocks he receives from other boys. Play, therefore, becomes important to the social psychologist:

> In short, play is the principal instrument of growth. It is safe to conclude that, without play, there would be no normal adult cognitive life; without play, no healthful development of affective life; without play, no full development of the power of will. [336]

Growth through play is evident in the social nature of the child: he produces on his own level the struggles and achievements of developed social life. Through play, the child gradually approaches the stern realities of adult living. Seashore says that play is the making of the social man—indeed 'we become like those with whom we play'. McDougall agrees [252] and considers that play has its share in the socialising influence of art: it provides a mutual understanding and sympathy, which develops into the collective life of a people.

Lehman & Witty

Lehman and Witty acknowledge the complexity of play, and that any definition of it must be partial and incomplete, for play has unlimited aspects, many variables and varieties of forms, the results of which are both subtle and far-reaching. They do not question the validity of previous theories—merely their completeness. They see that play is intertwined with the life process: the whole truth of play cannot be known until the truth of life is known. Play is not an isolated phenomenon: it cannot be explained apart from the background of life itself. Thus they have a tolerance towards all previous theories, accepting the elements of truth in each.

Perhaps Lehman and Witty are most famous, however, for their scientific investigations into play. We have already seen that play content varies according to environmental changes: that the child will utilise in his play any new object or machine that takes his fancy. They discovered a continuity in play—'characteristic traits of each period have their beginnings in preceding stages and gradually merge into succeeding ones'—and that play becomes more conservative as chronological age advances: older subjects engaged in a smaller number of activities, and with fewer distinct types, than the younger ones.

They saw basic sex differences. Boys engage more frequently in plays and games that are more vigorous and active, involve muscular skill and dexterity, contain competition, and are organised. Girls, on the other hand, engage more frequently in sedentary activities, and those involving a restricted range of action. They compared town and country children:

> Rural boys of ages $8\frac{1}{2}$ to $10\frac{1}{2}$ inclusive were found to engage in *fewer* activities than town boys of the same ages. Rural boys older than $10\frac{1}{2}$ in chronological age were found to engage in a *larger* number of play activities than town boys of corresponding ages. [233]

They found that negro children were more social in their play, and wrote poems more commonly, than white children. There were enormous individual differences in play behaviour but:

> Some of the variables which influence play behaviour and produce change are: age differences, sex differences, seasonal change, prevailing fashions in play, adult interests within a given community, social environment, playground space, material equipment for playing, etc. [233]

They also found that play interests reduced in number not only according to age, but also according to intelligence. Although gifted children displayed the normal versatility of play interest, they were also more solitary in their play than average children, and engaged more frequently in reading activities but less frequently in vigorous physical play.

PLAY AS COMPENSATION

Spencer seems to have been the first to mention the compensatory aspect of play, but the concept was developed by Robinson [316] out of 'depth' psychology. He considered that a weak child, surrounded by stronger playmates, could in his make-believe compensate for his lack of physical prowess and for any cramping in his environment. This relates to Freud's point that a child in play tries to master his environment; and also to Adler's idea that in the realm of imagination the child no longer feels subordinate.

Lehman and Witty's findings showed that children playing at school dramatically are often compensating for a feeling of intellectual inferiority resulting from some failure to succeed in the real school. They also found a marked desire for children to help their parents and Curti [79] saw this imitative desire as directly compensatory for, although children are constantly being exhorted to help mother, their inner need to do so is most often denied.

Jane Reaney

Reaney eclectically uses all the other theories of play, including Freud's concept of sublimation:

> It is a well-known fact that repression in early childhood is the cause of waste of energy and the development of morbid tendencies in adult life. If

each of the primitive instincts is a source of energy and its normal outlet is denied the energy is wasted. It is obvious that in many people an enormous amount of psychic energy is lost in this way. On the other hand if the primitive instinct is sublimated, that is, turned into a higher form of expression, this energy is conserved and used constructively. Thus many believe that the wonderful achievements of art are due to the sublimation of the sex instinct. [308]

So play is a make-believe action that compensates for the child's inability to directly express his energy. And the increasing ability to sublimate strong emotions through dramatic play is a sign of growing civilisation, or 'growing-up':

> Children can never play at fighting games for long without getting angry, while football matches between uneducated teams sometimes end in a free fight. On the other hand the highly trained team can take part in a fierce contest without showing or even feeling the slightest tendency to anger. In the case of the child and the primitive man the sublimation is not complete, while in that of the trained team it is. [308]

Imitation, says Reaney, makes play dramatic, and children's imitation of significant social customs produces folk-song games throughout the world. And she suggests that cooperative games give an outlet for the primitive instincts repressed in civilised life [307].

S. R. Slavson

Slavson relates the concept of compensation to the theory of Recreation. He sees play as the means whereby the child, in fantasy, attempts to master reality by scaling everything down into patterns he can comprehend. In this sense, play relates to Recreation in two ways:

> Reactive activities are frequently chosen because they compensate one for organic lacks and counteract emotional monotony. The need for new experiences and varying stimuli, denied in everyday living, are compensated by an overexciting and overstimulating leisure . . . There is, however, another type of compensatory recreation rooted in deeper emotional processes and in the unconscious . . . many persons choose recreation on the basis of weakness, feelings of inferiority, and unconscious strivings. Thus the boy who feels himself to be inadequate among his playmates may excel as a trapeze performer or baseball player . . . [343]

PLAY AS SELF-EXPRESSION

Mitchell and Mason stated that:

> ... play is explained by the fact that the individual *seeks self-expression* ... *all that is necessary to explain play is the fact that (man) seeks to live, to use his abilities, to express his personality.* The chief need of man is *life, self-expression.*
>
> [260]

In order to define this, they postulated a series of universal wishes—not instincts, but wishes which are the result of experience rather than fixed inborn drives. These are:

1. the wish for new experience—as in fighting, hunting, curiosity, roving, speed and creativeness;
2. the wish for security—as in flight, acquisition, imitation (from fear of social disapproval), and religion;
3. the wish for response—as in sociability, courtship and mating, parental love, boon friendship and altruism;
4. the wish for recognition—as in the desires for victory, proficiency, leadership, showiness, and undying fame;
5. the wish for participation—as in desires for membership of groups and affiliation with causes;
6. the wish for the beautiful—as in the aesthetic desires for beauty in colour, form, sound, motion and rhythm.

While the idea that play is a reflection of man's life may tie up with Burton's concept of play as part of the life process, Mitchell and Mason's method of getting there is very different. The theory of self-expression emphasises the conspicuous role of learned responses, of habits and attitudes, as the principal source of motivation in play.

The fact that man is naturally active, both physically and mentally, is all that is needed to account for play in the general sense. The specific form the play takes depends on a number of factors. The human organism has a characteristic physiological and anatomical structure which limits its activity and predisposes it towards certain definite lines of activity. The physical fitness of the organism affects the kind of activity it engages upon at any one time, and its psychological inclinations predispose it to certain types of play activity—primary physiological needs (like hunger, thirst and sex) and habits and attitudes acquired through interaction with the social environment, mean that the play forms of the group tend to become the individual's play habits.

Mitchell and Mason consider that man plays to feel the thrill of accomplishment and so he engages in an activity in which he can succeed: if an attempted play of a child is too difficult, he tends to drop it. But:

> When motives cannot be realised and desires satisfied by direct overt activity the individual seeks compensatory satisfaction through imagination, either in imaginative play or in day-dreaming or fantasy. [260]

Thus compensatory play is the result of the desire for self-expression when more adequate means seem impossible. In this sense, of course, work can be play, and play itself has its own aim:

> It is the presence of an aim or goal that gives meaning to an activity . . . Man is by nature a goal-seeking creature. [260]

If drudgery is activity with no adequate reward other than mere existence, and work is effort performed for rewards and satisfactions which are outside the activity, play is effort which contains its own satisfactions. Recreation is sought for relaxation, rest, physical and psychological balance, and escape; but play is different for it suggests growth, the perfecting of skills and the progression towards goals.

They also state a comprehensive classification of games, divided between competitive and non-competitive play:

A. COMPETITIVE
(*i*)   *Contests* (1) *Between individuals*—like swimming, track events, etc.;
                     (2) *Between groups*—like relay races, etc.
(*ii*)   *Games* (1) *Elementary games*—with simple organisation, and mainly running, dodging, and chasing—
                        (a) getting possession of a home, base or goal;
                        (b) tag games;
                  (2) *Personal Combats*—wrestling, boxing and fencing are games rather than combats;
                  (3) *Team Games,* usually with balls—
                        (a) throwing and striking: cricket, baseball, etc.;
                        (b) tennis games: badminton, racquets, squash, volleyball, etc.;
                        (c) football: rugby and association, hockey, polo, baseball, etc.;

(4) *Mental Competition*—chess, cards, etc., which are closely allied to social play.

B. NON-COMPETITIVE

(*i*)   *Hunting* (1) *Physical*—shooting, angling, trapping, etc.;
        (2) *Intellectual*—hunting for ideas, words (crosswords), etc.

(*ii*)   *Curiosity* — literally thousands: reading, puzzle-solving, etc.

(*iii*) *Roving* — hiking, riding, bicycling, sailing, etc.

(*iv*)   *Creative* (1) *using material objects*—arts and crafts;
        (2) *the non-material sphere*—drama, music, poetry, stories.

(*v*)   *Vicarious* — make-believe play, reading, films, day-dreaming, reverie.

(*vi*)   *Imitative* (1) *Free play*—trying to approximate to 'the proper way' to do things;
        (2) *Simple imitation*—whole group acts, like 'Follow my leader';
        (3) *Story plays*—stories created from the known with real movements imitated;
        (4) *Song Plays and Folk Dances*—often in imitation of social habits and actions, or features of courtship;
        (5) *Mimetic Exercises*—a correct movement shown by a leader and then a group imitates (as in swimming training).

(*vii*) *Acquisitive* — collections.

(*viii*) *Social* — from simple conversation to parties, dances and kissing games.

(*ix*)   *Aesthetic* (1) *Music*—listening, participating, composing;
        (2) *Art*—art and crafts;
        (3) *Religion*—ritual and worship;
        (4) *Nature appreciation;*
        (5) *Dramatics*—also pageantry, club and lodge ritual;
        (6) *Literature*—reading and composing;
        (7) *Rhythmic play*—song plays and dances.

Mitchell and Mason also state that play experience is the basis of the higher mental processes. Abstract knowledge is based on concrete knowledge, and the advancement of the individual is based upon his store of experience. Visualisation and abstraction is best done by the child who has many clear and vivid impressions. That experience is the basis for abstract thought can be seen from the original connection between the apple and gravitation—thus the wider the experience, the greater the power of clear image making.

Further, they call for a policy of education for leisure. With the changing nature of work-leisure patterns, there is a need for education for recreation. Education should be seen as a life-long process, and should not end with formal schooling. Such a programme of education for leisure should contain: (1) facilities and opportunities for those in need of recreation; (2) a general refinement of interests through adult education, and thus improved standards for theatre, sports, reading, radio and the mass media; (3) a conscious, constructive attitude to recreation.

PART FOUR

DRAMA THOUGHT & LANGUAGE

12 IMITATION, IDENTIFICATION & ROLE THEORY

Whereas instinct psychologists are concerned with the development of inherited characteristics, social psychologists have widened the whole scope of their approach to the individual who is seen as determined by environmental forces. All types of experiments, particularly in the United States, have continued in this field and have even affected psychoanalysts: Flugel, for example, examines the conscious and unconscious influence of the school, neighbourhood, local social situations, and the culture patterns upon the individual [110].

The environmental approach is known as Behaviourism, and the specific aspect which concerns man's behaviour in a learning situation is known as Learning Theory.

LEARNING THEORY

Classic Conditioning

Pavlov's classic experiments with dogs enabled him to provide the essential paradigm for the learning process. Food (Unconditioned Stimulus) produces salivating in the dog (Unconditioned Response). But if a buzzer (Conditioned Stimulus) goes many times before the US is presented, eventually the dog will salivate *before* the food is presented (Conditioned Response). Thus we have the paradigm:

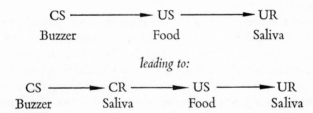

CS ⟶ US ⟶ UR
Buzzer   Food   Saliva

leading to:

CS ⟶ CR ⟶ US ⟶ UR
Buzzer   Saliva   Food   Saliva

Conditioning is, therefore, a simple type of learning: the animal has to learn to transfer the response from the US to the CS.

Instrumental Learning

Thorndike was the first to consider the process known variously as 'trial and error' learning, 'operant' or 'instrumental' conditioning. If the organism is in a situation where a variety of responses can be made and some need exists, it will act; thus a hungry rat in a puzzle box will go looking for food. But if a 'correct' response is rewarded in a way appropriate to the need (if the rat presses a lever and gets food as a result), he will learn to produce the 'correct' response—re-occurrence of the rewarded response increases with each rewarded trial. Thus:

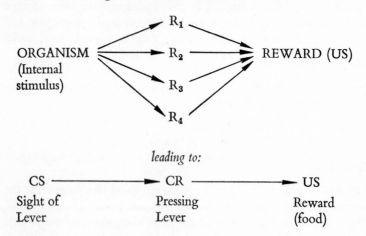

$$
\begin{array}{ccc}
 & R_1 & \\
\text{ORGANISM} & R_2 & \text{REWARD (US)} \\
\text{(Internal} & & \\
\text{stimulus)} & R_3 & \\
 & R_4 &
\end{array}
$$

leading to:

CS	CR	US
Sight of Lever	Pressing Lever	Reward (food)

In recent years, Instrumental Learning has become closely associated with Skinner [340] who emphasises reinforcement: that the connection between a stimulus pattern and a response is strengthened when it is reinforced.

Skinner also considers that Conditioning and Instrumental Learning represent two different kinds of learning behaviour: the first is a specialised form of behaviour which has little relevance to human beings; but the latter is the basis for most human learning. Certainly the latter ensures that the response is *instrumental* in obtaining the reward—thus Instrumental Learning is more 'active' than Classic Conditioning.

Hilgard and Marquis [172] describe three additional varieties of Instrumental Learning. The first is Secondary Reward Training, when an initially neutral stimulus acquires the power to reinforce learning. For example, Wolpe [391] allowed chimpanzees to put tokens in vending machines to secure grapes; but even when the machines were removed they continued to collect the tokens. Second, is Escape Training: an unpleasant stimulus will eventually make an animal learn to produce the 'correct' response in order to escape. And third, Avoidance Training: if a buzzer is sounded before a shock is given to the animal, he will learn to avoid the hazard.

Developments

Even in the early days of behaviourism, individuals had a variety of approaches. One of the earliest off-shoots of Watsonian behaviourism, for example, was Guthrie's Association Theory [158] which said that any combination or totality of stimuli which has accompanied a movement will be followed by that movement when the combination occurs again. Tolman [360] in his Sign-Gestalt Theory drew upon all psychology, and not merely behaviourism; he attempted to deal with goal-directed, whole acts of the organism and considered that what is learned is not a response or a movement, but 'what-leads-to-what' relationships.

More influential is Clark Hull's deductive system [187] which stems most directly from Watson and Thorndike. He considered that all behaviour is based on needs and drives and, as a result, all behaviour is motivated. There are two kinds of drives: (1) primary drives which are innate (like hunger, thirst, sex and avoidance of pain), are dependent upon certain bodily conditions and are endowments of the individual at birth; and (2) acquired or secondary drives which are learned through association with the primary drives so that any strong stimulus may acquire the characteristics of initiating or impelling action. Learning which reduces the drives (drive reduction) is stamped in—and this is reinforcement. A habit is a learned response over a considerable period of time, and is formed (or increases in strength) as a function of reinforcement, and as the need reduces. Habits are never 'unlearned': they can only increase or remain the same as they function only as a result of rewarded trials.

Stimulus generalisation is now accepted by most learning theorists. A person who responds to certain stimuli tends to generalise his responses to similar stimuli: these will be elicited by any stimulus which is similar to the original. This provides the necessary flexibility in human habits and learning, but the amount of generalisation depends on the degree of similarity. Generalisation of responses is also considered to occur according to similar principles. Thus human beings can transfer experience from one situation to another. But an over-generalised response is not reinforced and so behaviour is narrowed; it is this which is discrimination:

> ... generalisation ensures similar responses in spite of differences between the stimuli; discrimination ensures different responses in spite of similarities between the stimuli. [354]

IMITATION

Learning Theory has much to say about imitation which is a key factor within the process of dramatic play. It is also significant to education as a whole for it is inherent in the process of socialisation, and modern civilisation is relying more and more upon symbolic models for children to imitate—oral, written or pictorial instructions, or through a mixture of oral and visual devices (including films and television). Imitation (either in the formal classroom situation, or through dramatic play) is of vital importance to learning.

The approaches to imitation have been various. It was seen as an innate instinct by McDougall, Woodworth, Gabriel Tarde and others, but this is not satisfactory to behaviourists who have two basic ways of approaching imitation: Conditioning and Instrumental.

Imitation & Conditioning

Some follow Pavlovian Conditioning and will go no further. J. M. Baldwin said that imitation occurred when a stimulus started a motor process which tends to reproduce the stimulus and, again, the motor process:

> From the physiological side we have a circular activity—sensor, motor; sensor, motor; and from the psychological side we have a similar circle— reality, image, movement; reality, image, movement, etc. [19]

In other words, the child imitates to get the act started, and then circular reaction keeps it going. E. B. Holt [174] developed the reflex-circle hypothesis of imitative behaviour: when a child hears himself cry, simultaneous association results and a reflex-circle is established. When a child stimulates himself the behaviour is called iteration; but when a second person is the stimulus it is called imitation. F. H. Allport is similar to Holt, particularly concerning crying and babbling:

When others speak syllables to the child, they put into operation the ear-vocal reflexes which the child has already fixated by hearing himself talk. [9]

When an adult repeats an approximation of the child's babbling, together with a demonstration to which the word refers, the child is conditioned to repeat the word—and this is imitation. This is essentially the opinion of Humphrey, who stated it in terms of Classical Conditioning in 1921 [189], and also that of Gardner Murphy in his more modern biosocial approach:

Imitation at its most primitive level likewise appears to be a matter of conditioning; its mechanism is apparently based on the circular response. Some inner event or stimulus (S) makes one respond (R); one perceives (P) the R as it is carried out; all three events—S, R and P—overlap in time, so that each repetition of R leads to P and hence to another R . . . Having splashed the water for whatever reason, the two-year-old continues to splash it. On a later occasion, big brother in the same tub splashes it, and little brother does likewise. [271]

But:

Deliberate imitation is a more complex affair, involving closer perception of detail, greater integration of movement, and, above all, a set toward the end result, just as in the delayed reaction. [271]

The basic problem with this theory, as Miller and Dollard point out, is that it accounts for too much: there is no way of explaining how a reflex circle once started ever stops. It also fails to account for the emergence of novel responses during the model-observer sequence.

Miller & Dollard

Miller and Dollard [259] are the classic theorists for the second Learning approach to imitation. They consider that all human behaviour is learned—acquired rather than innate—and through the following paradigm:

DRIVE	→	CUE	→	RESPONSE	→	REWARD
want something		notice something		do something		get something

They consider imitation comes into the behaviour pattern as an acquired drive but, once generated, it acts exactly like a primary drive. And:

8

Imitation is a process by which 'matched', or similar acts are evoked in two
people and connected to appropriate cues. It can occur only under conditions
which are favourable to learning these acts. If matching, or doing the same as
others do, is regularly rewarded, a secondary tendency to match may be
developed, and the process of imitation becomes the derived drive of
imitativeness. [259]

They distinguish three types of imitation: (1) matched-dependent,
where the leader is able to read the relevant environmental cues but the
follower is not—this mechanism is important in the behaviour of
crowds or when young people match behaviour with older people;
(2) copying, where the response is slowly brought to an approximation
of the model, but the subject must know when he has done so in order
that his act is an acceptable reproduction of the model act; and (3)
same, where two people perform the same act in response to the same
cue—two people catching the same bus having read the same notice.

Imitation is vital in the learning of language. All societies are taught
special responses, which makes up the language of the group, and this
influences subsequent social learning. The baby's cry is a response to a
strong stimulus and he is rewarded by feeding. The tones of other
people's voices grow to have a reward value, say Miller and Dollard.
But the baby's first contact with formal language is learning to use
words spoken by others as cues for his responses—the sound 'No!' may
be followed by punishment. He learns that gesture accompanied by
sound is more likely to be rewarded. In fact, the child learns to talk
because society makes the effort worth while. It provides training in
connecting words to objects, and acts to words, and words into sequences of stimulus-producing responses; habits of grammar govern the
way in which other learned responses, words, and phrases are combined. The response to the spoken word as cue produces the appropriate word as a response; this becomes an anticipatory response, showing
that imitation has an important role to play in thinking and reasoning.

The function of reason is to shorten the process of trial and error.
Cue-producing responses are important in reasoning: a combination
of two separate items of experience (putting two and two together) is a
characteristic of simple reasoning; most reasoning is made up of longer
sequences of cue-producing responses and these are often learned by
the individual as part of his culture.

Miller and Dollard also see that imitation helps learning: it forces the
subject to respond to the proper cue more quickly than he otherwise

would. Copying is teaching a subject to respond independently to proper environmental cues and, in this sense, is particularly vital in learning a language. However, Mowrer can say:

> It might be said that Miller & Dollard were not really studying imitation at all, but simply discrimination in which the cue stimulus is provided by the behaviour of other organisms. Their rejoinder would probably be that imitation *is* 'simply discrimination' of the kind just described . . . [269]

C. W. Valentine

Valentine did not approach imitation from Learning Theory but from purely experimental psychology. He found that not all responses were imitative, and that the child did not imitate all people equally— he imitates some people but not others—and the key seems to be catching the child's attention who must then be interested in the imitatee. He summarises the imitation of young children as follows:

2. Actions to which there is already an innate tendency are imitated very readily within the first few months, e.g. sound making and smiling.

3. Actions which can serve no purpose perceived by the child and which are not based on instinctive impulses, are imitated freely between the ages of nine and twelve months.

4. There is sometimes a 'latent' period between the seeing of an action and the imitation of it, and sometimes the repetition of an action is necessary before imitation follows.

5. Primary, involuntary, or purposeless imitation seems to be due to the monopolisation of attention for a moment by some fascinating impression.

6. Some imitations seem to serve the purpose of helping the subject to realise or enter into the experience of the imitatee more vividly.

7. Some imitations are of a reflex type, if the term reflex can be applied where sight provides the only stimulus.

8. Experimental tests at twelve months and at two years suggest that the tendency to imitate any very interesting action is very strong in some children.

9. The imitatee is important: e.g. a child will sometimes imitate the mother but not another person.

10. There is some evidence that a child may wish others to join in the imitation. [365]

O. H. Mowrer & the Two-Factor Theory

Valentine in no way accounts for the phenomenon of imitation, he merely describes certain imitative characteristics. Learning theorists attempted to account for it but O. H. Mowrer considers:

> . . . according to the Miller–Dollard analysis, the only way a bird could learn to say 'Hello' imitatively would be to *say it* while noticing another bird (or person?) saying the same thing—and getting rewarded. The question is: How is the bird going to learn to make this highly improbable sound in the first place? A two-factor analysis of the process of word learning resolves this difficulty. [268]

Mowrer's two factors are: (1) Continuity—a bird becomes 'glad to see' and 'glad to *hear*' the trainer, and so the trainer's sights and sounds take on a secondary-reward value for the bird; and (2) Reward—should the bird, in making sounds, happen to produce one like the trainer's, this will have a secondary reward value. So imitation is:

> . . . a sort of automatic trial-and-error process, one which is dependent upon reward from another organism, or 'parent person', only in an indirect, derived sense. The response has become 'baited' so that whenever the bird makes it, satisfaction and reinforcement will be powerful and prompt—and self-administered!—provided appropriate motivation is present. [269]

Mowrer says that birds learn to talk only when a human teacher becomes a *love object* for them, thus drawing in the principle of reinforcement (from learning theory) and that of identification (from psychoanalysis).

IDENTIFICATION

Imitation & Identification

We must distinguish between imitation and identification. Talcott Parsons [288] said that imitation is the process by which *specific* items of a culture, individual pieces of knowledge, skill, and symbolic behaviour are taken over. In one sense it is a short cutting of independent learning, though it must be rewarding if the learnt act is to be reinforced. But specifically imitation does not imply any emotional relationship between the individual and the model.

On the other hand, identification implies the internalising of the values of the model; it implies an emotional relationship between the imitator and the imitatee so that value patterns are shared. We should also note that, in terms of social maturation, imitation is the basis upon which identification can be built:

> The social significance of the imitative responses of early infancy resides largely in their capacity for fostering adult-child interactions. [372]

Thus imitation is an early vehicle for playful communication between parent and child, and it is upon this empathy (which Sullivan has so well described) that later identification can develop.

In this sense, imitation would be an acceptable term for Conditioning or Instrumental Learning theorists. But Mowrer, finding classic behaviourism unsatisfactory, adds identification to the learning process.

Freud's Developmental & Defensive Identification

Freud at various times distinguished between two forms of identification: developmental, whereby the child introjects the qualities of the mother and, eventually, builds the superego; and defensive where, through fear, he identifies with the aggressor.

Developmental identification occurs when the nurturant mother begins to withdraw rewards she had previously freely given; the resultant threat of the loss of the loved object, says Freud [127], then motivates the child to introject her behaviour and her qualities. It is this introjection that Melanie Klein discovers at an even earlier age and by which the superego is acquired:

> In general, parents and similar authorities follow the dictates of their own superegos in the upbringing of children. Whatever terms their ego may be on with their superego, in the education of the child they are severe and exacting. They have forgotten the difficulties of their own childhood, and are glad to be able to identify themselves fully at last with their own parents, who in their day subjected them to such severe restraints. The result is that the superego of the child is not really built up on the model of the parents, but on that of the parents' superego; it takes over the same content, it becomes the vehicle of tradition and of all the age-long values which have been handed down in this way from generation to generation. [131]

Quite clearly, the identification with the parent which produces the superego is, for Freud, biological; but where behaviourists acknowledge it, it is as a precipitate of parental and other social conditioning:

The role which the superego undertakes later in life is at first played by an external power, by parental authority. The influence of the parents dominates the child by granting proofs of affection and by threats of punishment, which, to the child, means loss of love, and which must also be feared on their own account. This objective anxiety is the forerunner of the later moral anxiety; so long as the former is dominant, one need not speak of superego or of conscience. It is only later that the secondary situation arises, which we are far too ready to regard as the normal state of affairs; the external restrictions are introjected, so that the superego takes the place of the parental function, and thenceforward observes, guides and threatens the ego in just the same way as the parents acted to the child before. [131]

Defensive identification, on the other hand, is the outcome of the Oedipus complex for Freud [126] and then the child adopts the characteristics of the parent of the same sex. In this instance, it is fear of punishment rather than loss of love which provides the incentive for the boy to identify with his father. It is this form of identification which Anna Freud considered was one of the ego's mechanisms of defence: by pretending that he is the external aggressor, the child has no reason to fear. She gives a classic example of a girl who was afraid of the dark and ghosts (ghosts often being the intermediate link between the parents and the establishment of the ego):

Suddenly, however, she hit on a device . . . she would run across the hall, making all sorts of peculiar gestures as she went. Before long, she triumphantly told her little brother the secret of how she had got over her anxiety. 'There's no need to be afraid in the hall,' she said, 'you just have to pretend that you're the ghost who might meet you.' This shows that her magic gestures represented the movements which she imagined that ghosts would make. [119]

By impersonating the aggressor, the child transforms himself from the person threatened into the person who makes the threat.

Developmental Identification & Learning Theory

For Mowrer, as we have seen, learning involves both the conditioning and instrumental aspects (including reinforcement) of Learning Theory, but imitation—which he regards as essential for learning—is based upon identification. He uses this in the same sense as Freud uses developmental identification:

Words or other human sounds are first made by infants, it seems, because the words have been associated with relief and other satisfactions and, as a result, have themselves come to sound good ... Soon, however, the infant discovers that the making of these sounds can be used not only to comfort, reassure, and satisfy himself directly but also to interest, satisfy, and control mother, father, and others. [269]

Infants first produce words in order to 'recapture some of the pleasures which the parents have previously provided', and so:

In a very primitive and rudimentary sense, they are trying to re-present the mother, i.e. make her present again, in an autistic, quasi-magical way. This they do ... with *her sounds*. But then, as the infant thus learns to make conventional word sounds, the *second* stage of word functioning emerges. Now he utters a specifically meaningful word which serves, literally, to re-present the mother, recall, recapture, recreate her; and in so doing the infant reduces the necessity for relying upon the autistic, self-supplied satisfactions. Now, instead of merely *playing* with words, the infant makes them *work*.
[269]

But if identification is the attempt to 're-present' the mother, this is in fact the basic form of impersonation, of dramatic play. And this is understandable, for Mowrer shows that P. D. Courtney's Concept of Mediation [268] is central to this point: in the child's mind the mother becomes the link, the mediator, between his wants and their satisfaction and thus developmental identification begins to occur. The mother's behaviour and attributes take on secondary reward value and so, albeit in a quasi-magical way, he begins the elements of impersonation.

Sears, too, considers developmental identification as a form of behavioural development. He shows a series of developmental steps: (1) the child develops a dependency drive for the mother's affectionate nurture; (2) he imitates—behaves like—the mother; (3) he is so gratified by the imitation that it becomes habitual and, as a result, has the characteristics of a secondary motivational system:

Many symbolic acts performed by the mother (smiling, hugging, talking) become secondary rewards for the child, and when he performs these acts himself, he rewards himself. Thus his own performance of some kinds of identification behaviour is self-rewarding. So long as the mother does not actually punish him for such actions, and so long as she continues to use reasonably consistent symbols of love and approval, this process will continue. [335]

However, the strength of the identification will vary with the specific type of affectionate nurture given to the child: if it is continuous, the child will never have occasion to act like the mother; if it is punitive, he will not want to. Thus:

> The present hypothesis is that a secondary drive of identification produces the behaviour that is replicative of the parents' qualities, role behaviours and demands. In this sense, it is a process or mechanism. It has the effect of transmitting the values of the culture from one generation to the next, and of providing for the continuity, in a society, of persons appropriately trained for the roles of which the society is composed. [335]

Essentially, for Sears, the child's repeated association of imitation with direct or self-administered reward leads to identification becoming an acquired drive for which the satisfying response is acting like another person—impersonation, or dramatic play.

Defensive Identification & Learning Theory

Where Freud considered that the child was in competition with the father for the mother's affection, Whiting [386, 387] sees that rivalry may develop around any form of reward, material or social. The more the child envies the power or status of another person in connection with the rewards of which he feels deprived, the more he will pretend to be (take on the role of) that person. Identification, therefore, comes about through competition with, and fear of, the father: but not, as Freud considered, in the sexual field; rather, Whiting considers, it is in the field of nurture where the child competes with the adult for affection, attention, food and care.

Summary

Learning Theory, whether classical conditioning or instrumental learning, is limited to describing *some* of the mechanisms present in the learning process. Learning theorists normally explain imitation as a reflex circle or discrimination, both of which are unsatisfactory, and this has led Mowrer to postulate identification as the motivation for imitative learning.

Imitation is the process by which specific items of a culture are taken over, but with identification value patterns are shared. Developmental identification leads, through fear of loss of love, to the child imperson- ating the mother. Defensive identification leads, through fear of punishment, to the child impersonating the father. Social learning hinges on imitation; but imitation leads to identification. Thus it is that the process of social learning is inherently dramatic.

ROLE THEORY

Sarbin

Sarbin's development of role theory leans heavily on the initial work of G. H. Mead [253] and essentially considers that actions between persons are organised into roles, and that human conduct is the product of the interaction of the self and role.

With Kardiner and Linton, role theory regards culture as an organi- sation of learned behaviours and the products of behaviour which are shared and transmitted. Sarbin considers that all societies are organised around positions, and that the persons who occupy these positions perform specialised actions or roles. But the roles they perform are linked with the position and not with the person who is temporarily occupying that position.

Sarbin defines role as follows:

A *role* is a patterned sequence of learned *actions* or deeds performed by a person in an interaction situation. [328]

As to the acquisition of roles, role actions are learned in two ways: (1) by intentional instruction, and (2) by incidental learning.

Play is an incidental method of acquiring role behaviour, and Mead was one of the first to realise the importance of play in the adoptive learning of social roles. Dramatic play itself brings two results: (1) the acquisition of roles, and (2) the acquisition of skill in shifting roles. In fact, role theory sees imaginative impersonation as the keystone of social learning:

The imaginative processes are central in play acting. They are likewise central in covert processes, such as fantasy. The silent rehearsal of roles appropriate to real or imagined positions, and of roles appropriate to the position of the other, provides a large reservoir of experience. In all cultures, a good part of the content of imaginative behaviour is institutionalised in the form of folk tales, myths, and other story forms. The imaginative process is central likewise in that form of acquiring roles which has been variously named as identification, introjection, empathy, and taking-the-role-of-the-other. Dependent on the ability of the person (child or adult) to engage in *as if* processes, identification provides numerous avenues for acquiring roles. The number and kinds of persons with whom one may identify, of course, is limited by the number and kinds of persons in the environment and by cultural practises. [328]

The importance of the relationship between the imaginative process and role taking was seen as important by Mead and Moreno, both of whom tacitly acknowledged that imitation relates to identification which, through role taking, is in essence dramatic.

Role enactment, or impersonation, includes amongst other behaviours, gross skeletal movements, the performance of verbal and motor gestures, posture and gait, styles of speech or accent, the wearing of certain forms of dress or costume, the use of material objects, the wearing of emblems or ornamentation, and so on. Role enactment thus embraces the whole mechanics of the role-taking process. And the more roles in a person's behaviour repertory: '. . . the "better" his social adjustment—other things being equal'. On the other hand, absence of role-taking skills is influential in the development of paranoid disorders [54], while:

. . . deficiency in role playing means the incapacity to look upon one's self as an object (Mead) or to identify with another's point of view. [151]

Sarbin then delineates his 'Organismic Dimension'. As any role may be enacted with different degrees of organic involvement, it is possible to distinguish levels of intensity:

LEVEL I	*Role and Self differentiated*	e.g. casual role of customer in supermarket
LEVEL II	*Actor performing the motions necessary for portrayal of role*	e.g. employees who 'puts up a good front' to impress the boss
LEVEL III	*Actor 'living the role'*	But maintains some contact with the role in order to change tempo, intensity, etc.

LEVEL IV	*Hypnotic subject*	Behaviours: catalepsies, compulsive post-hypnotic actions, sensory and motoric changes, etc; more of the organism responding than in play acting
LEVEL V	*Hysteria* (overlaps with IV); afflicted with organic dys-function	e.g. hysterical seizures, hys-terical anorexia, hysterical paralysis, hysterical anes-thesia
LEVEL VI	*Ecstatic states*	e.g. ecstatic trances, pos-session, religious revivals, conversions, etc. teenage swooners
LEVEL VII	*Role of the moribund person*	e.g. object of sorcery or witchcraft (sometimes irre-versible)

Clearly with such a classification, we return to the concept of 'the mask and the face'; or, as Sarbin puts it:

. . . the self is what a person 'is', the role is what the person 'does'. [328]

Most of us act our roles in Levels I and II at some time every day; we are putting on our 'masks'. This is the logical development of childhood identification and, in fact, is an extension of the same process: we imitate specific items in the culture and so come to identify with our parents: thus we impersonate, or re-enact roles by which we adjust to society.

Imitation, Identification & Role Therapy

We have seen that, in his early work, Freud emphasised catharsis as a therapeutic treatment. Learning theorists concerned with imitation, identification and role theory disagree with this. Bandura, Ross and Ross [21] compared the effects of real-life models, human film-aggression, and cartoon film-aggression on the aggressive behaviour of pre-school children. They found that:

The children who observed the aggressive models displayed a great number

of precisely imitative aggressive responses, whereas such responses rarely
occurred in either the non-aggressive-model group or the control group.
[22]

Thus it is considered that in the social situation, learned patterns of
response to stress frequently originate from the child's observation of
parental and other models; during the course of a child's development,
parents usually provide him with ample opportunities to observe their
stress reactions and, so, to imitate them. Bandura and Walters [22]
consider that a child, presented with a model, normally responds in one
of three ways: (1) by a new response—exposed to aggression he may
repeat it; (2) by inhibitory and disinhibitory response—although not
precisely imitative, the response is in some respects similar (nonspecific
imitation); (3) an eliciting response—socially approved behaviour can
be readily elicited if appropriate models are provided (as with a
standardised speaker dropping back into original dialect within the
dialect situation).

Thus the recommended therapeutic situation is by role-playing, but
not quite in the way Moreno suggested:

> Role-playing may be a particularly effective means of producing behaviour
> change, since (at least in most experimental situations) the role player depen-
> dently accepts the assigned role and then is usually reinforced by approval for
> reproducing the behaviour of the model. Indeed, during the role-playing
> process, when his previous activities become a model for his own further
> behaviour, the agent may be receiving reinforcement both in his capacity as
> model and in his capacity of observer and imitator . . .
>
> In all cases, however, the essential learning process consists of the presen-
> tation of a model, symbolic or real-life, whose behaviour the observer
> matches. [22]

We meet, therefore, a crux problem. The therapeutic theory of
catharsis suggests that 'playing out evil in a legal framework' lets off
steam, that the cathartic discharge of emotion can produce a lasting
therapeutic change. (Though we have already seen, on p. 74, that
Freud in his later work did not think this was the only therapeutic
method.) On the other hand, Bandura and Walters, with a mass of
accumulated evidence, can say that:

> . . . evidence from controlled research studies of children indicates that far
> from producing a cathartic reduction of aggression, direct or vicarious

participation in aggressive attitudes within a permissive setting maintains the behaviour at its original level and may actually increase it. [22]

If acting aggressively, do the children tend to get rid of aggressive emotions (catharsis) or do they tend to increase their aggression role therapy)? Put another way, the problem becomes: if children use aggression in their play, will this lessen or increase their own aggressive behaviour?

There is no clear cut answer to this problem. But from the educational situation it appears as though, under certain conditions, both schools of thought may be right. Overinhibited children often benefit cathartically from dramatic play. So do some retarded and mentally backward children; yet it can also be said that these children, if provided with an anti-social model, are inclined to imitate, or identify with, the model. Certainly it appears that the Imitation—Identification—Impersonation model is the process by which the human child develops and, if human life worked like a calculating machine, no doubt all children watching aggression on television, or pretending to be a 'baddie' in their dramatic play, would grow up aggressively. And, indeed, behaviourist therapy, as summarised by Beech [25] would ask us to think so. But life does not work by cut-and-dried methods. Some children *do* show cathartic release in their play. And some children *do* learn aggression through imitation; but whether the lasting effects are quite as serious as Bandura and Walters imply is open to question. At the present stage of human understanding, the question must remain open.

13 THOUGHT

If the process of social learning is inherently dramatic, and through the impersonation of roles we adjust to society, the whole process of thought itself is related to the dramatic imagination. Thought is built up out of concept and human beings use concepts in two main ways: for creative thinking and memory learning. Both processes utilise dramatic play, overtly if we are children and covertly if we are adults.

Concepts

Concepts are ideas which group or classify experience—'representations that have some generality of application' [232]. Thus we put 'robin' and 'sparrow' into the classification 'bird'. In theory, an infinite number of concepts is possible but, in fact, they are usually based upon preliminary classifications of experience which have been found useful in some way. Thus we acquire a repertory of concepts: they tend to change with increasing age, becoming more complex, and more logical. Concepts vary in novelty and complexity with the individual but we all:

> ...(tend) to evolve concepts gradually, the occasional attainment of concepts without awareness of the concept itself, the development of inconsistent as well as consistent concepts, the tendency for concepts to be learned in a definite order, and the occurrence of varying degrees of concrete and abstract approaches to, and use of, concepts. [367]

Although it is often thought that concrete concepts (like 'birds' or 'boxes') are more easily learned than abstract concepts, (like the concepts of number), Mednick has shown [256] that this may not necessarily be true: rather, the variable appears to be the number of stimulus properties perceived by the subject.

Carroll [58] distinguishes primary and secondary concepts: (1) internal representations of classes or categories of experience for which, when the child has language, he learns the names; and (2) concepts built out of other concepts—they are built out of partial similarities in the *responses* to sensations (thus 'oppositeness' is built out of noticed instances). Bruner, Goodnow and Austin [45] examined types of concepts practically, showing their subjects some sets of designs which had variant figures and borders. Thus they postulate three types of concepts, from the easiest to the most difficult: (1) Conjunctive, where the criterion is a specified combination of attributes (thus, 'red figures with borders'); (2) Relational, where the criterion is a specified relation between attributes (thus, 'fewer figures than borders'); and (3) Disjunctive, where the criterion is any two or more alternative combinations or attributes (thus, 'either a red figure or one with two borders'). Modern research has shown [379] that the ability to discriminate positive from negative instances frequently precedes the ability to formulate the concept in words; also that information from positive instances can be assimilated and used more readily than information contained in negative instances. We should also note what Leon Festinger calls Cognitive Dissonance [107], which is:

> ... a state of affairs that occurs whenever two ideas are in marked conflict as when one is presented with an objective fact that appears to undercut one's cherished beliefs. Festinger shows that people are strongly motivated to reduce such cognitive conflict—either by changing their attitudes, seeking more information, or restructuring or reinterpreting the information available to them. [58]

Concept & Symbol

Concepts are based upon experience which is assimilated by sensation. Sense experience, in fact, conditions thought and all thought rests upon it. Thus Boulding can say:

> What I have been talking about is knowledge. Knowledge, perhaps, is not a good word for this. Perhaps one would rather say my *Image* of the world. Knowledge has an implication of validity, of truth. What I am talking about is what I believe to be true; my subjective knowledge. It is this Image that largely governs my behaviour . . . *The first proposition of this work, therefore, is that behaviour depends on the image.* [35]

Images are created by sense experience, and they themselves are the basis for conceptualising. Signs, such as words, come to be related to images and, in some cases, become synonymous with them. But in the initial instance, the percept of experience creates an image which, later, becomes associated with a word and 'binds itself' to it. Thus, in adult life, it often happens that the image and the word which represents it appear to become the same thing.

We have already considered the psychoanalytic approach to signs and symbols (pp. 69–70) and have noted that all symbols are images of sense experience. But the methods by which an image can be created are many: (1) perceptual, which accounts for the majority of images; (2) dream images; (3) images developing from a neutral matrix, like the voices which we sometimes hear in a sea-shell; (4) hypnagogic images, that occur as we are about to fall asleep; (5) hypnopompic images, occurring as we are about to wake; (6) hallucinations; and (7) eidetic images, which are so 'external' that they are confused with percepts (as occurred with Blake and Goethe). Man differs from all other animals in being free of immediate dependence on external stimulation; because of the imagistic nature of his thought, he lives in a symbolic world. Symbolic thought can initiate action and can organise, and becomes a factor in personality organisation. Structurally considered, however, when perceptual relationships are represented by signs—usually words, as shown in Osgood's Mediation Hypothesis [284]—the symbolic function emerges.

CREATIVE THOUGHT

The Creative Process

Behaviourism sees thinking as a chain of stimuli and responses, so that the essential factors in thinking are habit and past experience, repetition rather than reason [355]. But if a new thought is explained as the interaction of a series of old ideas by trial-and-error, this does not explain purely creative thought.

More interesting are Gestalt propositions in this field. According to Wertheimer, parts of a problem are determined by the structure of the whole, as the whole is by the parts:

1. There is *grouping, reorganisation, structurization,* operations of dividing into sub-wholes and still seeing these sub-wholes together, with clear reference to the whole figure and in view of the specific problem at issue . . .
2. The process starts with the desire to get at the *inner-relatedness* of form and size. This is not a search for just any relation which would connect them, but for the nature of their intrinsic inter-dependence . . .
3. Outstanding relations of this kind—sensible with regard to the inner structural nature of the given situation— . . . play a large role here . . .
4. There is the feature of the functional meaning of parts . . .
5. The entire process is one consistent line of *thinking.* It is not an and-sum of aggregated, piecemeal operations. No step is arbitrary, ununderstood in its function. On the contrary, each step is taken surveying the whole situation . . .

[383]

As Getzels and Jackson point out [144], while the Gestalt proposition is suitable to a situation where the problem has to be thought through, this is not the case in art or music where the completed creative thought is envisaged first and then the artist must attempt to make it concrete in terms of its parts.

Individual thinkers have also distinguished creative from non-creative thinking. Hadamard [162] considered that mathematical break-throughs were the result of insight, and this is supported by Koestler who shows [221] that great scientists like Copernicus, Kepler and Galileo resist the 'obvious' and use the 'illogical' for their creations.

Vinacke [368] distinguishes between realistic and imaginative thinking: the former adheres to logical and scientific criteria, and is dominated by reason and facts; the latter allows inner currents to play with perceptual data, allows free experiment to provide hypotheses, suggestions, fantasies, images and comparisons, and also strives towards barely conceived goals. Creative thinkers switch and mix styles in their actual thought processes. But if thought can be distinguished between realistic and imaginative, the imagination itself can be of two types: autistic, which does not relate to real conditions—as in fantasy, reverie and day-dreaming, and which is determined by inner stimuli (like needs, wishes and conflicts) as distinct from external stimuli; and genuine imagination which is characterised by free play based on external stimuli—the imagination concerns definite problems or tasks which act as a control factor.

There have been various discussions concerning the creative process used by specific artists [145, 361]: Stephen Spender delineates his own preparation (putting down ideas and notes), the sudden emergence of a germ of thought (inspiration), and the reworking of the material; Ben Shahn describes the same process for the painter—a chain of connective ideas responding to paint and colour, the rising of the image, and the reworking of the image; Henri Poincaré uses different terminology to describe the same basic pattern in creative mathematical thinking—conscious work (assembling data and making trials), unconscious work (fertilisation), and the working out with skills. Patrick [289] conducted experimental investigations with actual artists; his basic pattern for creative thought has been reworked by subsequent investigators [354] into the following: (1) Preparation—becoming familiar with the situation and materials; (2) Incubation—unconsciously the problem begins to be defined and fragments of it appear; (3) Illumination—

when the specific goal is envisaged and work is begun towards it, all of which can be affected by prior learning (there must be a necessary range of skills, habits and capacities), sensory cues (Freud used cheroots, and Spender coffee and tobacco, for concentration), the personality factors of receptivity, adventurousness, and motivation, and the ability to switch between realistic and imaginative thought; (4) Verification— or revision of results. But the sequence of events is far from invariable, and there is much overlapping.

Creativity & Intelligence

Getzels and Jackson [144] have made a major contribution to the understanding of creativity and its relationship to intelligence. Their researches show that creativity is as important a factor as intelligence for academic success.

Often, true giftedness is not rewarded with 'success' as it is commonly defined. The child may well grow up to learn that it is wiser to be 'successful' than to be 'gifted', and more virtuous to be 'President' than to be 'right'. The talented artist may well look futilely for an audience, while the successful man stares spellbound watching a Western on television. Getzels and Jackson question this whole moral standpoint: should education be for training or creativity? They ask:

> ... whether even the successful result may not after all be a Pyrrhic victory leading to the premature and unconditional surrender of play and fantasy to factualism and usefulness, an early surrender that makes itself felt later in the more or less irreversible separation of preconscious from conscious processes.
> [144]

They show that high creatives are more stimulus-free, fanciful, humorous, aggressive, violent, and less liked by their teachers than the high I.Q. group. Children who are highly creative:

> ... seem more expressive of impulses from within that are frequently inhibited, and descriptive of experiences from without that are often denied. The high creativity adolescent has a more playful—or if you will, more experimental—attitude toward conventional ideas, objects and qualities. Rather than dealing only in predetermined categories, as the high I.Q. adolescent is likely to do, he tends to use categories that he himself originates. Cereal does not only snap, crackle, and pop, it can also bend, sag, and sway.

Face cream does not only skid, it can also be skid-proof. The attainment of an ambition can mean not only success, it can also be just plain silly. [144]

They have, too, a comic aggression—against their school and teachers, their home and siblings, and against conventional forms and stereo-typed ideals.★

Thus they can say that what is needed is a change in the entire intellectual climate in which we—parents, teachers and children—function. And to this end they postulate the following differences:

1. Intelligent Thinking (as measured by I.Q., etc.)	v.	Creative Thinking
2. Independence and Unruliness	v.	Individuality and Rebelliousness
3. Morbid withdrawal (compulsive isolation)	v.	Healthy solitude (preferred separateness)
4. Irresolution and Indecisiveness	v.	Sense of Ambiguity and Ability to delay choice
5. Remembering and Information	v.	Discovering and Knowledge
6. Sense Perception	v.	Instinctive Perception
7. Censorship	v.	Evaluation
8. Unattainable Goal (leading to dejection and resignation)	v.	Difficult Goal (leading to aspiration and exertion)

★ Since this was written, an excellent short article has appeared in the *Times Educational Supplement* (10 March, 1967, p. 809) showing that, whereas various American studies have pointed to the view that intelligent and creative children were largely divergent groups, more recent British inquiries have questioned this. One such inquiry found 'no evidence that there existed any considerable group of children high in creativity but comparatively low in intelligence who had high scores in measure of school attainment'. A second considered that 'creativity should not be thought of as a separate intellectual mode'. It is clearly necessary to draw a distinction between the creative cognitive act, which is imaginative, and the intellectual cognitive act, which is the discovery of the inevitable pattern—the distinction between composing a poem and getting a sum correct—but whether these are exemplified by divergent groups is now open to question.

That there is increased interest in the whole problem of creativity is seen in the publication of the new quarterly, *The Journal of Creative Behavior* (Creative Education Foundation, Buffalo).

I am grateful to Dr Barbara M. McIntyre of Northwestern University, Evanston, Illinois, for bringing to my attention an excellent book on this subject for student reference: S. J. Parnes and H. F. Harding's *A Source Book for Creative Thinking* (Scribner, N.Y., 1962).

9. Information as educational objective   v.   Knowledge as educational objective (discovery)
   (repetition)

10. Sentimentality towards the 'cute'   v.   Honest appreciation of creative behaviour in the school situation
    and 'precious' without reference to
    intellectual merit

Here are a set of educational principles for the encouragement and development of creative thought and which underlie the whole approach of Dramatic Education.

Play & Creativity

That there is a direct relationship between play and the creative process, has much intellectual support. Freud, as we have seen, considered that creation is 'a continuation and substitution for the play of childhood'. Kris thought that creativity has a child-like quality and is a return to infantile modes of thought, while Kubie talks of 'toying' with preconscious material. Einstein, too, supports this view:

> The words or the language, as they are written or spoken, do not seem to play any role in my mechanisms of thought. The psychical entities which seem to serve as elements in thought are certain signs and more or less clear images which can be 'voluntarily' reproduced and combined.
>
> There is, of course, a certain connection between these elements and relevant logical concepts. It is also clear that the desire to arrive finally at logically connected concepts is the emotional basis of this rather vague play with the above mentioned elements. But taken from a psychological viewpoint, this combinatory play seems to be the essential feature in productive thought—before there is any connection with logical construction in words or other kinds of signs which can be communicated to others. [162]

The creative adolescent plays intellectually for the sheer pleasure of enjoying his fantasy. As Getzels and Jackson say:

> It is almost as if the creative adolescents experience a special delight in playful intellectual activity for its own sake. They involve themselves in the game-like task not because their teacher will like them for it, or because they anticipate a better grade, but seemingly because of the intrinsic pleasure that accompanies their use of fantasy. This delight in imaginative functioning—even in seemingly profitless situations—strikes us as reminiscent of the young

child's joy in exploring the world and testing his intellectual powers in make-believe and in acting 'as if'. [144]

Thus imaginative development in education should be based on dramatic play. It is this which allows free play with perceptual data and allows free experiment to take place in related fields—creative dance, creative music, creative art and creative language.

Synectics & Other Techniques

There have been a variety of recent methods for evaluating the scope of creativity. The validity of these 'creativity tests' is, however, in question for it is not known what inferences can be made about high scorers, nor do we know whether the tests have long-term or con-current validity.

'Brainstorming' is a technique for letting the unconscious flow freely [283] so that ideas come quickly and easily to the conscious. However, Taylor and others [353] have suggested that this reliance upon the unconscious inhibits creative problem-solving—and we have already seen that Kubie denies that the unconscious has a place in creative activity.

Probably of greater importance is the 'Synectics' of W. J. J. Gordon [150]. He considers that the creative efficiency of people can be markedly increased if they understand the psychological processes by which they operate and, further, that the emotional component of the creative process is more important than the intellectual, and the irrational more important than the rational.

Gordon specifically relates creativity and play:

Synectics theory implies that not all play is creative but that all creativity contains play. [150]

He cites Schiller and accepts Groos, but goes beyond them both:

Synectics maintains that the process of technical invention is the same as art. Conscious play, integrated with a desire for power over matter and pleasure at overcoming resistance, leads to technical inventions. [150]

Before they have been related to practice, all inventions are mere illusions and the motivation to put them into practice is (among other things) a desire for power over 'the way things are' through imagining 'the way things are *not*'. For:

> Play with apparent irrelevancies is used extensively to generate energy for problem-solving and to evoke new viewpoints with respect to problems. Play generates energy because it is a pleasure in itself, an intrinsic end. [150]

Modern space research is concerned with a world in which weight does not exist. Yet:

> . . . the imaginative game of conceiving this weightlessness world is in part 'play'—creating and trying to complete a world in some ways opposite to our own—as a child can create in the middle of the living-room floor a ship's bridge, a frontier ranch, or a battle. We (must) see how difficult it is for the average human adult to view the world as 'it-is-not', how important this view is for all invention, and the operational mechanisms by which this view can be attained. [150]

In this sense, the play involved in children's make-believe and scientific research can be controlled and disciplined. It involves the willingness to manipulate concepts, everyday and technical assumptions, together with playing with apparently irrelevant objects and things. It is the same with language:

> Play with words invigorates language and by implication reinvigorates perception as well as the way conceptions are used . . . Play with language not only livens metaphor, it also involves an oscillation between particulars and universals. [150]

Irrelevance itself is often creative. It can be an irrelevance of perception, idea or generality. It can be an irrelevant emotional factor: either the external object can be conceived as having autonomy, or there can be a Hedonistic Response—the warm feeling of 'being right' long before rationality occurs (as with Blake's intuition, or Einstein's vision of a possible solution). Or there can be a 'happy accident' where the creative thought 'just occurs'.

Thus Gordon can say that there are two basic processes involved in creation: (1) making the strange familiar, which is an analytic process for the understanding of a problem; and (2) making the familiar strange, which provides a new look to an old idea. The latter is done in three ways: by personal analogy, such as thinking of myself as a tin-can; by direct analogy, as with likening an organ to a typewriter; and by symbolic analogy which attempts to state the implications of a key word (such as considering 'focused desire' as the implication of 'target') in which case fantasy is encouraged. In all instances, play and 'make-believe' are involved in the creative process.

MEMORY LEARNING

To recall that 'William the Conqueror won the Battle of Hastings in 1066' or that '12 x 12=144' is an act of memory. The process involved has three phases: experience, retention and remembering.

PHASE ONE: TO EXPERIENCE (TO MEMORISE)
To commit a fact to memory must involve some experience or activity. I hear a tune; I see an incident; I drive a car. My senses have to be activated in some way or another before the act of memorising can even begin. The boy learning his tables or learning a piece of poetry will read and re-read the item, recite it and repeat it ('master it'). This is no passive or simple thing. It requires time and involves a complex of activities reulting from previous learning.

PHASE TWO: TO RETAIN
We have to retain the item we are trying to commit to memory over an interval of time occupied by many other activities, and perhaps over days, months or years. We know little about the methods of retention but experiences are probably retained by modifications to the nervous system (which may be of a structural kind when the retention is for a longer time than merely a few minutes).

PHASE THREE: TO RECALL (TO REMEMBER)
When we recall some experience we actually do something. The process of recall is an activity. We are re-experiencing. Should we be unable to recall our original experience (forgetting) it may be due to: (1) inadequate memorising; (2) failure to retain—though this is not thought to be a common feature; and (3) forgetting without a failure to retain, for we have all experienced the sudden recalling of a fact (often years later) that we thought we had forgotten.

We must note, in passing, that there is a correspondence between the process involved in memory and the process involved in imaginative identification and impersonation.

Memorising is based on sense experience, but two factors directly
effect it: meaning and repetition. James said:

Most men have a good memory for facts connected with their own pursuits.
The college athlete who remains a dunce at his books will astonish you by his
knowledge of men's 'records' in various feats and games, and will be a
walking dictionary of sporting statistics. The reason is that he is constantly
going over these things in his mind, and comparing and making series of
them. They form for him not so many odd facts, but a concept-system—so
they stick. So the merchant remembers prices, the politician other politicians'
speeches and votes, with a copiousness which amazes outsiders, but which the
amount of thinking they bestow on these subjects easily explains. The great
memory for facts which a Darwin or a Spencer reveal in their books is not
incompatible with the possession on their part of a brain with only a middling
degree of physiological retentiveness. Let a man early in life set himself the
task of verifying such a theory as evolution, and facts will soon cluster and
cling to him like grapes to their stem. Their relations to the theory will hold
them fast; and the more of these the mind is able to discern, the greater the
erudition will become. Meanwhile the theorist may have little, if any,
desultory memory. Unutilizable facts may be unnoted by him and forgotten
as soon as heard. An ignorance almost as encyclopaedic as his erudition may
coexist with the latter, and hide, as it were, in the interstices of its web. Those
who have had much to do with scholars and 'savants' will readily think of
examples of the class of mind I mean.
   In a system, every fact is connected with every other by some thought-
relation. The consequence is that every fact is retained by the combined
suggestive power of all the other facts in the system, and forgetfulness is well-
nigh impossible. [196]

A fact must be meaningful if it is to be memorised. We have all
experienced times when we have 'lacked interest' in committing something to memory and this is basically because the material has not had
interest, or value, or relevance to us. Play and dramatic activity have
direct relevance to us: these are the things we really *want* to do.
Utilisation of them, therefore, considerably helps the development of
memory. This is shown by what happens when we attempt to memorise what is not of any interest to us (such as nonsense material or
meaningless jumbles of words): we attempt to translate such material
into familiar terms—relating it to our previous experience. Dramatic
play is just such an exercise.
   William James showed that memorising is easier when the material
to be learnt can be related to material already familiar to us. Because

Darwin's existing material was already a concept-system, new related facts clung to it. The relevance to dramatic play is in its use of constructive imagination which provides new material with relevance to the individual.

Whether we subscribe to the Connectionist or Cognitive theories of learning, no one doubts that repetition plays a large part in our ability to retain. But to be really effective, repetition must be in some way active: the learner must be doing something in relation to the information—using it in some way. For example, reading-with-recitation makes for faster memorising than does reading alone, and Hunter says [191] that the reasons are: (1) the need to anticipate successive portions of the lesson ensures that the memoriser is actively involved in the task and does not lapse into inattentive re-readings; (2) he must engage in recalling the material, that is, he begins to practise just that activity which it is his ultimate aim to accomplish; (3) recitation provides the memoriser with immediate knowledge of results, giving him knowledge of his progress, mistakes and upon what he must concentrate; (4) it may encourage the memoriser by showing him his progress and spurring him on to constant improvement. This is, of course, another level of 'learning by doing'; the memoriser is externalising the material and making it 'work'. Not only is it more effective to recite what has to be learnt than merely reading it but it is even more effective to *act* it— witness that the learning of lines in a play is easier than the learning of lyric poetry.

But acting itself illustrates another important factor in effective memorising: learning by wholes. Gestalt psychology has shown that there is a general tendency of the mind to apprehend things in their relationship to one another, and that ability to learn in this way is generally accepted as a sign of intelligent behaviour. An actor, in memorising a role, familiarises himself with the play as a whole at the outset; he reads the whole play through, attempting to comprehend the basic elements of the plot, construction, characterisation, and so on. Then he comes to the understanding of his own role and its relationship to other characters, to the situation, etc. At first rehearsal, he 'walks it through' with the book in his hand, grasping the salient features of the part. In particular, he relates what he says to what he does: he might say one line sitting down, then he stands up to say the next—the relationship of word and action is a key matter in the process of memorising. Essentially, an understanding of and familiarity with the outline of the whole provides a context of meaning for each part; also, it provides a prompt recall of what comes next. But this method does have its drawbacks:

> Children often prefer the part method, and unpractised adults are often sceptical of the advantages of the whole method. With the whole method much more time and work is required before any results of learning are manifest . . . a learner gets the feeling of success sooner with the part method . . . The experienced and informed learner knows that the readings in the whole method are not a waste of time . . . While he must work longer before results are manifest, the final returns fully justify his patience and endurance. [217]

A clear example of learning by wholes is the Direct Method of learning languages. The child learns French by being placed in a series of situations so arranged that he is actively 'living' (or dramatically playing) the language. Thus he acquires the intonation and emotional tones of the language as well as the correct use of construction and vocabulary. The results are more permanent but need not be immediately manifest: 'understanding' is not necessarily 'knowing'. A boy may not immediately recall vocabulary by this method; but, with continuous activity, recall can be more effective in the long run. In the same way, a child may well appreciate and understand halves and quarters when he works at it with models and yet may not be able, at least for a while, to express this in figures in his Arithmetic book. Given continuous activity in the whole method, however, his learning is more permanent.

Whereas memorising is greatly affected by meaning and repetition, an important factor in recall is the image. When sense organs are acted upon by the appropriate stimuli, this leads to perception. Later, when we want to recall the perception 'in our mind's eye' we are said to image, or be imaging. It, too, is an activity, not something static, and there are considerable differences in people's ability to form these images. Visual imaging appears to be the most common and most vivid (as when we recall a friend by thinking of an image of his face); in order of frequency comes auditory, tactile, kinaesthetic, gustatory, organic and olfactory imaging. Although each one of us uses all these methods in imaging, we do not all use the same method for each specific image (and this can, incidentally, create difficulties for teachers who, with a class, may use one type of image when some individuals within the class may require to use another method of imaging). One or two other individual differences are of importance. It is generally true, for example, that our ability at imaging varies according to what we are trying to recall: it works better when we are trying to recall a concrete object (a face, a town) than with an abstract idea, argument or decision. This may be related to the fact that imaging appears to be more vivid with children than with adults. Also, people who are involved with much abstract thinking in their daily lives appear to have a less than average ability in imaging [142], but there are so many exceptions that this is very far from a rule.

There is no question of importance of imaging to the process of recall. The effectiveness of good visual aids in teaching is evidence of this; they make learning easier, and they also provide a picture which can be imagined later. Ideas such as thinking about past, future or possible objects or events need to be supported by images; many people, too, employ images of words, numbers and other symbols in mathematical or other abstract thinking:

> ... images are largely the result of out-of-school experiences; that is, experiences in which the children were intensely interested, and in which all their senses and a good deal of active movement played a part. Children form images as a result of doing things, not merely by hearing about them. This is one of the strongest arguments in favour of practical work, of 'learning by doing'. As methods of learning in school approach more nearly to methods of learning out of school we shall find that our pupils are not merely memorizing useful facts, but are developing images and ideas that will help them to understand a problem and to criticize a solution. [185]

We do not know for certain whether the capacity to form images can be increased, but we do know that the ability to recall images can be improved by several factors: purpose and interest; the frequency with which recall is continued; the strength with which the original experience created the image. The latter, of course, can be directly affected by dramatic play: in one sense, 'to live a fact is to know a fact'. But imaginative play is based on imaging and, thus, the frequency of such experience relates to the frequency of recall; if we, as teachers, direct and channel their play in ways which relate to experience that is valuable, the children will be recalling images which are valuable. With purpose and interest we return once more to motivation which, as play is so important a factor in the child's attitude, is the most powerful reason for the use of the dramatic imagination in learning.

Bacon said that acting is 'an art which strengthens the memory' [18].

It does so by making the material to be memorised more meaningful by aiding the process of repetition, and providing memorising in depth through over-all understanding (or learning by wholes). Further, dramatic play facilitates the recall of images which is vital in the process of remembering.

Thus thought, creative thought and memory learning are all directly related to the dramatic imagination.

14 THOUGHT & LANGUAGE

The development of concepts, creative thought and memory learning in children has a direct bearing upon our study. However, these topics are all so closely related to the development of language and speech that we need to consider the whole inter-relationship of thought and language before we can see how psycholinguistic maturation is affected by the dramatic imagination.

PSYCHOLINGUISTICS

Language & Concept

We have seen that concepts group or classify experience and we know that speech is indistinguishable from many thought situations—but not from all. Language is not always associated with concept: Kohler's chimpanzees solved problems without the use of language; the deaf child organises and classifies experiences much as the hearing child does. Yet there is, in many instances, a strong relationship between language and concept:

> ... some of the most important concepts for the solution of problems—concepts of identity, similarity, comparison of magnitudes, spatial position, temporal sequence, causation, and the like—are coded in the lexical and grammatical structure of a language. Nevertheless, many intellectual tasks can be performed without the use of linguistic codes. [58]

Words are signs without which much abstract thinking would be impossible. They transmit information and advice from past generations, they are an inherent part of the educational situation, and they are a major factor in the solution of problems and the performance of tasks.

Although many concepts are acquired without language, a word symbolises the formation of a particular concept. If we present the schoolchild with a picture of a kangaroo, read descriptions of it, and indicate the word 'kangaroo', a concept will be formed. And as there are approximately 10,000 words in all basic languages, mankind seems to be agreed on the concepts which have to be symbolised in words.

In the initial stages concepts appear to be formed by the infant without words. But, with maturation and the acquisition of language, the development of concepts appears to be related to words and the use of grammatical structure. Thus Carroll [58] considers the following to be the major concepts:

1. Noun forms (nouns, pronouns, noun phrases).
   Experience classified: objects, persons, ideas, and relations whose location or distribution in space, actually or metaphorically, can be specified.
2. Adjective forms (adjectives, adjectival phrases).
   Experience classified: qualities or attributes of noun forms, either on an all-or-none basis (presence/absence) or in terms of degree.
3. Verb forms (verbs, verbal phrases).
   Experience classified: events, relationships, or states whose location or distribution in time can be specified.
4. Adverb forms (adverbs, adverbial phrases).
   Experience classified: qualities or attributes applying to adjective or verb forms, either on an all-or-none basis or in terms of degree.
5. Preposition forms (prepositions, prepositional phrases).
   Experience classified: spatial, temporal or logical relations to noun forms.
6. Conjunctions.
   Experience classified: relationships between any two or more members of any class (or construction).

In the English language, the subject/predicate construction is typical and symbolises the class of experience used in communication situations. Moreover, grammatical structure of this kind aids thinking beyond the point at which language is used; its form permits the manipulation of complex concepts—Thinking and Language together make Reasoning possible, because the ability to reason is based on forming inferences in terms of language. This is perhaps best seen in metaphysics which followed an Aristotelian form until Bertrand Russell showed that this hinged on basic European forms of grammar, and so he delineated differing ways of thought. The sequences of words used in the grammatical structure of a language are important to thought, and two modern methods of approach to this problem are the 'finite state grammar' and Chomsky's 'phrase structure' [62].

As to the psychology of word usage, we know that some words are easier to learn than others. 'Content' words (like nouns, verbs, adjectives and adverbs) are easier to learn than 'functional' words (pronouns, conjunctions and prepositions) which are only necessary in order to make 'content' words 'work'. Psychologically, too, the formation of words (morphology) is important. The learning of plurals is not merely a matter of imitation: Berko showed [29] that we learn rules like, 'one mel plus one mel equals two . . .' The psychology of meaning has been extensively studied: Malinowski compared the relationship of thought and language in primitive and civilised societies and found that primitive language was a reflection of specific experience in particular communicative situations, but that civilised language is:

> . . . a condensed piece of reflection, a record of fact or thought. In its primitive uses, language functions as a link in concerted human activity, as a piece of human behaviour. It is a mode of action and not an instrument of reflection. [249]

The original association tests of Galton indicated that there were certain common responses to words—over 80% gave 'chair' as a response to 'table'—and so indicated that meaningfulness could be measured. Thus Osgood could postulate: a Semantic Differential which combined the association test with a rating scale, indicating a comparison of emotional responses to words; and a Factor Analysis which measured affective meaning according to evaluation (good/bad, clean/dirty, etc.), potency (large/small, strong/weak, etc.) and activity (fast/slow, hot/cold, etc.). With information of this type, it could be seen that there was such a thing as 'semantic satiation': continuous repetition leads to a reduction in meaningfulness, which can be seen when a word is measured on the Semantic Differential before and after repetition; this has importance for education for, when 'semantic satiation' occurs, learning is retarded.

Speech, too, has some relationship with the problem for, after all, language is based upon it. In the science of phonetics, a phoneme is a minimal sound unit used in a particular language (as with the 't' in 'sting'), while allaphones are variations of phonemes (as with the variation of the 't' sound in 'sting' and 'teem'). This has relevance to the fact the phonemes which occur most rarely in a language are learnt latest by the children speaking it—in English, for example, one of the last phonemic distinctions to be learnt is the distinction between 'f' and the voiceless 'th'.

> . . . we find that at age 3, 90% or more of the children could articulate the phonemes *n, t, g, m, b, d, w, h, p* and *k;* from 70 to 80% articulated correctly

f, ng, l, s, y; from 60 to 69% articulated *v, r, sh, j, ch;* while only 10 to 49% articulated correctly *z, th* (voiced), *th* (voiceless) and *hw.* By the age 6 the only sounds which were not correctly articulated by 90% or more of the subjects were *s, sh, th* (voiced), *z, zh, hw,* and *ch.* [57]

But the various intra-phonemic differences have little relevance linguistically: most people use words as fundamental units and the natural sub-divisions of these are syllables not phonemes.

Behaviourism & Language

Behaviourist psychologists have utilised the speech act as a major part of their stimulus-response analysis of learning. They consider that conditioning principles can apply to the process of producing and comprehending language. Speech is considered a social act with two functions: production of speech, and response to speech. In this sense it bears resemblance to communication engineering, and so Information Theory has developed [258]: a theory of information transmission which is essentially an extension of the general mathematical theory of probability and which has been of most use in the field of electronic communications systems. The communication process is described as a communication channel: there is a *source* where the message is generated and *encoded;* there is a *destination* where it is received and *decoded.* Thus psycholinguists can consider the message unit, the rules for combination, and the processes of acquiring and using the code. The human being's first steps in meaning (in decoding) are inseparable from the development of perception. Our first knowledge is from *proximal cues* (sensations) and then *distal cues* (visual, auditory) can antedate their presence—as with the sight of the bottle or the sound of the mother—and so become signs of objects [285]. But the majority of behaviourist researches have been concerned with language encoding (the verbal expression of ideas) and in two ways: the development of vocal skills— we shall examine the language and thought of the child below; and the development of semantic encoding—how do meanings become associated with vocal skills?

There have been a number of behaviourist approaches to this specific problem. Holt's associationist reflex-circle theory (stimulus—vocal response—self-stimulation—and so back to the vocal response) has support from Piaget. More generally accepted is the Reinforcement Theory: the child tends to learn whatever responses are 'reinforced'—

either by some immediate drive-reducing reward, or by some indirect secondary cue of an eventual reward. Speech and the development of language is largely a secondary reinforcement because parental language acquires secondary reinforcement powers [341].

This relates to the problem of imitation. For Miller and Dollard (see pp. 209–11) there is no imitative instinct but the child learns to copy in the early stages of language development when imitation is rewarded: he hears himself and responds vocally, then hears others and gives a response—and if this imitation is rewarded he tends to imitate the speech of others. Early vocalisations are used unselectively to express different needs and emotions; but learning to speak is a question of selecting a restricted group of sounds appropriate to each situation. Henle says that:

> . . . the vocal responses to a stimulus situation are initially more or less indiscriminate. Social selection gradually differentiates out of the response mass those sequences that are approved by the linguistic community. These sequences become increasingly numerous and increasingly complex. They are the 'data' of linguistic development—the growth of vocabulary and the complication of sentence structure. According to the theory of instrumental learning the data result from a great many processes of differentiation by social selection. [170]

Yet social reward is an insufficient explanation for the *need* to imitate speech, according to other behaviourists. Mowrer takes Cathy Hayes' famous description, in *The Ape in Our House* [168], to illustrate his point:

> Mrs Hayes says that Viki's imitativeness developed as a part of her *play*, i.e., as activity engaged in because it was self-rewarding rather than objectively instrumental. The same assumptions underlie what we have called the 'autism' theory of word learning. But just as Viki soon reached the point, with training, where she would imitate on command, so do children reach a similar stage with respect to the imitation of words . . . it will be clear that our view does not limit word learning to the autism principle; we hold that it is merely the mechanism whereby word acquisition *gets started* . . .
>
> Thus a child . . . first reproduces a word because of the indirect, autistic satisfaction which the word provides; but *then* the word may prove efficient in a more practical way in that it causes the parent again to supply the satisfaction with which his original pronunciation of the word was associated.
>
> [269]

Play provides the initial imitation, but subsequent imitations have a

9

secondary reward value. Yet, as we have already seen (pp. 211–12,
214–15), identification provides the motivation for the reinforcement
according to Mowrer. Church makes the same point: that speech
imitation is another version of dramatic play and impersonation:

> The pre-school child's play, which is clearly imitative, seems to serve the
> same function: by concretely re-enacting scenes from adult life, the child can
> grasp and identify with, if only partially, a style of life which he finds
> simultaneously alien, baffling, and attractive. Needless to say, there is a
> magical component in the dramatic play of young children, just as there is in
> the role-playing of older children and adolescents: but in both cases it is a
> magic that works. [63]

It seems that empathy, the emotional relationship of the child with his
mother, lies behind all communication; through this the child identifies
himself with her. Then, after play has provided the initial imitation
of her speech, identification provides the reward for subsequent
imitations. Imitation is the speech mechanism, the motivation for which
is an elementary form of impersonation.

Psychoanalysis & Language

Psychoanalysis has illustrated that speech was originally a far more
concrete activity than it now is: that the earliest kind of language
represented action. Indications of this have been observed in savages
and children: Freud, following Groos, saw that children treat words as
objects in the various games they play with them; and Frazer saw that
the savage attaches a considerable significance to words and especially
to names:

> Unable to discriminate clearly between words and things, the savage
> commonly fancies that the link between a name and the person or thing
> denominated by it is not a mere arbitrary and ideal association, but a real and
> substantial bond which unites the two in such a way that magic may be
> wrought on a man just as easily through his name as through his hair, his
> nails, or any other material part of his person. In fact, primitive man regards
> his name as a vital portion of himself and takes care of it accordingly. [116]

We have seen that fairy tales, like *Rumpelstiltskin,* can reflect similar
beliefs of children. It is thought by some that all words originally
possessed distinct motor and perceptual qualities, that roots probably

come from sounds associated with motor movements used in an instinctual act:

> Language in its preverbal beginning is no doubt a matter of natural motor movements of the entire body, as the arts of the dance and of the drama bear out. The attenuation of these movements—in accord with the development of thought as trial action—can be traced through verbalisations in song and poetry, the ancestors of all forms of literature. Pleasures in sound, rhyme and rhythm antecede the use of words for more abstract meanings and reflect the early infantile stages in the acquisition of language. Imagery, or metaphor, is an intermediate step in the development of meaning, and, like the comparable images of the dream, conjures up vivid sensory and motor memories as modes of primitive ideation. [213]

Thus, for Freudians, the unconscious consists of ideas only, which work by symbolic thought; the conscious also consists of ideas, and the idea of a corresponding word. Unconscious and abstract thought are conceived as opposite poles of the human thought processes.

ANTHROPOLOGY & LANGUAGE

Bearing upon the whole relationship of thought, language and speech are the ideas propounded by social anthropologists. From Frank Boas' original idea that:

> . . . language seems to be one of the most instructive fields of inquiry in an investigation of the formation of fundamental ethnic ideas . . . [34]

—was developed the Sapir-Whorf Hypothesis. Edward Sapir considered that:

> Language is a guide to 'social reality' . . . it powerfully conditions all our thinking about social problems and processes. Human beings . . . are very much at the mercy of the particular language which has become the medium of expression for their society. [250]

For Sapir, language is a self-contained, creative symbolic organisation which not only refers to experience but actually defines experience for us. Whorf extended this to the concept that language acts as a mould to thought: it is a sort of logic or frame of reference, forcing our thinking into *a priori* linguistic categories:

> . . . the linguistic system (in other words, the grammar) of each language is not merely a reproducing instrument for voicing ideas but rather is itself the

shaper of ideas, the program and guide for the individual's mental activity, for his analysis of impressions, for his synthesis of his mental stock-in-trade.

[388]

In this way language directs the perceptions of speakers and gives them habitual modes for analysing experience (this is called linguistic determinism).

Parts of language which can be separated from thought can be compared with the nature of the thought, and this is usually done with vocabulary, inflexion and sentence formation. Vocabulary reflects perception, and as one language differs from another in its vocabulary, each represents:

> . . . a complex inventory of all the ideas, interests, and occupations that take up the attention of the community. [250]

The world appears different to a person using one vocabulary than it would to a person using another: the Eskimo has many different terms for the colour of snow in contrast to the single English word 'white' showing that there is a relationship between the accessibility of linguistic terms and the psychological process of recognition; Euro-American children distinguish size, colour and shape later than children of the Navaho and there is a resultant difference in the order of emergence of these different concepts. Like vocabulary, the specific inflexion of a language calls attention to certain aspects of experience rather than to others. Thus:

> English stops with what from the Navaho is a very vague statement—'I drop it.' The Navaho must specify four particulars which the English leaves either unsettled or to inference from context:
> 1. The form must make clear whether 'it' is definite or just 'something'.
> 2. The verb stem used will vary depending upon whether the object is round, or long, or fluid, or animate, etc., etc.
> 3. Whether the act is in progress, or just about to start, or just about to stop, or habitually carried on, or repeatedly carried on . . .
> 4. The extent to which the agent controls the fall must be indicated . . . [220]

The forces that observation imposes upon the human being by the inflexion of his language constitute a mental 'set', or frame of reference. The same applies to grammar and sentence structure (as we have seen on p. 238). The differences in language structure between English and Hopi speakers means that English speakers see the world in terms of *things* (non-spatial entities conceived by spatial metaphor) while the Hopi folk see the world in terms of *events*. So, when vocabulary, inflexion and the structural elements of a language are compared with cross-cultural patterns, we find that there is a close relationship. English and Hopi speakers vary in the inflexions and structures used in respect of time: Hopi do not have different days but successive reappearances of the same entity and thus repetition is insistently present; English speakers, in contrast, emphasise sequence, chronology, history, mathematics and speed. The Navaho language is based upon action and action verbs, and we find that there is a corresponding emphasis upon movement in a culture which regards the wandering, restless universe as a dynamic flux. Thus:

> The Navaho speaks of 'actors' and 'goals' (the terms are inappropriate to Navaho), not as performers of actions or as ones upon whom actions are performed, as in English, but as entities linked to actions already defined in part as pertaining especially to classes of beings. [173]

The Navaho sees the universe as eternal forces with which he attempts to maintain an equilibrium; curing the sick is an attempt to put the individual or community back into harmony with the universe:

> It is done by re-enacting one of a complex series of religious dramas which represent, in highly abstract terms, the events, far back in Navaho history, whereby the culture heroes first established harmony between man and nature and so made the world fit for human occupation. By re-enacting these events, or some portion of them, the present disturbance, by a kind of sympathetic magic, is compensated and harmony between man and universe restored. The ill person then gets well, or the community disaster is alleviated, since these misfortunes were but symptoms of a disturbed relation to nature. [173]

And his ritual drama and habits of speaking serve somewhat the same purpose:

> Just as in his religious-curing activities the Navaho sees himself as adjusting to a universe that is given, so in his habits of speaking does he link individuals to actions and movements distinguished, not only as actions and movements, but as well in terms of the entities in action or movement. This division of nature into classes of entity in action or movement is the universe that is given; the behaviour of human beings or of any being individulated from the mass is customarily reported by assignment to one or other of these given divisions. [173]

And so Whorf can say:

> ... this 'thought world' is the microcosm that each man carries about
> within himself, by which he measures and understands what he can of the
> macrocosm. [388]

But we have seen that Erickson can say the same thing of dramatic
play, and the relationship is that both are man's methods of mastering
his environment.

Changes of language are taken as evidence of changes in concepts.
Normally the change in word meaning is from the practical to the
abstract, as with the Indo-European development:

> ... refined and abstract meanings largely grow out of more concrete
> meanings. Meanings of the type 'respond accurately to (things or speech)'
> develop again and again from meanings like 'to be near to' or 'get hold of'.
> Thus, *understand,* as we say, seems to have meant 'stand close to' or 'stand
> among'. [33]

The classic growth of language and concept from the concrete to the
abstract is found in the Greek language between Homer and Pericles
(as described by Havelock [170]). Homer's vocabulary contains the
seeds of abstraction: a god may symbolise a natural phenomenon but
he remains a god not a principle. At the Hesiodic level, a cosmogony is
not a cosmology—a narrative sequence in time is not a pattern of time-
less concepts. The Pre-Socratics attempted to achieve abstraction by
aggrandising words already available: thus 'cosmos' which originally
meant either 'woman's head-dress' and 'trappings of a horse's harness',
or 'decoratively' and 'orderly' (of ranks of soldiers), came with the
Ionians to mean 'world order'. The Pre-Socratics exploited concrete
words in attempting to achieve abstraction: Heraclitus moved from
the idea of 'one god' to 'one', and also selected out pairs of opposites
like day/night, war/peace, etc. By the time of Anaxagoras, the Greek
language was close to recognising temperature, humidity and the like.
But it was not until Plato and Aristotle that a word was given for a
quality. This same growth, in both concept and language, from concrete
to abstract is observable in the behaviour of children and has been
illustrated profusely by Piaget.

15 THE THOUGHT & LANGUAGE OF CHILDREN

Developmental Stages

For Piaget, the child perceives the world in ways that are essentially different from those of the adult, and he does this in various ways according to his stage of development. The stages of human development are seen as the gradual unfolding of the individual's ability to construct an internal model of the world around him, and to perform manipulations on this model so as to draw conclusions about the past and the future. The basic stages of a child's development are:

1. SENSORY-MOTOR INTELLIGENCE (0—2 years)
   This is a growth from neonatal, reflex actions to a relatively coherent organisation of sensory-motor actions. It is characterised by complete egocentrism (the world is conceived only from the child's point of view) and he learns by circular reaction from repetition on a trial-and-error basis. From simple imitations he comes to imitate complex models and to perform deferred imitation—reproducing an absent model through memory. His play develops dramatic qualities, is often ritualistic and symbolic. And, from only experiencing his own actions, he can eventually see the object as a thing apart.

2. PRECONCEPTUAL THOUGHT (2—4½ years)
   This is a growth from sensory-motor intelligence to an inner, symbolic manipulation of reality. It is still egocentric, but he can differentiate the inner symbol from external reality because images are created when he imitates; this leads to the child understanding signs (words). So he pretends by representing one thing by another. He plays constructional games, draws, understands letters and talks. Language is very important at this stage: he thinks out loud to tell himself what to do, for speech and action are linked. His stage of thinking is through preconcepts which are action-ridden, imagistic and concrete; thus he has difficulty in recognising stable identity in the middle of contextual changes:

   Again at 2:7 (12), seeing L. in a new bathing suit, with a cap, J. asked:

'*What's the baby's name?*' Her mother explained that it was a bathing costume, but J. pointed to L. herself and said: '*But what's the name of that?*' (indicating L.'s face) and repeated the question several times. But as soon as L. had her dress on again, J. exclaimed very seriously: '*It's Lucienne again*', as if her sister had changed her identity in changing her clothes. [294]

3. INTUITIVE THOUGHT (4½—7 years)
Thought is still tied to action and perception, and the child uses transducive reasoning—he proceeds from particular to particular. He finds difficulty in distinguishing various members of a class as separates; thus the appearances of varying insects at different times are interpreted as reappearances of the same insect; for instance, 'That is *the* slug'.

4. CONCRETE OPERATIONS (7—11 years)
Internal representative cognitive actions come to be grouped in systems: classifications occur, and the grouping of one class with another; seriation develops, and the child forms asymmetrical relations into a system. The concept of number begins: a collection of objects seen as equivalent. Concepts of time and space and the material world develop: by 8 years old, the child can coordinate relations of temporal order (before/after) with duration (longer/shorter lengths of time).

All these groupings are only mastered in concrete situations; the child works from the real to the possible, and he has to overcome the physical properties of objects and events (mass, weight, length, area, time, etc.) one by one.

Imitation develops: there is detailed imitation with analysis of the model; imitation is conscious; it is reflective—being used only as an aid to the fulfilment of the needs inherent in the child's activity—and so is controlled by intelligence as a whole. Symbolic play declines but games with rules increase.

5. FORMAL OPERATIONS (11 + years)
At this stage, the child makes his first break with the real: he can work with hypothesis and spontaneously seek laws. He is involved in propositional thinking: the entities of thinking are propositions not reality; hypotheses are confirmed or denied and then related to the external world:

He begins by organising the various elements of the raw data with the concrete-operational techniques of middle childhood. These organised elements are then cast in the form of statements or propositions which can be combined in various ways. Through the method of combinatorial analysis he then isolates for consideration the totality of distinct combinations of these propositions. These combinations are regarded as hypotheses, some of which will be confirmed and some infirmed by subsequent investigation. [108]

These divisions are not necessarily accurate according to age, but the sequence is invariable. And modern researches have shown that the developmental progress is the same in many cultures [85, 148, 242, 243], though some children reach each stage later and some, like modern American and British children, earlier.

Assimilation & Accommodation

Piaget considers that we inherit a specific method of functioning, a manner of thinking. It is not that we inherit *what* we think, but *how* we think. It is as if we are born with a basic pattern of intellectual structure which allows us to adapt to our environment. We adapt to the environment by modification of ourselves, and this is done by two mechanisms: assimilation and accommodation. Take for example the baby sucking. He has a cognitive structure which relates to his sequence of actions (a *schema*), but he gets better at sucking each day: he assimilates new experience to his schema by merging new elements into his earlier behaviour; he then accommodates the experience by generalising it, adapting it to the schema so that the schema itself alters and changes— and is ready for the next stage.

But play and imitation are directly related to the process of assimilation and accommodation:

. . . imitation is a continuation of accommodation, play is a continuation of assimilation and intelligence a harmonious combination of the two. [294]

For Piaget, therefore, play is assimilation of new experience—like the behaviourist's learned response or Freud's mastery of the environment. Imitation is a reproduction of familiar models: having assimilated the model by play, he then imitates its parts. The child cannot imitate visual models unless they are already understood—but he plays with them in order to understand them. Also, although assimilation (through play) and accommodation (through imitation) are described as separate, they must be thought of as being simultaneous.

Play

Play is pursued for mere assimilation, purely for functional pleasure. It proceeds by the exercise of activities for the mere pleasure of mastering them and acquiring thereby a feeling of virtuosity or power.

But Piaget can classify play activities into three types: practice, symbol and rule. Practice games begin in the first months of life and continue whenever a new skill is acquired: the child plays with a new set of bricks, practising with them and learning as he does so; the adult, having just acquired for the first time a radio or a car, finds it difficult to resist the temptation to use them merely for the fun of using his new powers. This type of play activity relates to Groos' 'pre-exercise' and, although it is essentially sensory-motor, it can also be used by the higher functions—like the child's game of asking questions just for the fun of asking, without interest in the problem or answer.

Secondly, symbolic games imply a representation of an absent object, since there is a comparison between a given and imagined element. It implies make-believe. The child pushing a box and imagining it as a car, is symbolically representing the car by the box, and this type of play occurs at the end of the first, or beginning of the second year; it does not occur with animals. This is the specifically dramatic form of play and Piaget says that when a child is pretending to go to sleep, or to wash, he is trying to use his own powers freely, to reproduce his own actions for the pleasure of seeing himself do them and showing them to others—to assimilate without being hampered by the need to accommodate at the same time.

The third type of play, games with rules, implies social relationships, for rules are regulations imposed by the group and their violation carries a sanction. They occur only rarely between the ages of 4 and 7, belong mainly to the 7—11-year-old, but continue in adulthood because they are the play activity of the socialised being.

While practice games are the first to appear, they are vicarious; they appear with each new acquirement but disappear after saturation. Although they diminish in importance with age, certain kinds last longer because they are bound up with situations which occur over a long period: fighting play, for example, occurs at various ages and in various forms. And practice play combines, in various ways, with symbolic play and games with rules. Symbolic play declines with age because the older child can satisfy himself by playing with real things, but games with rules continue as strongly as before. But, essentially, all forms of play are the human organism's attempts to assimilate experience:

> Play begins, then, with the first dissociation between assimilation and accommodation. After learning to grasp, swing, throw, etc., which involve both an effort of accommodation to new situations, and an effort of repetition, reproduction and generalisation, which are elements of assimilation, the child sooner or later . . . grasps for the pleasure of grasping, swings for the sake of swinging, etc. In a word, he repeats his behaviour not in any further effort to learn to investigate, but for the sheer joy of mastering it . . . [294]

Imitation

The child learns to imitate. It begins with a circular-reflex action (much as Holt sees it): the baby cries when he hears others cry; then, in the first 6 months, the reflex schemas are broadened—wailings and other vocalisations are reproduced for their own sake. But a model can only be imitated if it has already been assimilated to a schema:

> For instance, in obs. 12–14, J. did not imitate the action of opening and closing the hands until she had practised it as a separate action, in spite of the fact that prehension constantly involved this action. On the other hand, she very quickly imitated the action of separating the hands and bringing them together again, because she often made this movement herself within her field of vision . . . (the child) only imitates whole movements which he has observed and practised as separate schemas . . .
>
> Conversely, however—and this is the second conclusion—any schema practised as such can give rise to imitation provided that the movements the child has to make are within his field of vision . . . In our opinion everything depends on the baby's education. Left to himself, he gives to the study of his own actions the time that he would otherwise give to learning all kinds of tricks.
>
> This brings us to a consideration of imitation through training, or pseudo-imitation . . . we believe that this behaviour is distinct from imitation through direct assimilation and accommodation. It cannot explain true imitation, because it never lasts unless the training is prolonged and constantly kept up.
>
> [294]

Imitation is never, like play, a behaviour which is an end in itself. It is always a continuity of understanding, driven by a 'will to overcome'.

It is active experimentation but, in contrast to some behaviourist thinkers, Piaget never sees it as identical with intelligence.

Cognitive Symbolism

Central to Piaget's whole developmental psychology is that imitation (as part of accommodation) is the function that supplies the infant with his first 'signifiers', or elementary symbols. These early 'signifiers' internally represent for the child the absent 'significate', or object:

> What happens, Piaget believes, is that with the growth and refinement of the capacity to imitate the child is eventually able to make internal imitations as well as external, visible ones. He is able to evoke in thought, as opposed to actually carrying out in reality, imitations made in the past. This internal imitation takes the form of an image, broadly defined, and this image constitutes the first signifier (the significate being here the action, object, or word of which the image is the reduced and schematic replicate). [108]

His first signifiers are private rather than social. Verbal signs are at first difficult to grasp, and are unsuitable for the representations he is concerned with. And so the child comes to rely on nonverbal symbols and treats words as private symbols.

Before 4 years old, numerous spontaneous myths occur that are halfway between the symbolism of play and intelligence investigation: the child asks, What makes the sun? or, How are babies made? and creates his own myths of explanation; things are seen as products of human creation. At this age, too, thought is animistic—'There aren't any boats on the lake; they're asleep'; inanimate objects are seen as living. About the fifth year, this artificialism and animism evolves towards intuition—'We said the other day that the moon was made of air, like the clouds . . . Then how does it stay in the sky? Like balloons?' —which, although still imaginative, is a stage in the evolution of symbolic thought. Then comes the stage of magic-phenomenism— 'she stamped her feet in her room, saying: "I'm stamping because if I don't the soup isn't good enough. If I do, the soup's good" ',—by which time the child is abandoning egocentric preconcepts and arrives at a degree of objectivity comparable to the 'environmental reaction' of early Greek physics; this is a transitional stage between imaged preconceptual schemas and truly operational concepts.

Thus, for Piaget, play and imitation are basic to the growth of thought, and the development of symbolic thought is similar in its growth to that of primitive man.

THE RELATIONSHIP OF SPEECH & THOUGHT

Maturation

The mechanisms of speech and language develop with maturation. To begin with, the child speaks aloud when he thinks: sometimes it is socialised—he expects to be listened to and influence the hearer; but sometimes it is egocentric (and Piaget considers this is at its height about 3—5 years old) when it is not directed to the listener, nor does the child expect to be listened to. Egocentric speech slowly disappears and leaves all speech in the socialised form. But there is a medial position: silent speech:

> . . . all instances of movement in the speech muscles in accompaniment with reading or other forms of mental activity. [93]

It is interesting to note that silent speech can also occur at later stages, but: good readers engage in less silent speech than do poor ones; the reading of an easy text results in less silent speech than does the reading of a difficult one; and the reading of a clear text results in less silent speech than does the reading of a blurred one [93]. Yet silent speech is not quite the same thing as inner speech which is the real symbolic meaning behind the words that are spoken:

> Inner speech is to a large extent thinking in pure meanings . . . Its true nature and place can be understood only after examining the next plane of verbal thought, the one still more inward than inner speech.
>
> That plane is thought itself. As we have said, every thought creates a connection, fulfils a function, solves a problem. The flow of thought is not accompanied by a simultaneous unfolding of speech. The two processes are not identical, and there is no rigid correspondence between the units of thought and speech . . . The theatre faced the problem of the thought behind the words before psychology did. In teaching his system of acting, Stanislavsky required the actors to uncover the 'subtext' of their lines in a play. In Griboedov's comedy '*Woe from Wit*', the hero, Chatsky, says to the heroine, who maintains that she has never stopped thinking of him, 'Thrice blessed who believes. Believing warms the heart.' Stanislavsky interpreted this as 'Let us stop this talk'; but it could just as well be interpreted as 'I do not

believe you. You say it to comfort me', or as 'Don't you see how you torment me? I wish I could believe you. That would be bliss.' Every sentence we say in real life has some sort of subtext, a thought hidden behind it. [369]

In fact, inner speech is not necessarily speech at all: it is the thought content behind what is said. Overt development is from egocentric speech to silent speech, and from there to purely socialised speech.

BEHAVIOUR	AGES IN MONTHS					
	0	6	12	18	24	30
First noted vocalisations	xxxxxx					
First responds to human voice	xxxx					
First cooing	xxx					
Vocalises pleasure	xxxxxx					
Vocal play	xxx					
Vocalises eagerness and displeasure	xxx					
Imitates sounds		xxxxxxx				
Vocalises recognition		xx				
Listens to familiar words		xxx				
First word		xxxxxxxx				
Expressive sounds and conversational jargon			xxxxxxxxxxxxx			
Follows simple commands			xxxxxxx			
Imitates syllables and words			xxxxxxxx			
Second word			xxx			
Responds to 'no' and 'don't'			xxxxxxxxx			
First says more than 2 words			xxxx			
Names object or picture				xxxxxxxxxx		
Comprehends simple questions				xx		
Combines words in speech					xxxxxxx	
First uses pronouns					xxxxx	
First phrases and sentences					xxx	
Understands prepositions						xxx

Composite Table showing age in months at which selected items are reported in eight major studies of infant developments. [251]

Fig. 3

There is normally a sequence to the child's development of speech. In the first few months he coos and cries so learning, through appropriate reinforcement, the communicative character of vocal sounds. The exact nature of this reinforcement is the subject of some disagreement: Piaget and Holt think that the circular reflex is the basis and that it is self-reinforcing; Social Learning theorists think that the reward is socially conditioned; Mowrer considers it is based on identification. The beginning of language comprehension usually appears between 8 and 10 months when the child shows the first evidences of understanding symbolic gestures and sounds. The beginnings of symbolic communication appear towards the end of the first year (at the same time, approximately, as dramatic play). There is a gradual distinction between the more frequent phonemes (Lewis [239] shows that words with labials and dentals appear first), between words and phrases—but it is not until 4 or 6 years old that there is reasonable thought control over speech.

McCarthy's diagram illustrates the normal development of speech behaviour (see *Fig. 3*).

Soviet Approaches

Luria [246] considers that there is an interdependence between the functions of thinking and speech, and he stresses the importance of the influence of language on thought. In contrast, Piaget considers that each level of thinking does not correspond closely at each stage of growth to the growth of language. It should be said that Luria, like most Soviet psychologists from Pavlov on, stresses that growth depends on social conditions. Luria follows Vygotsky in considering that adults' speech has a strong formative function in the development of a child's mental processes. The properties of the mind are:

> . . . formed in the course of the child's relationship with adults and having later changed into the means of organising the mental processes themselves.
>
> [247]

Luria and Vygotsky both consider that the higher mental functions—complex perception, intelligent memorisation, voluntary attention and logical thinking—are formed in the course of the child's interaction with his social environment and, specifically, with adult speech. But, like Piaget, Luria considers that each particular development depends on the previous stage:

> Indeed, the formation of complex mental activity always requires strict consistency and succession of individual operations: sometimes, if only a single link of training is missed, if a certain stage in the development of the

necessary operation is not properly worked up, the entire process of further development becomes retarded, and the formation of higher mental functions assumes an abnormal character. [246]

This can lead O'Connor and Hermelin to postulate:

... words and symbols signifying things and events, may be the basis of the categorising which takes place in learning and which serves thinking. [281]

That thought is conditioned by language is, of course, a basic concept of social anthropology as maintained by Whorf and Sapir:

... a self-contained, creative symbolic organisation, which not only refers to the experience largely acquired without its help, but actually defines experience for us by reason of its formal completeness and because of our unconscious projection of its implicit expectations into the field of experience.
[327]

For Vygotsky, the primary function of speech is communication. The world of experience has to be greatly simplified in order to be translated into the signs of language but it is only through these signs that communication becomes possible.

Vygotsky distinguished the level of development necessary for verbal and written speech:

... the development of writing does not repeat the developmental history of speaking. Written speech ... (differs) from oral speech in both structure and mode of functioning. Even its minimal development requires a high level of abstraction. It is speech in thought and image only, lacking the musical, expressive, intonational qualities of oral speech. In learning to write, the child must disengage himself from the sensory aspect of speech and replace words by images of words ... It is the abstract quality of written language that is the main stumbling block, not the under-development of small muscles or any other mechanical obstacles.

... In conversation, every sentence is prompted by a motive ... The motives for writing are more abstract, more intellectualised, further removed from immediate needs. In written speech, we are obliged to create the situation, to represent it to ourselves. This demands detachment from the actual situation. [369]

Implications for Education

Vygotsky sees education as a combination of instruction and imitation. Imitation itself is basic to social learning:

> To imitate, it is necessary to possess the means of stepping from something one knows to something new. With assistance, every child can do more than he can by himself—though only within the limits set by the state of his development. [369]

And in the school situation, imitation is a basic method:

> In learning to speak, as in learning school subjects, imitation is indispensable. What the child can do in cooperation today he can do alone tomorrow. [369]

Piaget would consider that not merely imitation but play also is related to the development of thought, and so both ought to be related to the teaching situation. Educationalists following Piaget and, to a certain extent Vygotsky, would therefore let the children use the real actions which form the basis of learning: in the learning of fractions, for example, the children would cut a real object up into its component parts.

But if imitation and play are important for education, clearly symbolic or dramatic play has its special place. Despite the fact that Piaget distinguished symbolic play from practice play and play with games, he indicated in some detail that the symbolic or dramatic level of the imagination was a key factor: it is this which internalises objects, and which gives them significance to the individual. In one of Vygotsky's experiments:

> Identical pictures were shown to two groups of preschool children of similar age and developmental level. One group was asked to act out the picture—which would indicate the degree of their immediate grasp of its content; the other group was asked to tell about it in words, a task requiring a measure of conceptually mediated understanding. It was found that the 'actors' rendered the sense of the represented action situation, while the 'narrators' enumerated separate objects. [369]

Clearly learning through acting is a more elemental process than learning through language; the latter hinges on the former.

Thus we can say that modern theories of cognition and linguistics indicate that there is a fundamental process to learning: perception, imitation and play, concept. We perceive an action or a process. We imitate the various elements within it, and then describe it (in dramatic play if we are a child or in words if we are an adult). This process culminates in the formation of the concept as a whole. This has great significance at all stages of modern education. In modern Western civilisation, the normal process is the lecture method: a lecture is delivered by the tutor (to a group or singly) and then the student acts in relation to the given material—writes an essay or, with young children, draws a picture. But modern theories of cognition would indicate that this process is the reverse of what is required. The student should *watch* it, *do* it, *describe* it (in action and/or words), and then *theorise* about it. The 'describe' part would be acted with the young child, a mixture of mimic actions and words if an adolescent, and purely in words if an adult (for the dramatic imagination has become internalised).

So we see that the dramatic imagination is an inherent part of both thought and learning. To ignore it, as some older educational theorists would have us do, is to base learning on false premises. The basic paradigm:

PERCEPTION ——► ACTION ——► DESCRIPTION ——► THEORY
                                                (dramatic
                                                and/or
                                                linguistic)

is the dramatic method of learning and, as we have seen on pp. 231–6, is the most sure way to retain facts.

Dramatic Education is, therefore, not merely a way of looking at the education process (a philosophy), or a way of helping the individual develop (a psychology), or of assisting the individual to adjust to his environment (a sociology); it is the basic way in which the human being learns—and thus is the most effective method for all forms of education.

CONCLUSION

The dramatic imagination is at the centre of *human* creativity, and so it must be at the centre of any form of education that aims to develop the essentially human characteristics. That we have ranged wide over the related fields of philosophy, psychology, anthropology and other disciplines only means that they are some of the tools with which we can apprehend the human process. We have merely attempted to see how the varied branches of learning bear upon the dramatic impulse.

PART ONE

The essential characteristic of man when compared with the upper primates is his imagination, and this is essentially dramatic in its character. At the end of the first year of life the human child plays for the first time, developing humour and, in pretending to be himself or someone else, impersonates. This identification is the basic quality of the dramatic process whether, when we are young, we are pretending to be a lion or a cowboy or, when we are older, we are 'putting ourself in someone else's place' or imagining the possibilities inherent in a situation. It follows that the dramatic imagination, being such an all-important part of the human way of life, must be cultivated by any modern method of education.

This suggestion grows naturally out of the mainstream of Western European thought. Plato and Aristotle would base education on play; and, although Plato's idealism would banish the theatre from his Republic, Aristotle showed that man learned through imitation and that the theatre 'purges' man of impure emotions. Although Roman philosophers followed Aristotle's view of imitation, the early medieval Church opposed all forms of dramatic activity. But eventually, beginning with St Thomas Aquinas, the Church came to see the value of acting as relaxation and so, by the Renascence, drama was an inherent part of education 'to profit and delight'. After the dramatic recession of the eighteenth century, when education was more concerned with the formation of habits of mind, the Romantic philosophers brought education back to the mainstream of thought: Goethe encouraged both improvisation and performances in education, and Rousseau said that play and work should be synonymous. Darwin's theory of evolution showed that life was a growth, and play came to be accounted for in a number of ways: as 'surplus energy', as an instinct, and physiological studies saw it variously as recreation, relaxation, recapitulation of primitive culture patterns, and genetic transmission.

After various preliminary approaches during this century, a philosophy of Dramatic Education has evolved and this is in the mainstream of Western European thought. It starts with the child as a child (not as a miniature adult as in the eighteenth century) and it recognises the dramatic imagination as the essential human quality. Thus it encourages the child to express himself within the frameworks of creative movement, spontaneous speech and language, and impersonation and identification; in this way he can both learn and grow up—he can relate himself to his environment and see the relationship between ideas. The child comes to develop the human abilities to think and explore, to test hypotheses and discover 'truth'. Nothing has reality to the human being unless he realises it completely—lives it in the imagination—acts it.

As Dramatic Education is concerned with the life process, it ranges wide over related disciplines and impinges on almost all aspects of learning. Thus it is that the rest of this book discusses those aspects of other disciplines which most directly relate to Dramatic Education.

PART TWO

Dramatic play is a reflection of the child's unconscious and so we must approach psychoanalysis. The content of dramatic play is unconscious symbolic thought based on experience. The purpose of play is to reproduce in symbolic form the unsolved experiences of life and attempt solutions. Most analysts have discarded the earlier theory of free catharsis (non-directive therapy) and now consider repetition to be the key: play enables the child to re-experience events symbolically and, through repetition, gain mastery over them.

The origins of symbolic thought begin in the first months of life when fantasies of the 'good breast' and the 'bad breast' lead to projective identification—the basis for later identification. Then, with fantasies of destroying the mother, the child renounces immediate gratification and sublimates his instincts by displacing them on substitutes—the basis for later symbol formation and abstract thought. There is a natural growth from acting-out through fantasy to dramatic play; it is the latter which, becoming internalised and, thereby getting rid of associated action, becomes the adult's ability to think in abstractions. Essentially play is based on the child-mother relationship for this is the basis of imitation and later socio-emotional attachments; and, in adult life, any loss reflects the loss of the primary object and so recreates all the original related anxieties.

Of the various therapeutic methods, Psychodrama is the one whereby the individual improvises in theatrical form in order to recapitulate unsolved problems. Its educational importance lies in specific techniques which can help not only adjustment problems but also social and formal learning.

Psychoanalytic studies have also examined aesthetics. Where Freud saw art as the re-creation of unconscious symbols in 'the form of a dream', Ernst Kris considered it was preconscious (the daydream rather than the dream). Essentially art develops from play; with both the infant and the primitive man 'magic' and 'omnipotence of thought' lead to communication with others through artistic creation. But, because infantile experiences vary, different forms of art occur in adult life. The actor's specific exhibitionism is related to his need to make test-identifications, displacing tensions on to imaginary characters. The dramatist tries to resolve the world as he sees it and, often, creates infantile situations through the repetition compulsion—which accounts for the constant appearance of the Oedipus theme throughout dramatic history. The producer, identifying with his view of his parents' ideals, attempts to become the artistic parent, both to his artistic children (the actors) and in 'bringing up' the work of the dramatist as if it was his own child. Members of the audience identify in their unconscious with some aspect or person within the drama, just as in primitive enactments man made trial identifications with his god; in this sense, theatre is 'religious' and 'magical'; even in its most simple forms (puppets or the circus) it can provide identifications of an infantile nature.

PART THREE

Being a social activity, drama is inextricably linked with the nature and origins of society. The full range of dramatic play (from play to theatre) is observable in each civilised society. Situations in early childhood are reflected in both the adult character and the drama performed within the culture. All men in all societies have certain things in common, but each society develops its own specific characteristics in addition—or, as psychoanalysts put it, the infantile unconscious is wedded to the specific superego. In this way, although there is a basic similarity in the 'resurrection' dramas that are as far apart as the English Mummers' Play and the Bali Witch Drama, they also have differences: the ritual dramas are each society's version of a universal theme. A developed culture is based upon play: drama and ritual are the civilised versions of the mechanisms inherent in play; both the play of the child and the theatre of the adult are versions of the human being's attempt to find security. Also, civilised children and primitive men have certain patterns of thinking in common which are reflected in dramatic activity. There are far-reaching parallelisms in the dramatic patterns and religious beliefs of folk-lore, mythology, present-day savages and civilised children.

Drama is an important method of communication within a society and, as a result, the culture pattern and the dramatic enactment inter-relate. The origins and development of dramatic play show tribal, racial and cultural needs and patterns with which early dramatic practice is associated (the drama of the savage); these have relationships with modern children's play and traditional games. As drama and theatre developed, stable civilisations led to communal religious enactments within the framework of the ritual myth; thus the temple was established and the stylisation of ritual became liturgy. When the theatre emerged from the temple, and the bonds of ritual and liturgy were loosened, drama became more secular, although individual cultures developed in varying ways; priests and celebrants became actors and audience; and the ritual myth persisted in comedy as communal adjustment and in tragedy as ultimate experience. Each society possesses its own inherent dramatic patterns: medieval society had many such patterns; within our own society, folk plays and ballads, fairs and circuses, carnivals and fancy-dress dances, are all part of our own communal dramatic inheritance. Related to all dramatic studies are the concepts and notions of theatre which have varied through the centuries as they have been affected by human activities; and, as drama is the source of all art forms, the sociological approach must include the whole of the aesthetic inquiry.

Studies of social groups affect Dramatic Education. First, children's dramatic play occurs in groups and the nature of groups affect the play. Secondly, the participation of an audience is the characteristic difference between drama and other art forms. The culture patterns of the audience materially alter playwriting and acting, and there is a close interdependence between the nature of the playhouse, the audience and the performance.

Social psychologists consider that play is the method by which children approach the stern realities of adult living. As play is inter- twined with the life process, its content varies as the environment changes. Social psychological theories of play indicate that it can act as compensation, or as a way to master reality by scaling everything down to comprehensible patterns, or as self-expression.

PART FOUR

Although behaviourists have shown that imitation is a key factor in human learning, it can only begin on a basis of identification: the empathy between mother and child leads to an identification with the parent and a need to imitate. There are two types of identification: developmental, whereby the mother's qualities are introjected and the superego is built; and defensive, where, by fear of punishment, the child identifies with the aggressor. Thus social learning is dramatic in essence.

Role theorists, too, see imaginative impersonation as the basis of social learning. Dramatic play enables the child to acquire roles, and to develop skill in doing so; the better his ability, the better his social adjustment. In opposition to catharsis, however, role theorists suggest that imitation of aggression is likely to lead to permanent aggressive behaviour.

Creative thought processes are not accounted for by behaviourism because, in creativity, inspiration (or intuition, or illumination) is a necessary factor. Creative thought is based on play, and dramatic activity allows the necessary free play with perceptual data as well as free experiment within related fields.

Memory learning is considerably aided by dramatic play in the following ways: it makes the material to be memorised more meaning- ful, it aids the process of repetition, it provides memorising in depth through over-all understanding, and it facilitates the recall of images.

The development of speech, thought and language are interwoven. As with social learning, behaviourism cannot account for imitation in this field without recourse to identification; through the empathy of mother and child, the child identifies with her; play provides the initial imitation of her speech while identification provides the reward for subsequent imitations. Imitation is the speech mechanism, the motivation for which is an elementary form of impersonation. Further, language acts as a mould to thought. Language develops as thought develops, from the practical to the abstract—as instanced by historical developments and the growth of modern children.

Piaget indicates that dramatic play is directly related to the development of children's thought. With any cognitive structure (schema) there are two associated processes: play assimilates new experience to it, and then continues for the mere pleasure of mastery; imitation then takes place with the parts of the experience in order to accommodate these within the cognitive structure—play to accommodate, imitation to assimilate. Although imitation and play are directly related to the process of thought, and to the development of cognition, the dramatic imagination is the key factor—it is this which internalises objects, and which gives them significance for the individual. The fundamental paradigm for human learning is: Perception/Action/Description (dramatic and/or linguistic)/Theory.

Dramatic Education is not, then, training children to go on the stage. The idea of 'theatre', in fact, only enters as a method with older children and adults. Rather it is a whole new way of looking at the process of education. If dramatic play is such an important factor in a child's life as we have indicated, Dramatic Education asks that we centre the educative process upon it. We must examine our whole educational system in this light—the curricula, the syllabuses, the methods, and the philosophy upon which these are based. In all instances, we must start from acting: with young children, the spontaneous improvised make-believe inherent in them all; with older children and adults, the imagination which allows them to think dramatically—for both creative thought and memory learning are based on internalised identification. Dramatic Education asks that we start, as all liberal thinkers from Plato on would have us do, with the child. And it asks with Bernard Shaw:

> . . . whether it is possible to change this monstrous fraud of child schooling into the beginning of the education that ceases only in the grave, and is the unending recreation of its subject.

BIBLIOGRAPHY & REFERENCES

1. ABERCROMBIE, M. L. J.: 'Small Groups', in FOSS, B. M. (Ed.): *New Horizons in Psychology*. (Penguin, 1966).
2. ABRAHAM, K.: *Selected Papers on Psychoanalysis*. (Hogarth, 1927).
3. ADLAND, D. E.: *Group Drama*. (Longmans, 1964).
4. ADLER, ALFRED: *Social Interest: A Challenge to Mankind*. (Faber, 1938).
5. ADOLF, HELEN: 'The essence and origin of tragedy', *J. Aesth. & Art Criticism*, X, 1951; 112–125.
6. ALEXANDER, FRANZ: 'A note on Falstaff', *Psychoan.Q.*, 1933, 2; 592–606.
7. ALEXANDER, FRANZ: *Fundamentals of Psychology*. (Allen & Unwin, 1949).
8. ALFORD, VIOLA: *Sword Dance and Drama*. (Merlin, 1962).
9. ALLPORT, F. H.: *Social Psychology*. (Riverside, Cambridge, Mass., 1924).
10. ALTMAN, LEON L.: 'On the oral nature of acting out', *J. Am. Psychoan. Assoc.*, 1957, 5; 648–662.
11. ANAND, MULK RAJ: *The Indian Theatre*. (Dobson, 1950).
12. ANDERSON, G. L. (Ed.): *The Genius of the Oriental Theater*. (Mentor, 1966).
13. APPLETON, L. ESTELLA: *A Comparative Study of the Play Activities of Adult Savages and Civilised Children*. (Univ. of Chicago, 1910).
14. ARISTOTLE: *Poetics*. Trans. I. Bywater. (Oxford, 1920).
15. ARLINGTON, L. C.: *The Chinese Theatre from earliest times until today*. (Shanghai, 1930).
16. AUNG, MARING HTIN: *Burmese Drama*. (O.U.P., 1947).
17. AXLINE, VIRGINIA M.: *Play Therapy*. (Houghton, Mifflin, 1947).

18. BACON, FRANCIS: 'De Augmentis Scientiarum', in *Philosophical Works*, ed. J. M. Robertson. (Routledge, 1905).
19. BALDWIN, J. M.: *Mental Development in the Child and Race*. (Macmillan, 1895).
20. BALINT, EDNA: 'The Therapeutic value of play in the school situation'. *The New Era*. 1952, 33, 10; 243–246.
21. BANDURA, A., ROSS, D., *and* ROSS, S. A.: 'Imitation of film-mediated aggressive models', *J. Abn. Soc. Psych.*, 1963, 66; 3–11.
22. BANDURA, A., *and* WALTERS, R. H.: *Social Learning and Personality Development*. (Holt, Rinehart & Winston, 1965).
23. BATESON, GREGORY, *and* MEAD, MARGARET: *Balinese Character*. (New York Academy of Sciences, 1942).
24. *Bearings of Recent Advances in Psychology on Educational Problems*. London Univ. Institute of Education. (Evans, 1955).
25. BEECH, H. R.: 'Personality theories and behaviour therapy', in FOSS, B. M. (Ed.): *New Horizons in Psychology*. (Penguin, 1966).
26. BENDER, L. *and* SCHILDER, P.: 'Forms as a principle in the play of children', *J. Genet. Psychol.*, 1936, 49; 254–261.
27. BENEDICT, RUTH: *Patterns of Society*. (Routledge, 1935).
28. BERGLER, EDMUND: 'Psychoanalysis of writers', in RÓHEIM, GÉZA (Ed.): *Psychoanalysis and the Social Sciences*, 1. (Imago, 1947).
29. BERKO, J.: 'The child's learning of English morphology', *Word*, 1958, 14; 150–177.

30. BIERSTADT, E. H.: *Three Plays of the Argentine*. (N.Y., 1920).

31. BION, W. R.: *Experience in Groups*. (Tavistock, 1963).

32. BLACKHAM, H. J., BRITTON, JAMES, *and* BURTON, E. J.: 'A theory of general education', *The Plain View*. 13, 4, 1961.

33. BLOOMFIELD, LEONARD: *Language*. (Allen & Unwin, 1935).

34. BOAS, FRANK: 'Introduction', *Handbook of American Indian Languages*, Part I. (Washington, D.C., 1911).

35. BOULDING, K. E.: *The Image*. (Univ. Michigan, 1956).

36. BOWERS, FAUBION: *The Japanese Theatre*. (Peter Owen, 1952).

37. BOWERS, FAUBION: *Theatre in the East*. (Nelson).

38. BOYCE, E. R.: *Play in the Infants' School*. (Methuen, 1938).

39. BREUER, JOSEF, *and* FREUD, SIGMUND: *Studies in Hysteria*. (Hogarth, 1936; originally 1895).

40. BRILL, A. A.: 'Poetry as an oral outlet', *Psa. Rev.*, 18, No. 4, 1931.

41. BRILL, A. A.: *The Basic Writings of Sigmund Freud*. (Random House, N.Y., 1938).

42. BROWN, J. A. C.: *Freud and the Post-Freudians*. (Penguin, 1961).

43. BROWN, J F.: *Psychology and the Social Order*. (McGraw-Hill, N.Y., 1936).

44. BROWN, RADCLIFFE: *The Andaman Islanders*. (O.U.P., 1933).

45. BRUNER, J., GOODNOW, J., *and* AUSTIN, G.: *A Study of Thinking*. (Wiley, 1956).

46. BURTON, E. J.: *Teaching English Through Self-Expression*. (Evans, 1949).

47. BURTON, E. J.: 'The place of drama in education today. Living, learning and sharing experience', in *Art, Science and Education*. (Joint Council for Education Through Art, 1958).

48. BURTON, E. J.: *British Theatre: Its Repertory and Practice* 1100–1900. (Jenkins, 1960).

49. BURTON, E. J.: *The Student's Guide to World Theatre*. (Jenkins, 1963).

50. BURTON, E. J.: *The Student's Guide to British Theatre*. (Jenkins, 1964).

51. BURTON, E. J.: 'Drama as a first degree subject', (Paper privately circulated, 1965).

52. BURTON, E. J.: *Reality and 'Realization'. An Approach to a Philosophy*. (Drama & Educational Fellowship, 1966).

53. BUYTENDIJK, F. J. J.: *Wesen und Sinn des Spiels*. (Berlin, 1934).

54. CAMERON, N., *and* MAGARET, A.: *Behaviour Psychology*. (Houghton, Mifflin, 1951).

55. CAMPBELL, D. T.: 'Distinguishing differences of perception from failures of communication in cross-cultural studies' in, NORTHROP, F. S. C., *and* LIVINGSTON, H. H. (Eds.): *Crosscultural Understanding*. (Harper & Row, 1964).

56. CARR, H. H.: 'The Survival of play', *Investigation Dept. Psychology and Education*. (Univ. of Colorado, 1902).

57. CARROLL, JOHN B.: 'Language development in children', in SAPORTA, SOL (Ed.): *Psycholinguistics*. (Holt, Rinehart, N.Y., 1961).

58. CARROLL, JOHN B.: *Language & Thought*. (Prentice-Hall, 1964).

59. CHAMBERS, E. K.: *The Medieval Stage*. (O.U.P., 1903).

60. CHAMBERS, E. K.: *The English Folk Play*. (Clarendon Press, 1933).

61. CHEN, JACK: *Chinese Theatre*. (Dobson, 1949).

62. CHOMSKY, N.: *Syntactic Structures*. (Mouton, The Hague, 1957).
63. CHURCH, JOSEPH: *Language & the Discovery of Reality*. (Random House, N.Y., 1961).
64. CICERO: *De Republica*. Trans. Miller. (Heinemann, 1947).
65. CIRILLI, RENÉ: *Les Prêtres Danseurs de Rome*. (Geuthner, Paris, 1913) p. 114.
66. CLAPARÈDE, E.: *Psychologie de l'Enfant et Pédagogie Expérimentale*. Trans. M. Louch & H. Holman. (Longmans, 1911).
67. COGGIN, PHILIP A.: *Drama in Education*. (Thames & Hudson, 1956).
68. COHEN, J.: 'Analysis of psychological "fields"', *Science News,* 13; 145–158.
69. COLLIER, JEREMY: *Short View of the Immorality and Profaneness of the English Stage*. (1698).
70. COOK, CALDWELL: *The Play Way*. (Heinemann, 1917).
71. CORNFORD, F. M.: *The Origin of Attic Comedy*. Ed. T. H. Gaster. (Doubleday, 1961).
72. COURTNEY, RICHARD: *Drama for Youth*. (Pitman, 1964).
73. COURTNEY, RICHARD: (Ed.): *College Drama Space*. Institute of Education, London Univ., 1964.
74. COURTNEY, RICHARD: *Teaching Drama. A Handbook for Teachers in Schools*. (Cassell, 1965).
75. COURTNEY, RICHARD: 'Planning the School and College Stage', *Education:* 9.4.65., 725–728; 16.4.65., 799–802; and 21.5.65., 1075.
76. COURTNEY, RICHARD: *The School Play*. (Cassell, 1966).
77. COURTNEY, RICHARD: *The Drama Studio: Architecture and Equipment for Dramatic Education*. (Pitman, 1967).
78. CRUTCHFIELD, R. S.: 'Conformity and character', *Am. Psych.,* 1955, 10; 191–198.
79. CURTI, M. W.: *Child Psychology*. (Longmans, 1930).

80. DALRYMPLE-ALFORD, E.: 'Psycholinguistics', in FOSS, B. M. (Ed.): *New Horizons in Psychology*. (Penguin, 1966).
81. DAVISON, A., *and* FAY, J.: *Phantasy in Childhood*. (Routledge, 1952).
82. DE MOLINA, TIRSO: 'The Orchards of Toledo', in CLARK, H. BARRETT: *European Theories of Drama*. (Kidd, Cincinnati, 1919).
83. DE VEGA, LOPE: in CHAYTOR, H. J.: *Dramatic Theory in Spain*. (O.U.P., 1925).
84. DEL SORTO, J., *and* CORNEYTZ, P.: 'Psychodrama as expressive and projective technique', *Sociometry,* 1944, 8; 356–375.
85. DENNIS, W.: 'Piaget's questions applied to Zuni and Navaho children', *Psych. Bul.,* 1940, 37; 520.
86. DEUTSCH, F.: 'Mind, body and art', *Daedalus,* 1960, 89; 34.
87. DEWEY, JOHN: 'Educational principles', *The Elementary School*. (1900).
88. DEWEY, JOHN: *Art as Experience*. (Minton, Balch, 1935).
89. DOBRÉE, BONAMY: *Restoration Comedy*. (Oxford, 1924).
90. DOLLARD, J., *et.al:* *Frustration and Aggression*. (Routledge, 1944).
91. DURKHEIM, ÉMILE: *Suicide*. (Routledge, 1952).

92. EBBINGHAUS, H.: *Psychology: An Elementary Text*. Trans. M. Meyer. (Heath, Boston, 1908).

93. EDFELD, A. W.: *Silent Speech & Silent Reading*. (Almquist & Wiksell, Stockholm, 1959).

94. EDWARDS, OSMAN: *Japanese Plays and Play-fellows*. (Heinemann, 1901).

95. EHRENZWEIG, ANTON: *The Psychoanalysis of Artistic Vision and Hearing*. (Julian Press, N.Y., 1953).

96. EKSTEIN, R., *and* FRIEDMAN, SEYMOUR: 'The function of acting out, play action and play acting', *J. Am. Psychoan. Assoc.* 1957, 5; 581–629.

97. EMPSON, WILLIAM: *Seven Types of Ambiguity*. (Chatto & Windus, 1930).

98. ERICKSON, ERIK: 'Studies in the interpretation of play', *Genet. Psychol. Monog.* 1940, 22; 557–671.

99. ERICKSON, ERIK: *Childhood and Society*. (Penguin, 1965).

100. EVANS-PRITCHARD, E. E.: 'The Dance', in *The Position of Women in Primitive Societies and other essays in Social Anthropology*. (Faber, 1965).

101. EVERNDEN, STANLEY: 'Drama in Schools', (Private communication, 1966).

102. FENICHEL, OTTO: *The Psychoanalytic Theory of Neurosis*. (Norton, N.Y., 1945).

103. FENICHEL, OTTO: 'On acting', *Psychoan. Q.*, 15, 1946; 144–160.

104. FERENCZI, S.: 'Stages in the development of the sense of reality', in *Sex in Psychoanalysis*. (Badger, Boston, 1916).

105. FESTINGER, L. A.: 'Informal social communication', *Psych. Rev.*, 1950, 57; 271–282.

106. FESTINGER, L. A., SCHACHTER, S., *and* BACK, K.: *Social Pressures in Informal Groups*. (Harper, N.Y., 1950).

107. FESTINGER, L. A.: *A Theory of Cognitive Dissonances*. (Harper, N.Y., 1957).

108. FLAVELL, J. H.: *The Developmental Psychology of Jean Piaget*. (Van Nostrand, N.Y., 1963).

109. FLEMING, C. M.: 'The bearing of field theory and sociometry on children's classroom behaviour', in *Bearings of Recent Advances in Psychology on Educational Problems*. (London Univ. Institute of Education; Evans, 1955).

110. FLUGEL, J. C.: *Man, Morals & Society*. (Duckworth, 1945).

111. FORDHAM, FRIEDA: *An Introduction to Jung's Psychology*. (Penguin, 1953).

112. FOULKES, S. H., *and* ANTHONY, E. J.: *Group Psychotherapy*. (Penguin, 2nd ed. 1965).

113. FRANK, L. K.: *Projective Methods*. (Thomas, Springfield, Ill., 1948).

114. FRANKFORT, H., *and* H. A., WILSON, J. A., *and* JACOBSEN, T.: *The Intellectual Adventure of Ancient Man*. (Univ. Chicago, 1946).

115. FRAZER, J. G.: *The Golden Bough*, 3rd ed., 12 Vols. (Macmillan, 1907–15).

116. FRAZER. J. G.: *Taboo and the Perils of the Soul*. Part II of *The Golden Bough*, 3rd ed. (Macmillan, 1911).

117. FRENCH, J. R. P., JR.: 'Organised and unorganised groups under fear and frustration', *Univ. Ia. Child Welf.*, 1944, 20; 299–308.

118. FREUD, ANNA: 'Introduction to the techniques of child analysis', *Nerv. Ment. Dis. Monogr.* 1928, No. 48.

119. FREUD, ANNA: *The Ego and the Mechanisms of Defence*. (Hogarth, 1936).

120. FREUD, SIGMUND: *Totem and Taboo*. (Hogarth, 1913).

121. FREUD, SIGMUND: *Psycho-pathology of Everyday Life*. (Benn, 1914).

122. FREUD, SIGMUND: *An Outline of Psychoanalysis*. (Hogarth, 1920).

123. FREUD, SIGMUND: *The Ego and the Id.* (Hogarth, 1922).

124. FREUD, SIGMUND: *Group Psychology and the Analysis of the Ego.* (Hogarth, 1922).

125. FREUD, SIGMUND: *Beyond the Pleasure Principle.* (Hogarth, 1922).

126. FREUD, SIGMUND: 'The dynamics of transference', *Collected Papers,* II. (Hogarth, 1924).

127. FREUD, SIGMUND: 'Mourning and melancholia', *Collected Papers,* IV. (Hogarth, 1925).

128. FREUD, SIGMUND: *Inhibition, Symptom and Anxiety.* (Hogarth, 1927).

129. FREUD, SIGMUND: *The Future of an Illusion.* (Hogarth, 1930).

130. FREUD, SIGMUND: *Civilization and Its Discontents.* (Hogarth, 1930).

131. FREUD, SIGMUND: *New Introductory Lectures in Psychoanalysis.* (Hogarth, 1933).

132. FREUD, SIGMUND: *Moses and Monotheism.* (Hogarth, 1939).

133. FREUD, SIGMUND: 'Psychopathetic characters on the stage (1904)', *Psychoan.Q.* 1942, 9; 459–464.

134. FREUD, SIGMUND: 'Rumour', *Collected Papers,* V. (Hogarth, 1950).

135. FREUD, SIGMUND: 'The relation of the poet to day-dreaming (1908)', *Collected Papers,* IV, (Hogarth, 1953).

136. FREUD, SIGMUND: *Standard Edition of the Works of,* IV. (Hogarth, 1953).

137. FREUD, SIGMUND: *Standard Edition of the Works of,* VII. (Hogarth, 1953).

138. FREUD, SIGMUND: *The Interpretation of Dreams.* (Hogarth, 1955).

139. FRIEDMAN, JOEL., and GASSEL, SYLVIA: 'The chorus in Sophocles' *Oedipus Tyrannus*', *Psychoan.Q.,* 1950, 19; No. 2.

140. FROEBEL, F.: *The Education of Man.* (1862).

141. FROMM, ERICH: *Fear of Freedom.* (Routledge, 1952).

142. GALTON, SIR FRANCIS: *Inquiries into Human Faculty & Its Development.* (1883; repr. Eugenics society, 1951).

143. GASTER, T. H.: *Thespis.* (Doubleday, rev. 1961).

144. GETZELS, J. W., and JACKSON, P. W.: *Creativity and Intelligence.* (Wiley, N.Y., 1962).

145. GHISELIN, B. (Ed.): *The Creative Process: A Symposium.* (Univ. Calif., 1952).

146. GOMME, G. L.: *Ethnology in Folklore.* (1886).

147. GOMME, LADY ALICE: *Traditional Games,* I & II. (Dover, N.Y., 1964).

148. GOODNOW, J.: 'A test of milieu effects with some of Piaget's tasks', *Psych. Monog.,* 1962, 76; 1–22.

149. GOPAL, RAM: *Indian Dancing.* (Phoenix House, 1951).

150. GORDON, W. J. J.: *Synectics.* (Harper, N.Y., 1961).

151. GOUGH, H. G.: 'A sociological theory of psychotherapy', *Am.J.Sociol.,* 1948, 53; 359–366.

152. GOWEN, HERBERT, H.: *A History of Indian Literature from Vedic Times to the Present Day.* (Appleton, N.Y., 1931).

153. GRØNBECK, V.: *The Culture of the Teutons.* (1931).

154. GROOS, KARL: *The Play of Animals.* Trans. E. L. Baldwin. (Heinemann, 1898).

155. GROOS, KARL: *The Play of Man.* Trans. E. L. Baldwin. (Heinemann, 1901).

156. GROOS, KARL: 'Das spiel als Katharsis', *Zeitschrift Pedagogie* (1914).

157. GUHA-THAKURTA, P.: *The Bengali Drama, its Origin and Development*. (Kegan Paul, 1930).

158. GUTHRIE, E. R.: *The Psychology of Learning*. (Harper, N.Y., 1935).

159. H.M.S.O.: *Handbook for Teachers in Elementary Schools*. (1937 edition).

160. H.M.S.O.: *The Story of a School*. (1950).

161. HAAS, ROBERT BARTLETT, *and* MORENO, J. L.: 'Psychodrama as a projective technique', in ANDERSON, H. H., *and* J. L.: *An Introduction to Projective Techniques & Other Devices for Understanding the Dynamics of Human Behaviour*. (Prentice-Hall, 1951).

162. HADAMARD, J.: *The Psychology of Invention in the Mathematical Field*. (Dover, N.Y., 1954).

163. HADFIELD, J. A.: *Dreams and Nightmares*. (Penguin, 1954).

164. HADFIELD, J. A.: *Childhood and Adolescence*. (Penguin, 1962).

165. HALL, G. STANLEY: *Youth*. (Appleton, N.Y., 1916).

166. HARRISON, JANE E.: *Themis*. (Cambridge, 1912).

167. HAVEMEYER, L.: *The Drama of Savage Peoples*. (New Haven, 1916).

168. HAYES, CATHY: *The Ape in our House*. (Harper, N.Y., 1951).

169. HELLERSBERG, E. F.: 'Child's growth in play therapy', *Am.J.Psychother.* 1955, 9; 484–502.

170. HENLE, PAUL (Ed.): *Language, Thought & Culture*. (Univ. Michigan, 1958).

171. HERBERT, E. L.: 'The use of group techniques in the training of teachers', *Human Relations*, 14, No. 3. 1961.

172. HILGARD, E. R., *and* MARQUIS, D. G.: *Conditioning and Learning*. (Appleton, N.Y., 1940).

173. HOIJER, HARRY (Ed.): *Language in Culture*. (Univ. Chicago, 1954).

174. HOLT, E. B.: *Animal Drive*. (Williams & Norgate, 1931).

175. HOMANS, GEORGE C.: *The Human Group*. (Routledge, 1951).

176. HORACE: *Art of Poetry*. Trans. T. A. Moxon. (Everyman, 1934).

177. HORNEY, KAREN: *New Ways in Psychoanalysis*. (Norton, 1939).

178. HORNEY, KAREN: *The Neurotic Personality of Our Time*. (Norton, 1937).

179. HORNEY, KAREN: *Our Inner Conflicts*. (Norton, 1945).

180. HORNEY, KAREN: *Neurosis and Human Growth*. (Routledge, 1951).

181. HOURD, MARJORIE L.: *The Education of the Poetic Spirit*. (Heinemann, 1949).

182. HOURD, MARJORIE L., *and* COOPER, GERTRUDE E.: *Coming into their Own*. (Heinemann, 1959).

183. HOURD, MARJORIE L.: 'Some reflections on the significance of group work' *New Era*, No. 42, No. 1, 1961.

184. HOWARTH, MARY R.: *Child Psychotherapy*. (Basic Books, 1964).

185. HUGHES, A. G., *and* HUGHES, E. H.: *Learning & Teaching*. (Longmans, 2nd ed., 1946).

186. HUIZINGA, JOHAN: *Homo Ludens—a Study of the Play Element in Culture*. (Beacon, Boston, 1955).

187. HULL, C. L.: *Principles of Behaviour*. (Appleton, N.Y., 1943).

188. HULL, E. M.: *Folklore of the British Isles*. (Methuen, 1928).

189. HUMPHREY, G.: 'Imitation and the conditioned reflex', *Ped. Sem.*, 1921, 28; 1–21.

190. HUNNINGHER. B.: *The Origin of the Theatre*. (Hill and Wang, N.Y., 1961).
191. HUNTER, I. M. L.: *Memory*. (Penguin, rev. 1964).

192. ISAACS, SUSAN: *Intellectual Thought in Young Children*. (Routledge, 1930).
193. ISAACS, SUSAN: *Social Development in Young Children*. (Routledge, 1933).

194. JACKSON, L., *and* TODD, K. M.: *Child Treatment and the Therapy of Play*. (Methuen, 1946).
195. JACQUES, E.: *The Changing Culture of a Factory*. (Tavistock, 1951).
196. JAMES, WILLIAM: *Principles of Psychology*, I. (1891).
197. JOHNSON, SAMUEL: *The Rambler*. No. 156 (1751).
198. JONES, ERNEST: *Hamlet and Oedipus*. (Gollancz, 1949).
199. JONES, ERNEST: 'Psychoanalysis and anthropology', *Essays in Applied Psycho-Analysis*, II. (Hogarth, 1951).
200. JONES, ERNEST: 'Psychoanalysis and Folklore', *Essays in Applied Psycho-Analysis*, II. (Hogarth, 1951).
201. JONES, ERNEST: *Sigmund Freud: Life and Work*. (Hogarth, 1953-7).
202. JUNG, C. G.: *The Psychology of the Unconscious*. (Dodd, Mead, N.Y., 1916).
203. JUNG, C. G.: *Contributions to Analytical Psychology*. (Harcourt, Brace, N.Y., 1928).
204. JUNG, C. G.: *Modern Man in Search of a Soul*. (Harcourt, Brace, N.Y., 1933).
205. JUNG, C. G.: *The Integration of the Personality*. (Routledge, 1940).
206. JUNG, C. G.: *Introduction to a Science of Mythology*. (Routledge, 1949).
207. JUNG, C. G.: *Psychology and Religion*. (*Collected Works XI*). (Routledge, 1958).
208. JUNG, C. G.: *Two Essays on Analytical Psychology*. (*Collected Works VII*). (Routledge, 1958).

209. KABUKI THEATRE. (Japanese Embassy, Washington, 1954).
210. KALIDASA: *Various Works*. Trans. A. W. Ryder. (Dent).
211. KALVODOVA-SIS-VANIS: *Chinese Theatre*. (Spring Books, n.d.).
212. KANZER, MARK: 'Contemporary psychoanalytic views of aesthetics', *J. Am. Psychoan. Assoc.*, 1957, 5; 514-524.
213. KANZER, MARK: 'Acting out, sublimation and reality testing', *J. Am. Psychoan. Assoc.*, 1957, 5; 663-684.
214. KARDINER, A.: *The Individual and His Society*. (Columbia Univ., 1939).
215. KEITH, A. BERRIEDALE: *The Sanskrit Drama in its Origin, Development, Theory and Practice*. (Oxford, 1924).
216. KINCAID, ZOE: *Kabuki: The Popular Stage of Japan*. (Macmillan, 1925).
217. KINGSLEY, H. L.: *The Nature & Conditions of Learning*. (1946).
218. KLEIN, MELANIE: *The Psychoanalysis of Children*. (Hogarth, 1932).
219. KLEIN, MELANIE, HEIMANN, PAULA, ISAACS, SUSAN *and* RIVIÈRE, JOAN: *Developments in Psychoanalysis*. (Hogarth, 1952).
220. KLUCKHORN, C., *and* LEIGHTON, D.: *The Navaho*. (Cambridge, Mass., 1948).
221. KOESTLER, ARTHUR: *The Sleepwalkers*. (Macmillan, N.Y., 1959).
222. KRETSCHMER, E.: *Physique and Character*. (Kegan Paul, 1925).
223. KRIS, ERNST: 'On preconscious mental processes', *Psychoan. Q.*, 1950, 19; 542-552.
224. KRIS, ERNST: *Psychoanalytic Explorations in Art*. (Allen & Unwin, 1953).

225. KUBIE, L. S.: *Neurotic Distortion of the Creative Process.* (Univ. Kansas, 1958).

226. LABAN, RUDOLF: *Modern Educational Dance.* (Macdonald & Evans, 1948).

227. LANDAU, J. M.: *Studies in Arab Theatre and Cinema.* (Univ. Pennsylvania Press, 1957).

228. LANDIS, JOSEPH C. (Ed.): *The Dybbuk and Other Great Yiddish Plays.* (Bantam, 1966).

229. LAZARUS, MORITZ: *Die Reize des Spiels.* (Berlin, 1883).

230. LEE, HARRY B.: 'The values of order and vitality in art', in RÓHEIM, GÉZA: *Psychoanalysis and the Social Sciences,* 11 (Int. Univ. Press, N.Y., 1950).

231. LEE, JOSEPH: *Play in Education.* (Macmillan, N.Y., 1915).

232. LEEPER, R.: 'Cognition processes', in STEVENS, S. S.: *Handbook of Experimental Psychology.* (Wiley, N.Y., 1951).

233. LEHMAN, HARVEY C., *and* WITTY, PAUL A.: *The Psychology of Play Activities.* (Barnes, N.Y., 1927).

234. LESSER, SIMON O.: *Fiction and the Unconscious.* (Beacon, Boston, 1957).

235. LEVY, D.: 'Release therapy', *Am. J. Orthopsychiat.,* 1938, 9; 713–737.

236. LEWIN, K.: *Principles of Topological Psychology.* (McGraw-Hill, 1936).

237. LEWIN, K.: *Resolving Social Conflicts.* (Harper, 1948).

238. LEWIS, J. H., *and* SARBIN, T. R.: 'Studies in psychosomatics: the influence of hypnotic stimulation on gastric hunger contractions', *Psychosom. Med.,* 1943, 5; 125–131.

239. LEWIS, M. M.: *Infant Speech: A Study in the Beginnings of Language.* (Humanities, N.Y., rev. 1951).

240. LINTON, RALPH: *The Cultural Background of Personality.* (Routledge, 1947).

241. LOMBARD, FRANK ALANSON: *An Outline History of the Japanese Drama.* (Allen & Unwin, 1929).

242. LOVELL, K.: 'A follow up of some aspects of the work of Piaget and Inhelder into the child's conception of space', *Brit. J. Ed. Psych.,* 1959, 29; 104–117.

243. LOVELL, K.: 'A follow up study of Inhelder and Piaget's *The Growth of Logical Thinking'*, *Brit. J. Psych.,* 1961, 52.

244. LOWENFELD, MARGARET: *Play in Childhood.* (Gollancz, 1935).

245. LOWENFELD, MARGARET: 'The World pictures of children', *Brit. J. Med. Psychol.,* 1938, 18; 65–101.

246. LURIA, A. R.: 'Dynamic approach to the mental development of the abnormal child', *J. Ment. Def. Res.,* 1958, 2; 37–52.

247. LURIA, A. R.: *The Role of Speech in the Regulation of Normal and Abnormal Behaviour.* (Pergamon, 1961).

248. MALINOWSKI, B.: *Sex and Repression in Savage Society.* (Kegan Paul, 1927).

249. MALINOWSKI, B.: 'The problem of meaning in primitive languages', in OGDEN, C., *and* RICHARDS, I. A.: *The Meaning of Meaning.* (Routledge, 10th ed., 1949).

250. MANDELBAUM, D. G. (Ed.): *Edward Sapir: Culture, Language and Personality.* (Univ. Calif., 1957).

251. MCCARTHY, D.: 'Language development in children' in CARMICHAEL, L. (Ed.): *Manual of Child Psychology.* (Wiley, N.Y., 1946).

252. MCDOUGALL, WILLIAM: *Introduction to Social Psychology.* (Methuen, 1908).
253. MEAD, GEORGE, H.: *Mind, Self and Society.* (Univ. Chicago, 1934).
254. MEAD, MARGARET: *Coming of Age in Samoa.* (Morrow, N.Y., 1928).
255. MEAD, MARGARET: *Sex and Temperament in Three Primitive Societies.* (Routledge, 1935).
256. MEDNICK, S. A.: *Learning.* (Prentice-Hall, 1963).
257. MENZIES, I. E. P.: 'A case study in the functioning of social systems as a defence against anxiety: a report on the study of the Nursing Service of a General Hospital', *Human Relations,* 13, No. 2, 1960.
258. MILLER, G. A.: *Language and Communication.* (McGraw-Hill, N.Y., 1951).
259. MILLER, N. E., *and* DOLLARD, J.: *Social Learning and Imitation.* (Kegan Paul, 1945).
260. MITCHELL, ELMER D., *and* MASON, BERNARD S.: *The Theory of Play.* (Barnes, N.Y.; revised edition, Ronald Press, N.Y., 1948).
261. MIYAKE, SHUTARO: *Kabuki Drama.* (Japan Travel Bureau, N.Y., 1948).
262. MONEY-KYRLE, T. E.: 'Varieties of group formation' in RÓHEIM, GÉZA: *Psychoanalysis and the Social Sciences,* II. (Int. Univ. Press, N.Y., 1950).
263. MONTAIGNE: 'Customs' and 'Education of children', in *Essays.* (Dent).
264. MORENO, J. L.: *Who Shall Survive?* Trans. H. Lesage *and* P. H. Maucarps. (Nerv. Dis. Pub. Co., 1934).
265. MORENO, J. L.: *Psychodrama,* I. (Beacon House, N.Y., 1946).
266. MORENO, J. L.: *Psychodrama,* II. (Beacon House, N.Y., 1959).
267. MORRIS, BEN: 'How does a group learn to work together?' in NIBLETT, W. R.: *How and Why do we Learn?* (Faber, 1965).
268. MOWRER, O. H.: *Learning Theory and Personality Dynamics.* (Ronald, N.Y., 1950).
269. MOWRER, O. H.: *Learning Theory and the Symbolic Processes.* (Wiley, 1960).
270. MULCASTER, RICHARD: *Elementarie.* (1592).
271. MURPHY, GARDNER: *Personality: A Biosocial Approach to Origins & Structure.* (Harper, N.Y., 1947).
272. MURRAY, GILBERT: in HARRISON, JANE E.: *Themis.* (Cambridge, 1912).
273. MURRAY, GILBERT: *Aeschylus, the Creator of Tragedy.* (O.U.P., 1940).
274. MURRAY, GILBERT: in GASTER, T. H.: *Thespis.* (Doubleday, rev. 1961).
275. NEWTON, ROBERT G.: *Acting Improvised.* (Nelson, 1937).
276. NICOLL, ALLARDYCE: *Masks, Mimes and Miracles.* (Harrap, 1931).
277. NICOLL, ALLARDYCE: *The Development of the Theatre.* (Harrap, 1948).
278. NICOLL, ALLARDYCE: *History of English Drama,* I-V. (Cambridge, 1923–46).
279. NICOLL, ALLARDYCE: *Theatre and Dramatic Theory.* (Harrap, 1962).
280. NUNN, PERCY: *Education: Its Data and First Principles.* (Arnold, 1920).
281. O'CONNOR, N., *and* HERMELIN, B.: *Speech & Thought in Severe Subnormality.* (Pergamon, 1963).
282. ORDISH, T. F.: 'Folk Drama', *Folk-Lore,* II (p. 314 *et seq.*) and *IV* (p. 149 *et seq.*).
283. OSBORN, A. F.: *Applied Imagination.* (Scribner, N.Y., 1957).
284. OSGOOD, CHARLES E.: *Method and Theory in Experimental Psychology.* (Oxford, 1953).

285. OSGOOD, CHARLES E., *and* JENKINS, J.: 'Psycholinguistic analysis of decoding and encoding', in OSGOOD, C. E., *and* SEBECK, THOMAS A.: *Psycholinguistics: A Survey of Theory & Research Problems.* (Waverley, Baltimore, 1954).
286. OSGOOD, CHARLES E., *and* SEBECK, THOMAS A.: *Psycholinguistics: A Survey of Theory and Research Problems.* (Waverley, Baltimore, 1954).
287. OSGOOD, CHARLES E.: 'Psycholinguistics', in KOCH, SIGMUND (Ed.): *Psychology: A Study of a Science,* VI. (McGraw-Hill, 1963).

288. PARSONS, TALCOTT: *The Social System.* (Tavistock, 1952).
289. PATRICK, C.: *What is Creative Activity?* (Philosophical Library, N.Y., 1955).
290. PATRICK, G. T. W.: *The Psychology of Relaxation.* (Houghton, Mifflin, N.Y., 1916).
291. PELLER, LILI E.: 'Libidinal development as reflected in play', *Psychoanalysis,* Spring, 1955, 3; 3–11.
292. PHILLPOTTS, B. S.: *The Elder Edda.* (Cambridge, 1920).
293. PIAGET, JEAN: *Language & Thought of the Child.* (Harcourt, Brace, N.Y., 1926).
294. PIAGET, JEAN: *Play, Dreams and Imitation in Childhood.* Trans. C. Gattegno and F. M. Hodgson. (Routledge & Kegan Paul, 1962).
295. PLATO: *The Republic.* Trans. A. D. Lindsay. (Everyman, 1935).
296. PLATO: *Laws,* in *Dialogues.* Trans. B. Jowett (1892).
297. POPOVICH, JAMES E.: 'Development of creative dramatics in the United States', in SIKS, G. B., *and* DUNNINGTON, H. B.: *Children's Theatre & Creative Dramatics.* (Univ. Washington, Seattle, 1961).
298. PRICE-WILLIAMS, D.: 'Cross-cultural studies', in FOSS, B. M. (Ed.): *New Horizons in Psychology.* (Penguin, 1966).
299. PROGOFF, IRA: *Jung's Psychology and Its Social Meaning.* (Routledge, 1953).
300. POUND, EZRA, *and* FENOLLOSA, ERNEST: *The Classic Noh Theatre of Japan.* (Knopf, N.Y., 1917).

301. QUERAT,: *Les jeux des enfants.* (Paris, 1905).

302. RABELAIS: *Gargantua and Pantagruel.* (Dent).
303. RAGLAN, LORD: *The Hero.* (Methuen, 1936).
304. RANK, OTTO: *Trauma of Birth.* (Harcourt, Brace, 1929).
305. RANK, OTTO: *Will Therapy and Truth and Reality.* (Knopf, 1947).
306. READ, HERBERT: 'The limitations of a scientific philosophy', in *Art, Science and Education.* (Joint Council for Education Through Art, 1958).
307. REANEY, M. JANE: 'The psychology of the organised group game', *Psych. Rev.* Monog. Supp. 4, 1916.
308. REANEY, M. JANE: *The Place of Play in Education.* (Methuen, 1927).
309. REICH, WILHELM: *Character Analysis.* (Organs Institute, N.Y., 1945).
310. REIK, THEODOR: *Masochism in Modern Man.* (Grove Press, N.Y., 1957).
311. REIK, THEODOR: *A Psychologist Looks at Love.* (Rinehart, N.Y.).
312. REISMAN, DAVID: *The Lonely Crowd.* (Yale Univ., 1953).
313. RICHARDSON, J. E.: 'An experiment in group methods of teaching English composition', *Studies in Social Psychology of Adolescence.* (Routledge, 1951).

314. RICHARDSON, J. E.: 'Teacher-pupil relationship as explored and rehearsed in an experimental tutorial group', *New Era*, 44, Nos. 6 & 7, 1963.

315. RIVERS, W. H. R.: *Conflict and Dream*. (Routledge).

316. ROBINSON, E. S.: 'The compensatory function of make-believe play', *Psych. rev.*, 1920; 429–439.

317. RÓHEIM, GÉZA: 'Psychoanalysis of primitive cultural types', *Int. J. Psa.*, 1932, 13; 197.

318. RÓHEIM, GÉZA: *The Riddle of the Sphinx*. (Hogarth, 1934).

319. RÓHEIM, GÉZA: 'Psychoanalysis and anthropology', *Psychoanalysis and the Social Sciences*, I. (Imago, 1947).

320. RÓHEIM, GÉZA: 'Psychoanalysis and anthropology', in LORAND, SANDOR: *Psycho-Analysis Today*. (Allen and Unwin, 1948).

321. RÓHEIM, GÉZA: *Origin and Function of Culture*.

322. RÓHEIM, GÉZA: 'The Oedipus Complex, Magic and Culture', *Psychoanalysis and the Social Sciences*, II. (Int. Univ. Press, 1950).

323. ROTH, HENRY LING: *The Natives of Sarawak and British North Borneo*. (London, 1896).

324. ROUSSEAU, JEAN-JACQUES: *Emile*. Trans. Foxley. (Everyman).

325. SABATHCHANDRA, E. R.: *The Sinhalese Folk Play and the Modern Stage*. (Ceylon Univ. Pres, 1953).

326. SACHS, HANNS: *The Creative Unconscious*. (Sci-Art, Cambridge, Mass., 1942).

327. SAPIR, E.: 'Conceptual categories in primitive language', *Science*, 1931, 5; 578.

328. SARBIN, THEODORE R.: 'Role Theory', in LINDZEY, GARDNER: *Handbook of Social Psychology*, I. (Addison-Wesley, Cambridge, Mass., 1954).

329. SCHILLER, FRIEDRICH: *Essays, Aesthetical and Philosophical*. (Bell, 1875).

330. SCHNEIDER, DANIEL E.: *The Psychoanalyst and the Artist*. (Int. Univ. Press, N.Y., 1950).

331. SCHUYLER, MONTGOMERY: *A Bibliography of the Sanskrit Drama, with an Introductory Sketch of the Dramatic Literature of India*. (Univ. Columbia Indo-Iranian Series, No. 3, N.Y., 1906).

332. SCHWARTZ, EMANUEL K.: 'A psychoanalytic study of the fairy tale', *Am. J. Psychother.*, 10, 1956; 740–762.

333. SCOTT, A. C.: *The Classical Theatre of China*. (Allen and Unwin, 1957).

334. SCOTT, A. C.: *The Kabuki Theatre of Japan*. (Allen and Unwin, 1955).

335. SEARS, R. R.: 'Identification as a form of behavioural development', in HARRIS, D. B.: *The Concept of Development*. (Univ. Minnesota, 1957).

336. SEASHORE, CARL: *Psychology in Daily Life*. (Appleton, N.Y., 1916).

337. SEGAL, HANNA: *Introduction to the Work of Melanie Klein*. (Heinemann, 1946).

338. SHELDON, W. H.: *et al*: *The Varieties of Human Physique*. (Harper, 1940).

339. SIKS, GERALDINE BRAIN, *and* DUNNINGTON, HAZEL BRAIN: *Children's Theatre & Creative Dramatics*. (Univ. Washington, Seattle, 1961).

340. SKINNER, B. F.: *The Behaviour of Organisms*. (Appleton, N.Y., 1938).

341. SKINNER, B. F.: *Verbal Behaviour*. (Appleton, N.Y., 1957).

342. SLADE, PETER: *Child Drama*. (U.L.P., 1954).

343. SLAVSON, S. R.: *Recreation and the Total Personality*. (Association Press, N.Y., 1948).

344. SOLOMON, JOSEPH C.: 'Therapeutic use of play', in ANDERSON H. H., and G. L.: *An Introduction to Projective Techniques & Other Devices for Understanding the Dynamics of Human Behaviour.* (Prentice-Hall, N.Y., 1951).

345. SOUTHERN, RICHARD: *The Seven Ages of the Theatre.* (Faber, 1962).

346. SPENCE, LEWIS: *Myth and Ritual in Dance, Game, and Rhyme.* (Watts, 1947).

347. SPENCER, HERBERT: *The Principles of Psychology.* (Appleton, N.Y., 1873).

348. SPROTT, W. H.: *Human Groups.* (Penguin, 1958).

349. STEKEL, WILHELM: *Autobiography.* (Liveright, N.Y., 1950).

350. SULLIVAN, H. S.: *Conceptions of Modern Psychiatry.* (White, Washington, 1947).

351. SUTTIE, IAN: *The Origins of Love and Hate.* (Penguin, 1935).

352. TARACHOW, SIDNEY: 'Circuses and clowns', in RÓHEIM, GÉZA: *Psychoanalysis and the Social Sciences, III.* (Int. Univ. Press, 1951).

353. TAYLOR, D. W., BERRY, P. C., and BLOCK, C. H.: 'Does group participation when using brainstorming facilitate or inhibit creative thinking?', *Yale Univ. Industr. Admin. Psych. Tech. Rep.,* 1957.

354. THOMSON, ROBERT: *The Psychology of Thinking.* (Penguin, 1959).

355. THORNDIKE, E. L.: *Psychology of Arithmetic.* (Macmillan, 1922).

356. TIDDY, A.: *The Mummers' Play.* (O.U.P. 1923).

357. TILLE, A.: *Yule and Christmas.* (London, 1899).

358. TINBERGEN, N.: *The Study of Instinct.* (O.U.P., 1951).

359. TOLKEIN, J. R. R.: *Tree and Leaf.* (Allen and Unwin, 1964).

360. TOLMAN, E. C.: *Purposive Behaviour in Animals and Men.* (Century, N.Y., 1932).

361. THOMAS, VINCENT (Ed.): *Creativity in the Arts.* (Prentice-Hall, 1964).

362. TYLOR, E.: *Primitive Culture,* II. (Murray, 1871).

363. TYSON, MOYA: 'Creativity', in FOSS, B. M. (Ed.): *New Horizons in Psychology.* (Penguin, 1966).

364. URENA, P. H.: *Literary Currents in Hispanic America.* (Harvard U.P., 1945).

365. VALENTINE, C. W.: 'The psychology of imitation with special reference to early childhood', *Brit. J. Psych.* 1930, 2; 105–132.

366. VERISSIMO, E.: *Brazilian Literature—an Outline.* (Macmillan, N.Y., 1945).

367. VINACKE, W. E.: 'The investigation of concept formation', *Psych. Bul.,* 1951, 48; 1–31.

368. VINACKE, W. E.: *The Psychology of Thinking.* (McGraw-Hill, N.Y., 1952).

369. VYGOTSKY, L. S.: *Thought & Language.* Trans. E. Hanfmann & G. Vakar. (Wiley, 1962).

370. WALDER, ROBERT: 'The psychoanalytic theory of play', trans. Sara A. Bonnet., *Psychoan. Q.,* 1933, 2; 208–224.

371. WALEY, ARTHUR: *The No Plays of Japan.* (Allen & Unwin, 1922).

372. WALTERS, R. H., and PARKE, R. D., in LIPSITT, L. P., and SPIKER, C. C.: *Advances in Child Development and Behaviour,* II. (Academic Press, 1965).

373. WANGH, MARTIN: 'The scope of the contribution of psychoanalysis to the biography of the artist', *J. Am. Psychoan. Assoc.*, 1957, 5; 564–575.

374. WARD, WINIFRED: *Creative Dramatics.* (Appleton, N.Y., 1930).

375. WARD, WINIFRED: *Stories to Dramatics.* (Children's Theatre Press, 1952).

376. WARD, WINIFRED: 'Let's Pretend', *Junior League Magazine*, LX Feb., 1953.

377. WARD, WINIFRED: *Playmaking with Children.* (Appleton, N.Y., 2nd. ed. 1957).

378. WARD, WINIFRED: 'Creative dramatics in Elementary and Junior High schools', in SIKS, G. B., *and* DUNNINGTON, H. B.: *Children's Theatre & Creative Dramatics.* (Univ. Washington, Seattle, 1961).

379. WATSON, P. C.: 'Reasoning', in FOSS, B. M. (Ed.): *New Horizons in Psychology.* (Penguin, 1966).

380. WATTS, A. F.: *The Language and Mental Development of Children.* (Harrap, 1944).

381. WEISSMAN, PHILIP: *Creativity in the Theater.* (Basic Books, 1965).

382. WELSFORD: *The Court Masque.* (Cambridge, 1927).

383. WERTHEIMER, M.: *Productive Thinking.* (Harper, 1954).

384. WEXBERG, ERWIN: *Individual Psychology.* (Cosmopolitan, N.Y., 1929).

385. WHITE, R., *and* LIPPIT, R.: 'Leader behaviour and member reaction in three "social climates" ' in CARTWRIGHT, D., *and* ZANDER, A.: *Group Dynamics.* (Tavistock, 1960).

386. WHITING, J. W. M.: 'Sorcery, sin and the superego', in JONES, M. R.: *Nebraska Symposium on Motivation.* (Univ. Nba., 1959).

387. WHITING, J. W. M.: 'Resource mediation and learning by identification' in ISCOE, I., *and* STEVENSON, H. W. (Eds.): *Personality Development in Children.* (Univ. Texas, 1960).

388. WHORF, B. L.: *Collected Papers in Metalinguistics.* (Dept. of State, Washington D.C., 1952).

389. WICKHAM, GLYNNE: *Early English Stages*, I. (Routledge, 1959).

390. WILES, JOHN *and* GARRARD, ALAN: *Leap to Life!* (Chatto & Windus, rev. 1965).

391. WOLPE, J. B.: 'Effectiveness of token rewards for chimpanzees', *Comparative Psych. Mon.*, 12, No. 5.

392. WOLTMAN, ADOLF G.: 'The use of puppetry as a projective method in therapy', in ANDERSON, H. H., *and* G. L. (Eds.): *An Introduction to Projective Methods and Other Devices for Understanding the Dynamics of Human Behaviour.* (Prentice-Hall, N.Y., 1951).

393. WOLTMAN, ADOLF G.: 'Concepts of play therapy techniques', *Am. J. Orthopsychiat.*, 1955, 25; 771–783.

394. WOOD, WALTER: *Children's Play and its Place in Education.* (Kegan Paul, 1913).

395. YAJNIK, R. K.: *The Indian Theatre: Its Origins and Later Development under European Influence, with special reference to Western India.* (Allen & Unwin, 1934).

396. YORK, ELEANOR CHASE: 'Values to children from creative dramatics', in SIKS, G. B., *and* DUNNINGTON, H. B.: *Children's Theatre & Creative Dramatics.* (Univ. Washington, Seattle, 1961).

397. ZIMMER, HENRICH: *The King and the Corpse*. (Bollinger Series, XI Pantheon, N.Y., 1948).
398. ZUCKER, A. E.: *The Chinese Theatre*. (Jarrolds, 1925).
399. ZUNG, CECILIA S. L.: *Secrets of the Chinese Drama*. (Harrap, 1937).

400. WAY, BRIAN: *Development Through Drama*. (Longmans, 1967). This appeared while the present volume was printing. A most valuable work, it extends the 'child drama' approach in a number of ways, in particular: (a) the concept that personality development is non-linear (p. 11 *et seq.*), which relates to the philosophy of Marshall McLuhan; and, (b) some valuable comments on the relationship of rhythm, emotion and logic (pp. 112–17).

INDEX

Lévy-Bruhl, 127
Lewin, K., 133, 186, 187
Lewis, M. M., 255
LIFE & DEATH THEME: 20, 63, 69,
    102, 147, 154, 156, 158, 159, 163, 180
Lillo, G., 18
Linguistic determinism, 243–6, 256
Linton, R., 130–1, 133, 186, 217
Liturgy, 13, 150, 155, 158, 159, 262
Locke, J., 18
Louis XIV, 17
Lowenfeld, M., 75, 78–9
Loyola, I., 15
Luria, A. R., 255–6
Luther, M., 12
Lyly, J., 15

Macready, W., 41
Maenads, 159
Magic, 56, 64, 67, 84, 86, 101, 107, 109,
    115, 119, 137, 139, 141, 143, 144,
    145, 146, 147, 149, 151, 154, 160,
    162, 165, 180, 215, 242, 245, 252, 261
Maintenon, Mme de, 17
Malim, W., 14
Malinowski, B., 133, 141
Marie Antoinette, 17
Marlowe, C., 15
Marriage, 125, 128, 133, 136, 137, 140,
    144–5, 156, 172, 179, 198
Mask, 7, 115, 119, 150, 151, 152, 155,
    161, 165, 169, 172, 174, 176
Maturation, 62, 76, 83, 89, 213, 237,
    247–9, 253–6
McCarthy, D., 254–5
McDougall, W., 25, 33–4, 195, 208
McIntyre, B. M., 227 fn
McLuhan, M., 278
Mead, G. H., 217–18
Mead, M., 134–7, 142, 168
Mediation Hypothesis, 224
Memory: learning, 55, 222, 231–6,
    263, 264; recall, 55, 231, 235;
    spontaneity &, 98
Menzies, I. E. P., 189
Merrill, J., 42
Miller, C., 70
Miller, N. E., et al, 209–11, 241
Milton, J., 17
Mime & professional performers, 12,
    161, 169, 170, 171, 172–3, 175, 176,
    177
Mimesis, see Drama Origins

Minturno, 15
Mitchell, E. D., et al, 33, 198–201
Molière, J. B. P., 112
Money-Kyrle, T. E., 80, 81, 181
Montaigne, 16
Montessori, 20
Moore, E., 18
More, Sir T., 15
Moreno, J. L., 91–9, 184–5, 218, 220
Morris, B., 189, 190
MOTHER THEME: anthropology &,
    134–8, 139–42; actor &, 108; art &,
    129; empathy, 133, 213, 242, 263;
    Great Mother, 67; group &, 182;
    identification &, 212–17, 263; matri-
    archy, 128–9; play &, 73, 89, 261;
    producer &, 111–12; psychoanalysis
    &, 63, 64, 69, 70, 76, 81–3, 84, 85,
    116, 126, 144, 146, 260–2 (see
    Oedipus); Perchta, 165; psycho-
    drama &, 93; (see WITCH
    THEME)
Mourning, 81, 82, 89, 139
Movement & Dance: 8, 9, 10, 14, 15,
    17, 21, 30, 31, 32, 35, 36, 37, 38, 45,
    46, 87, 94, 143, 145, 149, 150, 151,
    152, 153, 154, 155, 156, 157, 159,
    163, 165, 166, 167, 173, 175, 176,
    183, 184, 200, 229, 243, 245; creative,
    2, 45, 47, 48–9, 56, 98, 260
Mowrer, O. H., 211–12, 214–16, 241–
    242, 255
Mulcaster, R., 14
Mummers, 164–9, 172; Mummers'
    Play, 137, 156, 166, 168, 262
Murphy, G., 209
Murray, G., 160, 162
Music & Song, 8, 9, 14, 32, 36, 37, 45,
    46, 56, 87, 150, 151, 152, 156, 161,
    162, 165, 173, 174, 176, 200
Muths, G., 34–5
Mystery cycles (see Theatre emer-
    gence, medieval Europe)
Myth, 67, 68, 71, 115, 126, 131, 135,
    138, 142, 144, 147, 148, 156, 159,
    161, 162, 166, 176, 217, 252 (see
    Theatre origins, ritual myth)

Narcissism, 64, 109, 117, 141
Near East: Assyria, 159; Babylon, 158,
    164; Canaan, 156; Hebrew, 156, 158;
    Hittite, 156, 158; Syria, 158 (see
    Theatre origins)